Michael MacDonagh

Irish Life And Character

Michael MacDonagh

Irish Life And Character

ISBN/EAN: 9783744713665

Printed in Europe, USA, Canada, Australia, Japan

Cover: Foto ©ninafisch / pixelio.de

More available books at **www.hansebooks.com**

IRISH LIFE AND CHARACTER

BY MICHAEL MACDONAGH
Author of "The Book of Parliament"
and "Bishop Doyle a Biographical
and Historical Study"

NEW YORK
THOMAS WHITTAKER
2 and 3, BIBLE HOUSE
London: HODDER AND STOUGHTON

Preface

I HOPE I have achieved the object which I have had in view in writing this book, namely, to give a clear, full and faithful picture of Irish life and character, illustrated by anecdotes and by my own recollections and experiences during a twelve years' connection with Irish journalism.

Hitherto no attempt has been made to do for Ireland what Dean Ramsay, in his ever popular *Reminiscences of Scottish Life and Character*, has done so well for Scotland. There is no complete collection of real, genuine Irish anecdotes which throw light on the character, customs, manners, and ways of thought of the Irish people. Many of the anecdotes passing current as Irish entirely lack the Irish note, the Irish spirit; and therefore, while they may excite strangers to laughter, they make no appeal whatever to the understanding and sympathy of those who have any knowledge of Ireland and the Irish nature, except, perhaps, to arouse a feeling of annoyance or disgust. They are simply extravagant exaggerations and burlesques of certain phases of Irish character. None of these manufactured stories will be found in this book. While most of my anecdotes are new and fresh, some of them have, no doubt, been met with or heard of before, but I have admitted into my collection only anecdotes that are truly genuine, really humorous, and certainly characteristic of the Irish people.

The face of Ireland, as seen in these pages, is always puckered with a smile. I think I have shown that the world-wide reputation for humour, conscious and unconscious, which the Irish people enjoy is well founded. But I should be disappointed if the book were regarded simply as a collection of droll stories. I hope it will lead to a better understanding by other nationalities of the characteristics of the Irish race; to a wider recognition and appreciation of their many good qualities, to a kindlier tolerance of their faults and follies, which are mainly due to the chequered history of the race,—to the wayward circumstances of their unhappy past.

MICHAEL MacDONAGH.

Contents

CHAPTER		PAGE
I	THE OLD IRISH SQUIRE	1
II	DUELLING	26
III	FACTION-FIGHTING IN IRELAND	52
IV	SOME DELUSIONS ABOUT IRELAND	61
V	"BULLS" FROM IRISH PASTURES	76
VI	IN THE IRISH LAW COURTS	107
VII	FROM THE WITNESS TABLE AND THE DOCK	126
VIII	"AGIN THE GOVERNMINT"	141
IX	IRISH HUMOUR	154

CHAPTER		PAGE
X	IRISH REPARTEE AND SARCASM	170
XI	WILD FLOWERS OF SPEECH FROM IRELAND	182
XII	LOVE-MAKING IN IRELAND	202
XIII	THE HUMOURS OF IRISH POLITICS	223
XIV	ON THE WAY TO ST. STEPHEN'S	243
XV	AT ST. STEPHEN'S	255
XVI	THE ULSTER IRISHMAN	286
XVII	THE IRISH CARDRIVER	301
XVIII	THE IRISH BEGGAR	315
XIX	IRISH COLLOQUIALISMS AND PROVERBS	325
XX	THE SUNNINESS OF IRISH LIFE	339
XXI	AT THE GATES OF DEATH	371

Chapter I

THE OLD IRISH SQUIRE

DURING the Dublin autumn season the Irish country gentleman, up from his estate in Galway, Kerry, or Kildare, is a familiar and a wholesome figure in the streets of the Irish metropolis. There is no mistaking him. He stands out conspicuously, in his rough-tweed suit, leggings, and bowler hat, with ruddy features and soft brogue, from the crowd which forms the permanent society of Dublin. Meet him in Grafton Street (the Regent Street of the Irish metropolis), and you see with him three or four daughters, tall, well-set up, healthy and vivacious girls, by whom he is enticed into many a shop devoted to modes and millinery, to the sad depletion of his purse—not very ample or well filled in times of agricultural depression. Later on in the afternoon he may be seen at the Kildare Street Club—about which he is positive, as well he may, that Pall Mall cannot show him anything better—loitering on the steps flicking his leggings with his riding crop, or at its bow windows gazing at the passers-by in Nassau Street, or across the verdant stretches of the park of "Old Trinity," where he spent many a gay and light-hearted hour in his undergraduate days. He strikes you as a healthy, good-humoured fellow, with a liberal stock of animal spirits. There is always a merry twinkle in his bright, clear eye, and a smile is ever playing about the corners of his soft, yielding mouth : and that he is fond of a good joke and story the loud, hearty bursts of laughter which at night ascend from the hospitable dinner-tables of Merrion Square and Fitzwilliam Square sufficiently testify.

But though fun and frolic and light-hearted gaiety still hold sway during the season, on the banks of the Liffey, when the country gentleman is in town, and though you will get the most genuine welcome, the very best he has to give, and excellent sport, if you visit him in Clare, Wexford, or Westmeath, the Irish squire of to-day is, as a rule, a very different personage from his grandfather, who lived at the opening of the century. The lapse of time inevitably brings changes; evolution is remorseless, and if that national light-heartedness to which every Irishman is heir still survives in undiminished gaiety in the Irish Squire of to-day, he has lost all of the "recklessness," and he has lost much—happily not all—of the "rollicking" characteristics of his forefathers. He no longer plays rough, practical jokes or fights duels, or consumes enormous quantities of whiskey punch at night. Intimate association with England and Englishmen has gradually led to the assimilation by the Irish country gentlemen of English gravity of manner and English sobriety of thought, to some extent at least; for he is still very different—and proud he is of the fact—from the ordinary Englishman. He keeps accounts, and safely invests his money—which his forefathers never did—with the result that he leaves to his heir an estate comparatively free of mortgages.

In the social history of Ireland during the hundred years from the middle of the eighteenth century to the Great Famine of 1847 — which event separated by a broad, black funereal line, as it were, Old Ireland from New Ireland, and brought the *regime* of the old Irish squire to an end—three national characteristics are very conspicuous. These are, the ostentatious mode of living, the extravagant hospitality of the gentry; their embarrassed circumstances (the one, of course, being the necessary consequence of the other), and their extraordinary passion for duelling. I do not propose to dwell on the dark side of these social characteristics. The hospitality of the gentry often degenerated into coarse debauchery, their chronic incapacity to pay their debts was the ruin of many an honest trader, their love of "blazing," as duelling was popularly called, was responsible for much bullying and blackguardism. But there is a bright side—a very droll side—to the picture, and it is to the fun and frolic to which those three social qualities gave rise that I propose to draw attention in this and the subsequent chapter.

"I'll cut you off with a shilling, you young bla'guard," said an Irish squire of the old days to his son, with whom he had a quarrel. "Where will you get the shilling?" retorted the youth. The chronic state of impecuniosity in which the Irish gentry of a century ago existed was due to their reckless mode of living and prodigal hospitality. It was essential to a man of standing and popularity in his county that there should be no lack of feasting and drinking under his roof-tree. "Economy!" exclaimed an old squire, on whom a friend had been urging the necessity of retrenchment, "Economy! faix, it isn't a bad thing if it doesn't descend to meanness." The suspicion of parsimony, or even thrift and prudence, was sufficient in those days to lead to a man's ostracism from society. For money the gentry had to depend solely on their tenants. Investment of capital in securities was a thing undreamt of; and there was, therefore, no source of income but the rents of the estates. The tenants were as improvident as the landlords. Their modes of farming, too, were so primitive that they did not produce from the land more than half the crops it could be made to yield if properly worked. At the best of times, it is to be feared, the tenants were spasmodic in the payment of their rents. Their feudal devotion to "the ould shtock" was deep-seated and whole-hearted. Their cudgels—or rather " shillelaghs "—were always at the service of their landlords. But, while they were ready to shed their blood in profusion, or run risks in getting their skulls cracked, at the call of the landlord, they did not respond to the demand for the rent with the same alacrity, perhaps for the excellent reason that the "ould stocking"—the Irish peasant's deposit bank—was always empty. But the tenants kept the landlords well supplied at least with whiskey, for those were the days when "poteen" was manufactured in private stills on every hill-side; French smugglers lay off the coast at all times with cargoes of claret; and if these sources of supply failed through any cause, the " drinkables " were ordered from Dublin or London on credit.

An old Irish nobleman, when dying, was told by the clergyman that life and its vanities would soon pass away, and he was, therefore, exhorted to repent. "Repent! For what should I repent?" cried the old lord. "I don't remember that during the whole of my long life I ever denied myself anything." Nor did those Irish gentlemen of the old school deny their friends anything. The smoke of the "turf" fires in the kitchens went up continuously, day and night, for visitors called at all hours of the night, as well as of the day, and if they did not need food they were certain to require "hot wather" for the inevitable whiskey punch. The fare was coarse, but good and plentiful. The carcases of a couple of cows, sheep, and pigs were always hanging in the slaughter-house, convenient to the kitchen, and were sliced up into joints, steaks, cutlets, hams and rashers as required. There was also an abundant supply of fowl of all kinds, and of eggs, and butter. But the chief thing was to keep the cellar well supplied with claret, port, and whiskey. It was little many of the guests cared for the food. "You have a very small appetite, Mr. O'Brien," said a hostess to a guest at a dinner table. "I have, indeed, a very poor appetite, ma'am," replied O'Brien, "and what little I have I reserve for the dhrink." "The dhrink" most popular with all classes was "poteen,"—"the whiskey that never paid the king sixpence," as the phrase went. General Mathew (an ancestor, by the way, of Father Mathew, the great temperance advocate) thus eulogised "poteen" in a speech delivered in the Irish House of Commons: "The Chancellor on the Woolsack drinks it; the Speaker in his chair drinks it; the Judge on the bench drinks it; the Peer in his robes drinks it; the Beggar with his wallet drinks it; I drink it; every Man drinks it."

Our forefathers were remarkable for conviviality, and for an exalted sense of hospitality as a social duty. But these estimable qualities were often so abnormally developed that the first duty of a host was supposed to fill his guests with food and drink—especially drink—to a most appalling point of excess. A host was "a mane man entirely" if he neglected to compel his guests to indulge far beyond their natural capacity in the consumption of wine and whiskey. "Do you know Daly of Dalystown?" asked one Galway squire of another. "I used to know him," said the other. "He's too stingy for me. Sure, I never left his table comfortably drunk."

That a guest should leave the house sober was considered either a gross breach of hospitality on the part of the host, or a rank offence against what was due to a host on the part of the guest. Some hosts took very extreme measures to protect themselves from the insult of a guest leaving their tables steady on his legs. The late Mr. S. C. Hall states in his *Retrospect of a Long Life*, that his father, while quartered with his regiment in the city of Limerick early in this century, was invited to a dinner given by a county magnate. After dinner the host placed a loaded pistol on the table, and swore he would shoot the first of his guests who rose to go. "You must all fall under the table drunk," said he. Hall escaped from the room by watching his opportunity and leaping out of the window! No attempt at shirking the bottle or decanter, as it passed round the table, was then allowed. If a guest left the room for a time, a piece of paper was dropped into his glass for every round the decanter or bottle had gone in his absence, and on his return he was compelled at once to wipe out the score. One favourite device of those who desired to go to bed sober was to pour the wine or whiskey—while pretending to drink it—down behind the stiff stock or cravat which was then worn high to the chin, and to simulate intoxication. The liquor instead of rising to their heads, descended to their boots.

The capacity of the old Irish squires for getting outside enormous quantities of "the dhrink" is almost incredible in these sober days. A gentleman of the old school once complained to a friend, in a tone of protest against Providence, that he could not take more than three bottles of claret at dinner. "Thank God, I can take my five or six bottles comfortably," said the friend in a tone of deep thankfulness and contentment. "Ah," said the other, "you began to make your head early. I didn't come in for my property till I was a middle-aged man." Two gentlemen, neighbours in County Cork, after a hearty dinner washed down with plenty of claret, betook themselves, as was the custom, to whiskey-punch. After drinking until a reasonable hour, the guest was, as a favour allowed to go, as he had to attend a fair at a distance early the next morning. On passing his friend's house on his way to the fair about five o'clock, he saw the servant going to the yard pump for a kettle of water. Suspecting the purpose for which the water was required, he said, " Well, Tom, is your master still at the punch?" "Bedad he is, sur," replied the servant; "this is the twelfth kittle since yer honner left him lasth night!" Sir Frederick Flood, a notable Irish squire, was in London, at the beginning of the century, as a delegate from the Irish Protestants to Pitt on some great question of the day, when one evening as he was dining with the Prime Minister the conversation turned on the drinking habits and powers of consumption of the Irish gentry. Sir Frederick said his usual allowance was four bottles of claret every night, and he often drank five. " What! Sir Frederick," cried Pitt in astonishment, though he could take "a dhrop" himself, by all accounts, "do you mean to say you could drink five bottles of claret without any help?" "Oh, I had the help of a bottle of port," was the reply. A favourite toast at those drinking bouts was: "Here's to our host. May he live to eat the hen that scratches over his grave!"

The landlords were, as I have said, always in debt; but, happily for them, the fact that a man was heavily in debt was regarded in Ireland, during the period of which I write, as indisputable evidence of what the peasantry called "blood and breedin'." "*He* a gentleman," said a squire in whose presence a man who paid his way was mentioned with respect. "Why, the fellow never owed a hundred pounds in his life." Many of the landlords, before the Great Famine, owed more than the income and substance of their estates would fetch if sold in the market to the highest bidder. Yet they managed, thanks partly to the prestige of their position and partly to many amazing and amusing expedients, to fare sumptuously to the very last. Old Lord Leitrim, who was up to his neck in debt, wanted nothing that luxury could demand. Some of his friends seated round his festive board one night ventured, while some excellent claret was going round, to remonstrate against his extravagance. "Now poteen punch would have done us very well," they said. "I know all that, my dear fellows," said his lordship. "Nothing would delight me more than to regale you with whiskey punch, if I could, but consider the expense."
"The expense," cried the astonished guests, hold-

ing up their bumpers of the finest claret, and remembering that their host had at his command an unlimited supply of "the rale Mountain Dew," which was extensively manufactured on his estate. "Yes, the expense," continued his lordship. "Where are the lemons to come from? I get this wine direct from London on credit; but I would have to obtain the lemons from the local shopkeepers for cash. No, I cannot do that; ready money for lemons would break me in no time."

Diverse indeed were the devices to which these embarrassed squires resorted to satisfy their weakness for the pleasures of the table. A landlord who was repeatedly solicited by a Dublin wine merchant for the benefit of his custom, wrote the following candid letter in reply:—

"MY DEAR SIR,—I am not rich enough to pay for your wine myself, but I should be very happy to serve you in another way. If you will send me a list of your best customers, I will see what I can do to cultivate their acquaintance."

Charles Manners, fourth Duke of Rutland, was appointed Lord Lieutenant of Ireland in 1784, and died while still in office in October, 1787, at the early age of thirty-three years. He was noted as a man of pleasure, which, indeed, was his chief recommendation for the exalted post of Viceroy of Ireland. It was hoped by Downing Street that he would be able to keep in good humour the Irish squires, members of the Houses of Commons and Peers, who were then becoming rather restless politically.

While staying at an inn at Kilbeggan, he insisted, one night after dinner, on knighting the landlord, named Cuffe. Next morning, when his head was cooler, he repented of his action, and having sent for Cuffe, told him to put out of his mind what had passed the night before; that as the whole affair was a joke, the sooner it was forgotten the better. "I should be well plased to obleedge yer Ex-cel-lency for it's all wan to me," was the reply of the new knight; "but I unfortunately mintioned the matter to Leedy Cuffe; and she would part wid her life before she'd give up the title." And so Sir Christopher and Lady Cuffe the worthy pair were styled to the day of their death. The same Viceroy was entertained to dinner by the Mayor of Cork. Happening to praise some wine which was making the circuit of the table, he was rather astonished at the Mayor coolly replying: "Well, me lord duke, it *is* good claret, but nothing to be compared with a better quality in me cellar!"

Even the judges on the bench were not free from the prevailing baneful habit of indulging to excess in strong drink. A well-known judge who lived at the opening of the century had a strange

habit while sitting in court of sucking one end
of a quill pen, while the other end rested in a
large black ink-bottle on the bench in front of
him. But the mystery was explained when it
was discovered one day by accident that the
bottle was filled with brandy. His lordship found
it impossible to get through his judicial labours
without the aid of stimulants. There is another
amusing anecdote of a lawyer who was induced
by his wife to take a pledge against intoxicating
liquors. On one occasion he was engaged in an
important criminal case tried in Green Street
Court House, Dublin. The Court sat till very
late in the evening, and the lawyer found very
little sustenance in his glasses of milk. He told
his sad plight to a lawyer friend in court. "You
did not make a vow against eating liquor?"
asked his friend. "Nonsense!" said he; "how
could that be done?" "I'll show you," replied
the friend. He left the court, and soon returned
with a plate of fresh rolls. There was a full
noggin, or a quarter of a pint of whiskey, ab-
sorbed in the hot inside of each roll! The
lawyer was in capital form during the remainder
of the sitting.

An old member of the Irish Bar told me that
many years ago when he was a junior, just beginning his career, he got a brief in a case in which a
Dublin Insurance Company resisted payment of

a policy for a large sum on the life of an old country gentleman on the plea that he had caused his death by excessive drinking. Among the witnesses examined on behalf of the next of kin (who brought the action to recover the amount), was an old friend of the deceased, who, to prove that drinking did not hasten death swore that for the past eighteen years of his life he had been in the habit of taking every night four-and-twenty tumblers of whiskey-punch, and felt not a bit the worse for it. "Recollect yourself, sir," cried the cross-examining counsel for the company. "Four-and-twenty tumblers of whiskey-punch. You swear to that! Did you ever drink five-and-twenty?" "I'm on my oath," replied the witness, "and I'll swear no further than that, for I never keep count beyond the two dozen. There is no saying how much beyond it I might drink to make myself comfortable; but four-and-twenty's my stint!"

About the time that these habits of excessive drinking were happily waning, but while their influence still touched the imagination of the people, an English gentleman who was introduced by a friend to the well-known Kildare Street Club, Dublin, said to a waiter in the reading-room of the Club: "Bring me *Punch*." In a few minutes the attendant appeared, not with the London comic journal, but with "the ingredients," namely, a small decanter of whiskey, hot water, sugar, and a lemon. I remember reading an anecdote, with a similar moral, in an account given by a lady of a visit she paid to the West of Ireland, about the middle of the century. She arrived with another lady late one evening at an hotel in Clifden, and asked the servant to bring them a jug of hot water to their bedroom. The jug of water duly arrived; but on the tray also were two glasses of whiskey, some sugar, and a lemon.

Major O'Gorman, M.P. for Waterford, one of the drollest Irish members that ever appeared at St. Stephen's, was also one of the last survivors of those good old times. A friend of mine told me that he met the Major at a supper party in Dublin; and in the early morning accompanied him to the Imperial Hotel, Dublin, where he was staying. The Major asked the waiter to let them have some whiskey and hot water in the coffee room. "You can have plenty of whiskey, Major," said the waiter; "but not a drop o' hot wather." "What?" roared the Major in indignation. "No wonder ould Ireland is going to the dogs when hot water is not to be had in a hotel in Sackville Street, Dublin, at three o'clock in the morning." I have heard another story of the famous M.P. A young lady who sat beside him at dinner said to him: "Do you mix much in Waterford society, Major?" The association of ideas induced by the word "mix," and the spectacle of the well-spread table before him, betrayed the Major. "Well, a matter of about twelve tumblers," was his immediate reply.

During a debate on the Sunday Closing (Ireland) Bill, in the House of Commons, early in the Seventies, Mr. Blake, an old Irish member who sat for Waterford, stated that when he was a young man he had an uncle who regularly took twelve tumblers of whiskey-punch daily. This habit of his aged relative greatly troubled him, so he resolved to write and remonstrate with him. The following was the letter he sent :—

"MY DEAR UNCLE,—I write to say how pleased I should be if you could see your way to giving up your twelve glasses of whiskey a day. I am sure you would find many advantages in doing so, the greatest of which would be that, as I am persuaded, it would be the means of lengthening your days."

After a brief interval, the uncle replied as follows :—

"MY DEAR NEPHEW,—I am much obliged to you for your dutiful letter. I was so much struck by what you said, and, in particular, by your kind wish to lengthen my days, that last Friday I gave up the whiskey. I believe you are right, my boy, as to my days being lengthened, for, bedad, it was the longest day that I ever remember."

Of course the extent to which these drinking habits prevailed amongst the gentry was well known to the peasantry. One result of that knowledge was that a singular idea of what indicated wealth existed among the lower classes. Two Tipperary labourers were overheard discussing the amount of fortune of their landlord, a well-known Irish judge, who lived about sixty years ago. "Och, he's very rich, intirely," said one. "He has a hundhred a quarter, maybe." "Arrah, go on wid yer hundhred a quarter," said the other. "He has a hundhred a week, if he has a shillin'." "Glory be to God, do ye tell me so'," exclaimed the first labourer. "An I niver saw him drunk yet as long as he is comin' here!"

Up to the year of the Great Famine these old squires and landlords exercised almost feudal powers over their tenants. Before the establishment of the Petty Sessions Courts, they heard and disposed of all petty criminal and civil cases arising on their estates. Some of them had strange and ludicrous modes of dispersing justice. Maurice Nugent O'Connor, an old Roscommon landlord, used to hear cases sitting under a tree near his house, and all criminals were condemned to be ducked in an ornamental lake close by. William Carleton, the novelist, mentions in his autobiography, the case of Sir William Richardson, of Augher Castle, Co. Tyrone. If two men had a quarrel, and one summoned the other before him, he settled the case—if he saw that the parties were well matched in age, strength, and vigour—by furnishing each man with a cudgel, and conducting them to the backyard of the Castle, setting them to belabour each other. "This," says Carleton, "made the people—fighters as they were—worship him." If two neighbours had a dispute, one would say to the other, "Come, ye scoundhrel, are ye willin' to go before Sir William!" "Never say it again. I'm yer man," was generally the reply. But this method of administering justice became too popular. Disputes abnormally increased, demanding for their settlement more time than Sir William Richardson could afford; and as he was growing old, he thought it better to resign his magisterial powers.

One of those old squires who continued to adjudicate in cases even in the days of his dotage, once gave a remarkable decision. Two men had a quarrel. One picked up a stone and flung it at the other, who saved himself by dipping his head, and the missile went through the window of a house. The two men were brought before the squire by the owner of the broken window. The squire was fairly puzzled to decide which of the men should bear the cost of the damage. 'It is true," said he, "that Tom Brady flung the stone, but he did not intend to break the window, and the window would not have been broken if Mick Healy had not dipped his head. The fairest way, then, is to divide the cost between ye."

Some of them, too, were rather badly educated. One old squire wrote to his doctor thus:— "Dear doctor, will you come to see me in the morning. Bring some stuff for the gout with ye." The doctor arrived next morning, examined his patient, and said, "Why, it isn't gout you have at all—it's rheumatism, and you told me to bring you gout medicine!" "Sure, doctor, I know it's rheumatism as well as yourself, and I would have tould you so in the letter, only there wasn't wan in the house that could spell the word." And how proud they were! There was The MacDermott, Prince of Coolavin—the representative of an ancient Celtic family — who, in 1776, was invited by the Lord Lieutenant to dine at Dublin Castle. He arrived late and sat himself down at the foot of the table, near the door. The Viceroy sent one of his aides-de-camp to request The MacDermott to sit beside him at the head of the table. "Tell his Excellency,' was the reply, "that wherever The MacDermott sits is the head of the table." The Prince of Coolavin had a small property in Co. Sligo, out of which he had an income of a few hundred a year. But he always dined alone in awful majesty. Neither his wife, though she was well born, nor his children, though presumably they had some of the royal blood of the MacDermotts, were permitted to sit at table with him. On one occasion a large party, including the Lord Lieutenant, came down from Dublin to visit him. He met them at the door of his house. "O'Hara, you are welcome," said he to one. "Sandford, I'm glad to see your mother's son—she is an O'Brien," he said to another; and addressing the bulk of the party, he added, "As to the rest of ye, come in as ye can."

Numerous were the expedients to which the embarrassed gentry had to resort in order to avoid the service of writs issued by creditors. They fortified their mansions; they organised their tenantry to defend them, and directed them to keep a sharp look-out for the enemy—the process-server. Every stranger seen approaching "the big house" was stopped, and subjected to the closest examination. If a process-server were discovered in him, he was compelled to eat, not only the paper copy of the writ, but the parchment original, and was then soused in a dirty bog-hole.

But, notwithstanding all these precautions, the resourceful "limb of the law," by resorting to ingenious and amusing subterfuges, often succeeded in properly serving his obnoxious blue document. A process-server who held for a long time a writ against a landlord happened to learn that his intended victim was very partial to a goose egg for his breakfast. Well, one morning the squire, when taking his customary early walk, espied a goose-egg on the pathway in front of his hall-door. "Ah," said he, "I'll go bail that was left by the grey goose that always has such consideration for my breakfast." He picked up the egg, and seeing a piece of paper near it he naturally took that up also and examined it. Instantly a voice cried out from behind a bush close at hand, "That's the copy, yer honner, and here's the original!" It was the process-server! The landlord rushed back to the house for his pistols, but the process-server "showed the heels of his brogues," and was out of sight in no time.

A noted Clare process-server named Tom MacNamara effected "personal service" in a still more amusing fashion. The landlord against whom the writ was issued kept himself closely confined to his house. He went abroad only on Sunday, on which day service was not legal. It used to be said of him in the district, "Faix, he's so pious that he never stirs out only on Sunday." On the other days of the week he kept a number of men armed with sticks constantly prowling about the place, to persuade any process-server who thought of approaching the house to turn back. One day these "shillelagh boys" were greatly incensed on encountering a force of police, with a prisoner, on their way to the house for the purpose of obtaining a committal order from the landlord, who happened to be a magistrate. The hearts of the boys went out to the man in the clutches of the law, and it was only on the entreaty of the prisoner himself that they refrained from a rescue. On arriving at the house the police and the prisoner were ushered into the presence of the squire in the parlour. The man was suspected of being a "Terry Alt," or a member of a local agrarian conspiracy, and the police applied for a remand in order that they might inquire further into his antecedents. "Indeed yer honner," said the prisoner plaintively, "I niver did harm to man or mortal. I'm a poor, honest labourin' man, as the characther from his riverence, Father Meehan, will show; and his riverence has known me since I was the height of yer honner's knee." "Have you the character about you?" asked the magistrate. "I have, yer honner," said the prisoner, taking a paper from his pocket and handing it to the magistrate. When the magistrate unfolded the paper he turned deadly pale. "That's the copy, yer honner; here's the original," said the prisoner, who was no other than Tom MacNamara; and, turning to the police, he added, "I'm under your protection." He was marched out of the house, safe and sound.

A solicitor who had vainly endeavoured to serve a writ on a landlord hit upon the following plan: Having sealed a stone bottle with an imposing crest, and marked it "poteen," he forwarded it by an intelligent lad of sixteen, who was previously well instructed, as a present from a friend, with instructions to be delivered to himself. The bait took. "There is a note, I believe, in the wrapper, sir," observed the messenger; "and perhaps it would require an answer." The landlord undid the newspaper in which the present was folded, and took out an envelope. "There's a writ in that, sir," cried the youngster; "you're served!" and bounded out of sight in an instant. The squire looked as if he was converted into stone. Molly, who had let the boy in, foamed with rage at being made the involuntary instrument of a ruse through which her "poor masther" was "sarved with a paper out of the Coorts."

Motions to substitute personal service of the writ by serving the defendant with two letters through the post—one registered and the other unregistered—and by posting copies of the writ upon the defendant's hall-door, or upon the gates of the Catholic and Protestant Churches of the parish, were of common occurrence in the superior Courts, Dublin. Before the application was allowed there had to be a sworn affidavit from a process-server, showing that an attempt to personally serve the writ was attended with danger to his life. In one case the process-server quaintly deposed in his affidavit that "on calling at the house of the defendant the latter appeared at the upper window with a musket, or blunderbuss, and presenting said musket or blunderbuss at this deponent, threatened that if this deponent did not instantly retire he would send this deponent's soul to hell, which this deponent believes he would have done had not this deponent precipitately retreated."

But it often happened that substituted service, and even the verdicts, judgments, and decrees of the Courts, which followed, were of little use in enabling creditors to obtain what was due to them. The sheriff, being often in league with the debtor, refrained from levying the execution. This was sometimes done for friendship sake, but — as is shown in the following letter, which was addressed by the sub-sheriff of Mayo to the wife of a landlord, many years ago—something more substantial than personal regard occasionally inspired the remissness of the executive officers of the law in carrying out the decrees of the Courts :—

"DEAR MADAM,—I have by this post received the two writs as expected from Dublin. I settled the execution against your husband. I received the two bullocks, but, as cattle are down, there is a balance due. A Dublin wine merchant has just handed me an execution for £617, and insists upon accompanying me to your place. I have, therefore, named Wednesday; on which day you will please have the doors closed against us. As the plaintiff may again be officious, I would recommend his being ducked in a bog-hole when returning; and a city bailiff, whom you will know by his having a scorbutic face, and a yellow waistcoat, should, for many reasons, be corrected. Pray take care that the boys do not throw stones, as I may be hit; and warn them not to go too far in handling the wine merchant and the bailiff, as manslaughter, under the late Act, is now a transportable felony. Tell your Uncle Ulick I have returned *non est inventus* to his three last; but he must not *show*. After we return *nulla bona* on Wednesday next. I will come out and arrange matters.

"Believe me, my dear Madam, truly yours,

"A. B."

Chapter II

DUELLING

WITH all this reckless extravagance, excess, and dissipation—due to an exaggerated sense of hospitality — contemporary authorities agree that the old Irish squire was a thorough gentleman—a man of polished manners, of high intellectual culture, and with a scrupulous regard for personal honour. It was this latter trait which made the old Irish squire a noted duellist. A challenge was immediately given and readily accepted on the smallest provocation.

But, apart from questions of personal honour, it is not to be wondered at that dinner or supper parties, at which strong drink was indulged in to the amazing degree the stories in the previous chapter indicate, gave rise to many a duel. "What are you doing?" asked a Galway gentleman of his neighbour, whom he saw practising pistol shots in his garden. "I've a dinner party of friends this evening," said the other, "and I am getting my pistol hand into practice." Nor is one surprised to hear that a dying Irish squire, at the beginning of the century, thus addressed his eldest son—" God bless you, me boy! I leave you nothing but debts and mortgages; but I'll give you one piece of advice—never drink with your back to the fire, and never fight a duel with your face to the sun." These stories may be considered humorous exaggerations. They are, however, by no means improbable in a state of society such as I am attempting to depict in these pages.

No man who was not in Holy Orders could dare —if he had any regard for his position in society— to shelter himself behind law, religion, and morality, and refuse a challenge to a duel. It would mean— such was the extravagant point to which it was deemed necessary to uphold the obligations of honour—his instant expulsion from any club or *coterie* to which he might belong. A refusal to fight when challenged led in every case to one inevitable conclusion—that it was due to cowardice. Therefore, rather than run the slightest risk of such a dishonourable charge, many a man willingly faced the pistol in the hand of a " dead shot " for the most trivial cause of quarrel. Indeed, in some cases the challenged was utterly oblivious of ever having given his adversary the faintest cause of offence. A Galway gentleman who attended a county dinner was surprised to receive next morning a challenge from another gentleman whom he had met at the social gathering, but with whom he was unconscious of having had any cause for quarrel. However, he accepted the challenge, and in the encounter had the good luck, not only to escape unhurt himself, but to "wing" his adversary. Going over to shake hands with his prostrate foe—in accordance with the usual custom—he said, " I have no recollection of ever having uttered a word to offend you!" "Oh, bedad, you're the wrong man, sir," exclaimed the other. "The fellow I meant had but one eye!"

The story of a County Clare duel, which I heard from a descendant of one of the parties in the encounter, shows how in these good old days a social party, such as a dinner or supper, often ended in a duel. About eighty years ago the sub-sheriff of the County of Clare was Mr. Samuel Spaight, who lived at Six-mile-bridge, a few miles outside Limerick. Several neighbours, including a Mr. Bridgeman, dined with him one evening. While the punch was circulating after the dinner, a servant of the house told Mr. Bridgeman that he was wanted outside. At the hall door he saw his own herdsman, who told him that a number of his cattle had been sent to the pound for trespassing by order of Mr. Spaight. Bridgeman, highly incensed at this proceeding, returned to the dining-room and said to the host, "Sam, are you aware that my cattle have been sent to the pound?" "Quite well aware of it," replied Spaight. "I told my steward not to allow any man's cattle to trespass on my property." "Then you and your property be d——!" cried the enraged owner of the impounded beasts. "If I was not in my own house and you not one of my guests, I'd pound you also," retorted the master of the house. "Don't let your fastidiousness stop you, my tight fellow," said Bridgeman. "If you are willing to come out, I am at your service," said the host, rising from the table. A duel with pistols was there and then arranged, two of the other guests agreeing to act as seconds; and as the night was lit by a brilliant moon, it was decided that the encounter should take place forthwith. On the lawn in front of the house the twelve paces were measured, and at the word "fire" host and guest blazed at each other. The guest escaped unhurt; but the host received a bullet in his leg which lamed him for life.

In fact, no gentleman was considered to have taken his proper station in life until he had "blazed," or, as it was sometimes said, "smelt powder." The barrister in the Courts, the fashionable man in society, the politician in Parliament—all saw in duelling the readiest road to the realization of their ambitions for social, legal, or political advancement. Many eminent members of the Bar undoubtedly owed their success to their reputation for skill in the use of the pistol, rather than to their eloquence or their legal acumen. It was wittily said of the famous Lord Norbury that he "shot up" to the Judicial Bench; and even Henry Grattan, the great statesman and orator, who was not especially distinguished as a "fire-eater," summed up the whole wisdom of worldly success in the advice—"Be always ready with the pistol!" The indifference and levity with which duelling was regarded is humorously illustrated by the following authentic story of John Philpot Curran, one of the leaders of the Irish Bar and subsequently Master of the Rolls. He was discovered early one morning by a friend, under the hands of his hairdresser, undergoing all the laborious process of being powdered and curled. "I am dressing for the Provost's ball," he explained, when, in reality, he was about to "meet" Hutchinson, the Provost of Trinity College at twelve paces in the Phœnix Park. A popular place of resort for duellists was "the Fifteen Acres"—so called, in Irish fashion, because it consists of nine acres—in the Phœnix Park. An attorney of the city, penning a challenge, must for the moment have thought he was drawing up a lease, for he invited his antagonist to meet him "at the place called the Fifteen Acres, be the same more or less"!

The expert use of the pistol formed part of every young gentleman's training. One old and faithful servant adopted a very practical method of teaching "the young masthter" how to shoot. Having placed the loaded pistol in the youth's hand, old Martin stooped behind a low wall twenty paces distant, then jumping up suddenly, he cried, "Now, Masther Tom, one, two, three—fire!" bobbing down again before "Masther Tom" had succeeded in hitting him. After a week's practice a bullet through the domestic's hat showed the improvement which had taken place in the youth's shooting. "Well done, Masther Tom!" he cried exultantly. "Thry agin; an' if ye can get up the hand a little quicker maybe ye might hit me in the shouldher!"

In those days duelling pistols were kept at all well-equipped inns. A favourite, but gruesome order to the waiter at night was, "Call us at six; pistols for *two*; breakfast for *one*." This story is told of an innkeeper who was counting out the change of a sovereign to a customer — "Twelve shillings, 13, 14 (a shot is heard outside). "John"—to the waiter—"go and see who's kilt; 15, 16, 17" (John returns, saying, "It's Captain Kelly, sur")— "poor Captain; he was a very good customer of mine—18, 19, 20 shillings. There's your change, sir." Sometimes the duel was fought in a room of the hotel, the combatants standing at the top and bottom of a long dining-table. Charles Lever relates in one of his novels a funny story of a duel, which I am tempted to quote, as I have been informed on good authority that it is founded on fact. It was the custom of the novelist to turn to excellent account in his works all the strange experiences which befell himself while acting as a dispensary doctor in the west and north of Ireland, and all the humorous anecdotes he was told by landlords, peasants, priests and parsons. Here is the story:—An English gentleman on his first visit to Ireland was sitting in the first-floor room of an hotel in Galway, enjoying the wing of a fowl, when his plate divided with a sharp crack, and the wing, which he had just then under his knife and fork, flew up to the ceiling. His consternation and bewilderment were by no means relieved when a minute later the excited waiter rushed into the room exclaiming, "He's safe! he's safe!" "Who is safe?" inquired the anxious traveller. "Misther Mulcahy, sir," said the waiter. "Sure, the Captain, Heaven bless him! fired in the air." It then became apparent to the Englishman that a duel had been fought in the room beneath him, and that one of the combatants had magnanimously pointed his pistol upwards instead of towards his adversary! While staying at the Railway Hotel, Westport, I was shown the room in which a most comical duel was fought by two attorneys who had quarrelled one night over their whiskey punch. Their seconds, who happened to be noted Mayo wags, loaded the pistols with powder and red currant jelly. The attorneys blazed at each other, scattering the jelly right, left, and centre; and their horror on finding, as they thought, their brains dashed all over the place made a most ludicrous scene.

But it may be asked did the law do nothing to stop duelling? Nothing whatever. It is true the laws against duelling were very severe; but they were rarely if ever put into operation. Now and then when a duel ended fatally a prosecution was instituted; but, as a rule, no conviction followed. Every man on the Grand Jury, every barrister in Court, and the judge on the Bench was probably a duellist. In the case of a prosecution after a fatal duel, the judge would leave it to the jury to decide whether there had been any "foul play," with a direction not to commit for murder otherwise. Towards the close of the century there was a motion for a criminal information arising out of a duel in the Court of King's Bench Division, before the Chief Justice, Lord Clonmel; and the judicial view of duelling is set out in the following interesting extract from the judgment:—

" There are cases where it may be, and when it is, prudent for a man to fight a duel—cases in which the law does not afford him redress—cases of persevering malignity, cases of injured honour, cases of a wounded spirit; and a wounded spirit who can bear? In cases of this complexion the Court will never interfere with its discretionary authority against a man. But in all those cases where a man seeks to bring himself into notice by provoking a combat—when an aspiring upstart seeks to put himself on a level with, or to humble, his superior—cases where there has been no provocation, no sufficient ground to force a man of prudence to have resource to the *ultima ratio*, or cases (as frequently happens in this country) where a man seeks to decide a contested right or a claim of property by this sort of wager of battle—in all these cases the Court will lend its discretionary arm, and bear more or less heavily upon the party, according to the nature of his transgression."

Again, in the case of the King *v.* Fenton, for the murder of a Major Hillas in a duel, tried at the Sligo Assizes in 1812, Judge Fletcher thus capped his summing-up to the jury:—"Gentlemen, it is my business to lay down the law to you, and I will. The law says the killing of a man in a duel is murder, and therefore in the discharge of my duty I am bound to tell you it is murder. But I tell you at the same time a fairer duel than this I never heard of in the whole course of my life." It is hardly necessary to add that the accused was acquitted.

A fatality was happily a rare occurrence in a duel. There was no desire to kill in those encounters; "good hits but no lives lost" was the bulletin most hoped for. But if a death did occur it was regarded as a misadventure for which, if the duel had been fought fairly according to the rules of the game, no punishment was deserved. In Cork, however, the survivor in a fatal duel was hanged. "For what on earth did they hang the man?" asked one Galway squire of another. "For the want of a Galway jury," was the reply.

How could there be convictions for duelling—even if the Crown took action—when there were on the Bench noted "fire-eaters" like John Toler, Lord Norbury, the Chief Justice of the Common Pleas? Toler was born at Beechwood, Co. Tipperary, the second son of a squire. When the father was dying, he called his son John to his bedside and said, "The estate must go to your elder brother. All I can afford to give you is fifty pounds and these"—drawing from beneath his pillow a pair of handsome silver-mounted pistols. "Now, Jack," he continued, "be always ready to keep up the credit of the family and the honour of an Irish gentleman." Toler went to Dublin, and got called to the Bar. He had no legal knowledge, he made no pretence of eloquence, he had no family influence, but he was a man of reckless courage, and by a dexterous use of his pistols on opponents of the Government he rapidly outpaced, in the race for promotion, men of great ability and learning, but ill adepts at the use of these instruments of forensic and Parliamentary advancement. Curran never conveyed more truth in a witty epigram than when he said, " Norbury has shot himself up to the Bench ! "

As a judge, Toler was as truculent and as bellicose as he had been at the Bar and in Parliament. He often intimated to a counsel who pressed him hard in Court that he would not seek shelter behind the Bench, or merge the gentleman in the Chief Justice! " Name any hour before my Court opens to-morrow, sir," he would roar at any barrister who presumed to dispute his rulings. Norbury was also a humorist (a *rôle* in which we shall find him in a subsequent chapter), and one specimen of his fun at the expense of Daniel O'Connell may be appropriately quoted here. In 1815, Sir Robert Peel, who was then Chief Secretary for Ireland, took affront at some expressions in a speech by O'Connell, and challenged the great agitator. It was arranged that the duel should take place in France, and thither Peel went. But O'Connell delayed *en route* in London, in order that he might receive news of the health of his wife, whom he had left very ill in Dublin, and the police, having got information of the affair, arrested him and bound him over to keep the peace. The duel was thus prevented. It was whispered that O'Connell might have passed over to France undetected had he pleased. While the matter was still the talk of Dublin, a case in which O'Connell appeared as counsel came before Lord Norbury. " Pardon me, my lord," said O'Connell, in answer to some remark from the Bench, "I am afraid your lordship does not apprehend me." "Pardon me also," retorted Norbury ; "no one is more easily apprehended than Mr. O'Connell"; and, pausing for a moment, he added slowly, in sarcastic tones, "whenever he wishes to be apprehended."

About the same time another public character had declined a challenge to a duel on the plea of his daughter's illness. The two cases were the subject of the following impromptu verse by Chief Baron Bushe :—

"Two heroes of Erin, abhorrent of slaughter,
　Improved on the Hebrew command,
One honoured his wife, and the other his daughter,
　That his days might be long in the land!"

But O'Connell had shown earlier in that year (1815) by his encounter with D'Esterre — the most famous of the Irish political duels—that he was ready "to meet his man," and also "to take good care of himself," as the duelistic expressions went in those days. He truly described himself at this time as "the best abused man in the country." But few could equal him in the matter of abuse. He described the Dublin Corporation— in those days an Orange and Anti-Catholic body— as "the beggarly Corporation," and D'Esterre, a member of the Council, challenged him to a duel. As D'Esterre was noted as ' a dead shot," it was confidently expected by O'Connell's opponents that he would be killed. The parties met early one winter's morning in a field near Naas, in Kildare. Major McNamara, a Clare landlord and a Protestant, known as "Fireball" (owing to the number of duels he had fought), was O'Connell's second. Charles Phillips, a well-known Irish barrister, and author of *Curran and his Contemporaries*, also accompanied O'Connell as a friend to the field. O'Connell called him aside and said: "Phillips, this seems to me not a personal, but a political, affair. I am obnoxious to a party, and they adopt a false pretence to cut me off. I shall not submit to it. They have reckoned without their host, I promise you. I am one of the best shots in Ireland at a mark, having as a public man considered it my duty to prepare, for my own protection, against such unprovoked aggression as the present. Now, remember what I say to you. I may be struck myself, and then skill is out of the question; but if I am not, my antagonist will have cause to regret his having forced me into this conflict." The parties, each supplied with a brace of pistols, were placed on the ground at twelve paces distant, with directions to fire as they chose, after a given signal. D'Esterre theatrically disclaimed all hostility to his Roman Catholic fellow-countryman, and crossed his pistols upon his breast. Then the signal was given; the antagonists fired together, and D'Esterre fell mortally wounded.

This affair caused O'Connell much mental anguish to the day of his death. He often referred to it as the one act of his life which he most bitterly regretted. Immediately after the duel he wrote to Mrs. D'Esterre, expressing his profound grief for being the cause of the death of her husband, asking her forgiveness, and offering to settle on her an annuity of £150 for life. The Corporation, however, induced her not to accept O'Connell's offer, and settled on her an allowance out of their own funds. O'Connell, shortly after, publicly announced his determination never again to send or to accept a challenge to a duel. He was once taunted in the House of Commons with having refused to fight a man whom he had caustically assailed with his tongue. "There is blood upon these hands," he exclaimed, "and I have registered a vow in heaven against duelling." But he continued to use language of his political opponents which in other circumstances would have brought showers of challenges upon his head. In 1835 he thus described his erstwhile Radical friend, Benjamin Disraeli: "He possesses just the qualities of the impenitent thief who died upon the cross, whose name, I verily believe, must have been Disraeli"; and Disraeli, stung by the taunt, wrote to young Morgan O'Connell (who a short time before publicly announced his willingness to accept the responsibility for his father's language) to perform "the vicarious duty of yielding satisfaction for the insults which your father has too long launched with impunity on his political opponents." But Morgan O'Connell in this instance declined to stand up to be shot at for the sake of his father.

Many a political duel also arose out of the violent language which was used in the Irish House of Commons during the exciting quarter of a century which preceded the Union in 1800. Here, as an illustration, is an extract from a speech by Toler, attacking Ponsonby, an eminent and eloquent member of the Patriot Party led by Henry Grattan: "What, has it come to this in the Irish House of Commons, that we should listen to one of our own members degrading the character of an Irish gentleman by language which is fitted but for haranguing a mob. Had I heard a man uttering out of doors such language as that by which the honourable gentleman has violated the decorum of Parliament I would have seized the ruffian by the throat!"

Sir Boyle Roche, the celebrated maker of "bulls," while speaking once in the House, was interrupted by the affected coughing of a hostile group of members, on the other side of the Chamber. He took a handful of pistol-bullets from his pocket, and holding them out said, "These are infallible pills for a cough, if any of those honourable gentlemen opposite will care to try them." Such "pills" were in fact administered for the cure of all sorts of political complaints. It was no unusual thing for two disputing politicians in "the old House in College Green" to retire to the Phœnix Park or Ballsbridge by break of day, and settle the difference between them with pistols.

One of the most remarkable of those encounters was that in which Henry Grattan and Isaac Corry, the Chancellor of the Exchequer, were the antagonists. During the debates on the motion for the Union in 1799 Corry assailed Grattan, and Grattan, a master of scornful invective, thus replied: "I will not call him villain, because it would be improper, and he is a Privy Councillor. I will not call him fool, because he happens to be Chancellor of the Exchequer. But I say that he is one who has abused the privilege of Parliament and freedom of debate by uttering language which, if spoken out of the House, I should answer only with a blow. I care not how high his situation, how low his character, how contemptible his speech, whether he be a Privy Councillor or a parasite, my answer would be a blow!" Hardly had Grattan resumed his seat when a challenge was conveyed to him on behalf of Corry. The parties met next morning in a field at Ballsbridge, just outside Dublin, and fought with pistols in presence of a large crowd. The directions were that they should fire two shots at each other. Grattan escaped uninjured; but he hit Corry with his first shot, and fired the second in the air. " I then went up to him," said Grattan, describing the affair in after years. " He was bleeding, and he gave me his bloody hand. We had formerly been friends, but he was set on to do what he did."

This passion for duelling prevailed not only among the makers of the law, and the administrators of the law, among statesmen and among judges, it existed also among the subordinate agents of " law and order " in Ireland. Sir William Gregory relates in his autobiography a good story which he heard from his grandfather, who was Under-Secretary for Ireland for many years. A duel was arranged between two Galway gentlemen named Sir Val Blake and Mr. Robert Burke, and the place selected for the meeting was a field close to old Gregory's gate. As he was shaving in his room one morning he heard shots fired; and rightly guessing that a duel was being fought, he hastily donned a dressing-gown and ran out to try to put a stop to it. As he was making towards the field he heard more shots, and a voice exclaiming, " Gentlemen, this is all child's play. Let us finish the business properly. Let each second advance his man two paces, and I'll engage they won't miss." " And who are you, sir, to give such bloody counsel?" said old Gregory, who had now arrived on the scene. "Who am I, sir?" said the other in indignant tones. "I'll have you to know, sir, that I'm Mr. Hickman, the Clerk of the Peace for the County of Clare."

Another anecdote will show how duelling was regarded by the ladies of the period. The Kilkenny Militia were stationed in Galway in 1798. Captain Rawson not only refused to obey an order of the Colonel of the Regiment to take a firing-party to the Green and shoot down in batches of ten a number of unfortunate peasants who had been implicated in the Rebellion of that year, but publicly administered a flogging to that officer at the door of the Tholsel for having given such an order. The Colonel sent him a challenge, which, however, Rawson refused to accept, as he was about to be married. But when he called at the lady's house on the morning arranged for the ceremony, she told him she would never marry a man on whose honour rested the stain of having refused a challenge to a duel. Rawson immediately rushed to the barracks, fought the Colonel in the square, wounding him, and in two hours returned to the house to find awaiting him the most willing of brides.

The most extraordinary affair in the history of Irish duelling took place in County Leitrim in 1786. Robert Keon, an attorney practising in Leitrim, had a quarrel with George Nugent Reynolds, a country gentleman residing in the same county. The parties subsequently met outside the Court House at Carrick-on-Shannon, and Keon struck Reynolds across the shoulder with his whip. Reynolds then sent Keon a challenge to a duel, which Keon accepted. A singular circumstance in connection with the affair is that it was agreed between the seconds that no ball ammunition was to be brought to the field on the day of meeting, which agreement was communicated to the principals and had their sanction. Honour was to be satisfied by Keon and Reynolds simply blazing at each other with blank powder. Reynolds rode to the field on the day of meeting, October 16th, 1786, accompanied by his second, Mr. James Plunkett. Keon was already on the ground. On alighting from his horse, Reynolds approached Keon, and courteously taking off his hat said, "Good-morning." Keon immediately replied, "D—— you, you scoundrel! why did you bring me here?" and raising a pistol he held in his hand, he fired and shot Reynolds through the head. The unfortunate gentleman instantly fell and expired. Keon was arrested, and in due time was brought to trial at Carrick-on-Shannon, before Lord Clonmel, for the murder of Reynolds. The defence, which was sustained by the prisoner's brother and some other persons who were present on the field, was that Reynolds attempted to horsewhip Keon, and that striking the pistol, it went off accidentally. The jury convicted the prisoner. After the death sentence had been pronounced by the judge, a lady who was sitting in a retired part of the Court, in black and heavily veiled, rose, and flinging back her veil, exclaimed, " I have fled from my home. I have travelled on foot a hundred miles to hear this sentence. The blood of my murdered husband cried to Heaven for vengeance, and its cry is heard." Two days after the trial Keon was led out of prison to be publicly executed in one of the streets of Carrick-on-Shannon. A clergyman accompanied him on the execution cart. Arrived at the gallows, Keon stood up, and seemed to be about to address the assembled people, when suddenly he caught sight of the widow of Reynolds at a window of a house overlooking the scene. She stood there dramatically looking at him, and pointing her finger downwards, as if to hell. The wretched man spoke not a word. He gave himself to the executioner, and in a few minutes was writhing at the end of a rope.

The duel between Standish O'Grady, a country gentleman of good family, and Captain Roland Smith in 1830—probably the last fought in

Ireland — was also attended by many singular circumstances. One day as O'Grady was riding down Nassau Street, Captain Smith and his friend Lieutenant Markham were driving in a cabriolet up the street. As they were passing each other, the two horses got into close and rather dangerous proximity, and O'Grady gave the animal attached to the cab a flick with his whip to turn him off. Smith immediately jumped out of the cab, saying to Markham, " If we submit to this we shall have to leave Dublin "; and following O'Grady, who rode on, thinking no more of the incident, he gave him a slash with his whip, and then returning to his cab, drove away. O'Grady sent Smith a challenge. The parties met at Harold's Cross. O'Grady was mortally wounded, and died two or three days afterwards. Smith and Markham—who had acted as his second—were arrested, and indicted "for killing Mr. Standish O'Grady in a duel," before Lord Plunket and Judge Vandeleur. They were convicted of manslaughter, and sentenced to two years' imprisonment. Before the prisoners were removed from the dock, Smith threw his arms around Markham's neck and sobbed, " Oh, Henry! see what I have brought you to!" Lord Plunket, who seemed moved by the scene, said to the prisoners, " Nothing affecting your character as gentlemen or men of honour has been proved against you." After serving six months' imprisonment both the prisoners were released.

But, as I have said, these encounters were happily rarely fatal, and left no bitterness between the combatants. I knew one celebrated Irish duellist, The O'Gorman Mahon, M.P. Mr. Gladstone asked him how he felt when challenged. "I cannot tell you," replied the old swashbuckler; "I was never challenged. I was always the challenger." I had once the good fortune of having an interesting conversation with him on the subject of duelling. A short time previously I had seen the pair of pistols with which it was said Major MacNamara, of Clare—he who had acted as O'Connell's second in the duel with D'Esterre, and succeeded the Liberator in the representation of Clare in 1830, and is even now popularly known among the peasantry of Munster as "Fireball MacNamara"—had fought as many as twenty duels. The handles of the pistols had, according to custom, a notch for every duel in which they had been used, two notches being made when the duel had proved fatal. I noticed that the double notches were very few and far between, so that even MacNamara, although he had the reputation of being a "dead shot," did not often kill his antagonist. I asked The O'Gorman Mahon why it was that duels were so rarely fatal. The answer was certainly surprising. It was that the nearer the antagonists were to each other the less danger they ran, and that, with a view to preventing a fatality, the seconds were accustomed to place their friends only ten or twelve paces apart. As The O'Gorman Mahon put it, "The fellows stood nine or ten yards apart and blazed at each other like d—— fools." He did not approve, it will be seen, of lessening the risks of duelling. The explanation given of this curious fact by The O'Gorman Mahon was that when a man has to look straight almost into the muzzle of his antagonist's pistol he is apt to become nervous and to shoot blindly. The circumstance has, however, been scientifically explained. It has been calculated by experience of the course taken by bullets on leaving the pistol that at *nine* yards there might be comparative safety; at *twelve* yards danger might be expected, and that at *fifteen* yards a hit was practically certain.

But if the duels were rarely fatal, they were always fruitful in good jokes. A witty Dublin barrister was consulted by a physician as to calling out a person who had insulted him. "Take my advice," said the lawyer, "and instead of calling him out, get him to call you in, and have your revenge that way. It will be much more secure and certain." A "squireen," or upstart, went to an old squire in his neighbourhood for advice as to sending a challenge. "Healy of Loughlinstown," said he, "has threatened to pull me by the nose whenever he meets me. What would you advise me to do?" "Has he really used that threat?" asked the squire. "Oh, yes, there is no doubt in the world about it" replied the other. "Well," said the squire, in sarcastic and contemptuous tones, "I'll tell you what to do. Soap your nose well, and it will slip through his fingers." But perhaps the greatest contempt that was ever expressed by one man for another was contained in the rejection by an old Irish gentleman of a challenge. "Fight with *him*!" he exclaimed; "I would rather go to my grave without a fight!"

John Egan, an Irish lawyer—a big, brawny fellow, commonly known as "Bully Egan," from his proportions and his swagger, quarrelled with his contemporary at the Bar, John Philpot Curran, who was a man of slight and diminutive stature. A duel, of course, followed. On the ground Egan complained that the disparity between his immense girth and height and Curran's few feet gave his antagonist a great advantage. "I might as well fire at a razor's edge as at Curran," said Egan, "and he may hit me as easily as a turf stack." "I'll tell you what, Egan," replied Curran; "I wish to take no advantage of you whatever. Let my size be chalked upon your front, and I am quite content that every shot which hits outside that mark shall not count." There is a laughable story current in journalistic circles in Ireland in relation to a duel in which the editor of the *Limerick Chronicle*—a very old and influential newspaper—figured several years ago. Like many members of his craft, the editor's sight had got dimmed in the trying work of writing out matter to fill his columns; and he had recourse to spectacles. But his opponent's second objected to his wearing the glasses at the duel, on the ground that it gave him an unfair advantage. "Sure," said the newspaper man, "I couldn't see to shoot me father without them, much less Captain O'Grady." In another duel one of the parties had his eye shot out. His antagonist was very much concerned about what he called "the accident." "How do you feel?" said he to the wounded man. "Can you see at all with the eye that's knocked out?"

Of course, excuses were occasionally offered for refusals to stand up at twelve paces to be shot at. Some of these were characteristically humorous. A Dublin lawyer who received a challenge pleaded that the only provision for his family was a policy of insurance on his life for £5,000, which would be forfeited if he came by his death in a duel. "Tell him," said his antagonist, "that I'll give him a mortgage on my estate for the money, so that he can meet me with an easy heart." Another refusal of a challenge ran: "Dear Sir,—I must decline to meet you with pistols. I have no desire to leave my poor old mother, who is now in her seventy-fifth year, an orphan!"

Chapter III

FACTION-FIGHTING IN IRELAND

WHAT the pistol was to the Irish gentry in the old duelling days, the stout ash cudgel or blackthorn shillelagh was, till more recent times, to the Irish peasantry—it was the arbiter in personal quarrels, family feuds, disputes about trespass, right of way, boundaries, and local contentions between baronies or parishes.

The scene of the bloodiest faction fights was the celebrated Donnybrook Fair, which was held in the early part of the century, a few miles outside Dublin. The fair opened on the first Sunday in August and lasted a week. It was attended by people from all parts of Ireland. Many went to buy or sell, but most "feelin' blue-mouldy for want of a batin'," visited the fair solely for the purpose of "joinin' in the dischussions with shticks." In a song still very popular with the Irish peasantry we are told that—

"At Donnybrook Fair
An Irishman, all in his glory, is there
With his sprig of shillelagh and shamrock so green.

He steps into a tent, and spends half a crown,
Comes out, meets a friend, and for love knocks him down,
With his sprig of shillelagh and shamrock so green!"

High above the noise of buying and selling, and haggling and wrangling over a few shillings in the price of a cow or horse, were heard the warhoops, "Who dare say boo! Who dare tread on the tail of me coat!" exclaimed by bands of men, or factions, dancing through the fair, trailing their coats in the mud behind them, shouting, yelling, screaming, and excitedly waving their sticks over their heads. When two rival parties met, they belaboured each other with might and main amid a terrific din of cries and exclamations, and the rattle of sticks in fierce collision. A "servant bhoy" who never missed a visit to Donnybrook was advised by his master one year to stay at home. "You always come back, Denny," said the master, "with a broken head. Don't go to-day, and I'll give you half a crown." "Well, now, yer honner, does it stand to raison that I'd take half a crown for the batin' I'm to get at the fair?" replied Denny.

An Irish judge, who lived about the middle of the century, made a tour in Wales. In one large town which he visited the assizes were just being held, and remembering his own experiences as a judge, he saw with astonishment that the calendar contained not a single case of homicide or assault.

He happened to mention this gratifying circumstance to his tipstaff on his return. But the tipstaff looked at the matter from an entirely different standpoint. "Is that so, sir?" he exclaimed; "well, what a mane-spirited people the Welsh must be!" The warm and excitable temperaments of the people, their pugnacity, their love of fighting and dare-devilry, were—as this story indicates—the main causes of faction-fighting in Ireland. Just as a gentleman who had not "blazed"—that is, fought a duel—was thought little of in society, so among the peasantry, by whom all the faults and follies of the gentry were absurdly imitated, a man "was no great shakes" unless he had cracked a neighbour's skull.

As a rule, little or no animosity lay behind these faction fights. Often there was but the slightest cause of quarrel between the parties engaged. They simply fought for the pure love of fighting—to "let off steam," to give vent to pent-up feelings. Sometimes, however, these accidental and causeless encounters at fairs, horse-races, or hurling matches often developed into bloody family or barony feuds. Two of the most noted factions in Ireland, which existed as recently as fifteen or twenty years ago, were the "three-year-oulds" and the "four-year-oulds" of County Limerick. Many, many years ago—so far back is it that the date cannot be accurately fixed—two County Limerick farmers had a dispute at a fair over the age of a cow. One, the owner, asserted that she was a three-year-old; the other, the proposed buyer, was positive she was a four-year-old. They came to blows in the excitement of their controversy, and their respective relatives and friends at the fair joined in the fight. But the quarrel did not end there. For several generations their descendants —one side being known as "three-year-oulds" and the other as "four-year-oulds"—cracked each other's skulls because of that ridiculous difference of opinion long, long ago as to the age of a cow. The members of the rival factions lived amicably enough on the same countryside during most of the year. It was generally at a local fair at Pallas Green, when the parties had "a drop taken," that they came to blows. The challenge was given by a member of one or other of the factions indulging in what was called "wheeling," which consisted in shouting, "Who dare strike a Ryan?" or "Who dare strike a Bourke?" and forthwith the Bourkes fell on the Ryans, or the Ryans on the Bourkes.

I have often seen members of these County Limerick factions, when they met together at social parties, in a public-house, or in a railway carriage, showing to each other their scarred skulls, and boasting of the number of stitches their craniums contained, just as a war-worn veteran would proudly display the wounds which showed how he had been in the hottest part of many an engagement. One old Doon farmer, to whom I had done some little service, when I was connected with a Limerick newspaper, offered me his *shillelagh*. "It's been in our family for three generations now, and I don't know how many skulls were cracked with it be me grandfather, me father, and meself. There's no work for it now, thank God! for we've given up faction-fightin'!" The oaken stick hung above the kitchen fireplace. It was about three feet long. At its end was a big knob, and the handle contained a looped piece of leather, which was slipped round the wrist, to prevent the weapon being wrested or struck from the hand in the scrimmage. I did not accept the old faction-fighter's offer.

A friend of mine, a barrister, was in Abbeyfeale, County Limerick, attending Quarter Sessions, about fifteen years ago. Standing at the hotel door in the evening, the head constable of the police rushed past. "What's the matter, Head?" asked my friend, pulling him up. "Oh, a grate dale intirely!" he cried, with a look of concern in his face. "There'll be ructions in the town to-night." "Why?" asked my friend, much astonished. "Oh, the Fi'garlds are all drunk, and they're 'wheelin'' for the Moriartys, and lookin' for thim," said the head constable. "And what have they again the Moriartys?" said my friend. "The ould story," replied the policeman. "For betrayin' the cause of Ireland." In the sixteenth century the Moriartys—according to local tradition—betrayed the great Earl of Desmond (the head of the Fitzgeralds) to the English; and ever since the Fitzgeralds "have it in"—as the phrase goes—for the Moriartys in Limerick and Kerry!

These faction fights were no child's play. They were usually fought with a grim determination. There is a story told of a man who, having got his head battered in a faction fight, bound it with a piece of rope to keep it together, and entered the *mêlée* again, until his head was irreparably displaced. "You have been in many 'ructions,' I suppose, Pat?" said a landlord to one of his tenants. "Oh, a great many, yer honner," replied Pat unaffectedly. "And I suppose you fight grimly—you never give in, I mean?" "I always fight till I die," said Pat. Happily these "ructions" did not give much occupation to the coroner. They provided the local dispensary doctors with many a hard day's work; but as a rule that was all. And even if a "bhoy" was killed he was not without something to console him for his untimely end. "You had a narrow escape of being killed by that blow, my man," said a doctor to a peasant as he was binding up his wounds after a faction fight. "Faith, if it killed me, I'd have the satisfaction of seeing Mick Mahoney swing or transported," said the peasant. Some curious verdicts have been returned by juries in inquests on men killed in faction fights. One was "the deceased met his death by the visitation of God under suspicious circumstances." Another was, "We find that Tom Cusack was killed by the fall of a piece of timber on his head."

Prosecutions, of course, often followed these fights. The famous Daniel O'Connell so successfully defended a man who was accused of killing another in one of those "ructions" that the prisoner was acquitted. As he was leaving the dock, the man exclaimed, "Och, counsellor, I've no way here of showin' yer honner my gratitude; but I wish I saw ye knocked down in me own parish, an' maybe I wouldn't bring a big faction to the rescue." In a case of aggravated assault, arising out of similar proceedings, the prisoner pleaded that he only gave the man "a pat on the head." "I suppose," said the judge, "you spell that 'pat' with a capital P?" After one terrible faction fight in the County of Limerick, the whole countryside was arrested. An *alibi* was clearly proved on behalf of one of the prisoners; but, nevertheless, he was found guilty with the others. On being directed to stand up in the dock to receive sentence, he loudly protested, "Wasn't it as clear as noonday that I was at home in bed at the time of the fight?" "Hold your tongue, sir," said the judge sternly. "You're just as guilty as any of them. You know you would have been there if you could. Three years' imprisonment with hard labour."

Faction-fighting is now practically dead in Ireland. The death-blow has been given it partly by the spread of education and partly by the great political movements. During the agitation for Catholic Emancipation, led by Daniel O'Connell in the Twenties, treaties of peace were established between most of the then existing factions; and the Land League movement of 1879-81 extinguished the feuds between the "Three-Year-Olds" and the "Four-Year-Olds" in County Limerick, and the "Magpies" and the "Blackhens" in the neighbouring county of Tipperary. In some instances the reconciliation between barony, parish, or family factions has been attended by religious ceremonies. In the case of one faction between families and their relations on each side—which were always the most implacable—peace was publicly established in the local Catholic chapel one Sunday after Mass. Two old men, the leaders of the rival factions, advanced to the front of the altar. They stood for a few seconds silently and with bent heads, and then grasped each other's hands as if with a painful effort. The next moment one of them dashed himself down on the floor, and in a voice broken with passionate sobs cried out: "*Avic Mochree!* me murdered son! I've clasped the hand that shed the last drop of your blood!"

Chapter IV

SOME DELUSIONS ABOUT IRELAND

THERE is a story told of an Englishman who after spending a week in the East of Ireland—the portion of the country most subject to English influences—returned home and said to his friends, "I assure you I did not meet or see a single real Irishman the whole time I was in Ireland." What sort of an Irishman had this visitor expected to see in Ireland as plentifully as blackberries in the country's hedges? Why, of course, the Irishman with which English comic papers, English novels, and the English stage had made him so familiar.

In the English comic journals—especially those which "lift" their pictures from New York and Chicago papers—the Irishman is usually represented as an uncouth-looking barbarian, arrayed in rags, that any self-respecting scarecrow would turn up his nose at—a tattered, frieze, swallow-tail coat, a collarless shirt and torn knee-breeches; a face with broad, distorted lineaments, relieved only by a latent expression of mingled foolishness and fun;

a mouth extending from ear to ear—the yawning sepulchre, it is suggested, of untold hogsheads of whiskey; no nose to speak of; on his wild shock of hair a battered *caubeen*, or hat, in the band of which the inevitable clay pipe is fixed; and in his hand a bit stick or shillelagh. The audiences of the variety theatres are introduced to an Irishman of an exactly similar type, in dress and equipment, with the equally preposterous additions, perhaps, of red hair and whiskers and an almost unintelligible gibberish. That type of Irishman, or anything approaching to a resemblance to him, is not—as the English visitor of my story discovered—to be met with in Ireland. I never yet met a countryman who, even in his most frolicsome moments, carried his pipe in the band of his hat. The Irish, like the English, smoke their pipes in their mouths, and as for the average Irish face, it is, by common consent, well formed, cheerful and animated.

Of course every race is made a butt for ridicule by some other nation. All its characteristics are more or less grossly caricatured. Look at the pictures of John Bull in the Parisian comic journals. He is represented as a big-bellied fellow, with a silly, ugly face, protruding teeth and a retreating forehead. Scotsmen and Welshmen, as well as Irishmen, are held up to ridicule. We therefore must not be too squeamish or captious about an occasional jest. It is mainly done for fun, though sometimes the fun descends to scurrility and calumny. The stage Irishman, bad as he is, regarded as a representative of national characteristics, has the saving virtue of being always entertaining in his own ridiculous blundering way; and despite his formidable bludgeon and his broad platter face, with its fringe of red hair, he is considered a lovable character, on the whole, by the audience.

Ireland is no longer the *terra incognita*, the land of unknown marvels, it once was to England. Early in the century it was believed in England that there were no spiders in Ireland. The functionary who then showed visitors over Westminster Hall used to assert that there were no cobwebs in the oaken roof because the wood came from Ireland. The Edgeworths in their *Essay on Irish Bulls* recount a conversation, on the subject of Ireland, between an Englishman, a Scotsman, and an Irishman, travelling in the Bath coach. The conversation is, of course, imaginary; but some of the delusions which then prevailed in England in regard to Ireland are thus set forth by the Englishman:— "What little knowledge I have of Ireland has been drawn more from observation than from books. I remember when I first went over there, I did not expect to see twenty trees in the whole island. I imagined that I should have nothing to drink but whiskey; that I should have nothing to eat but potatoes; that I should sleep in mud-walled cabins; that I should, when awake, hear nothing but the Irish howl, the Irish brogue, Irish answers and Irish bulls; and that if I smiled at any of these things a hundred pistols would fly from their holsters to give or demand satisfaction. But experience taught me better things." But though Ireland is now better known to England, many of these delusions—such is the force and vitality of tradition—still linger among the English people.

The Queen in her interesting book, *Leaves from the Journal of our Life in the Highlands,* gives her impressions of the two brief visits she paid to Ireland in 1849 and 1861. Her Majesty evidently was also on the look-out for the Irishman of the stage and fiction. At Carton, the seat of the Duke of Leinster, she saw the Irish jig danced by the peasantry. "It is quite different from the Scotch reel," she says; "not so animated, and the steps different, but very droll. The people were very poorly dressed in thick coats and the women in shawls," and she adds, "There was one man who was a regular specimen of an Irishman, with his hat on one ear." The fact that the Irish are entirely different, in temperament, manners, habits, ideas, from the English also struck Her Majesty. Cork was the first place she saw on her first visit to Ireland in 1849. "It is not at all like an

English town, and looks rather foreign," she graphically writes. "The crowd is a noisy, excitable, but very good-humoured one, running and pushing about, and laughing, talking, and shrieking. The beauty of the women is very remarkable, and struck us much—such beautiful dark eyes and hair, and such fine teeth; almost every third woman was pretty, and some remarkably so. They wear no bonnets, and generally long blue cloaks. The men are very poorly, often raggedly dressed, and many wear blue coats and short breeches, with blue stockings."

The Irish, I will admit, are to other nationalities a strange and incomprehensible race. John Bull has not only lived beside Paddy, but has attempted to govern him, for more than seven hundred years, and he does not quite understand him yet. Indeed, it is a question whether John will ever make Paddy out. The manners, customs, and ideas of the people of Ireland have always been, and probably ever will be, the sources of wonder, bewilderment, and dismay to the Anglo-Saxon people. This is shown in the invented stories, supposed to be illustrative of Irish life and character, current in English and American journals. Most of them are silly, stupid, and preposterous. Some of them are humorous in their way, but even these lack, as it were, the Irish accent—the Irish attitude of mind, the Irish idiom, and the Irish turn of phrase, are missing—and they are, therefore, to an Irishman, at least, obviously bogus. I came across the following anecdote quite recently in an American newspaper:—" An emigrant sailing ship left Queenstown with a large number of Irish passengers. The ship was scarcely under way when a young Irishman appeared on deck in great consternation, and ran from side to side of the vessel, crying 'Och! och!' 'What's the matter with you?' asked the mate. 'Oh troth,' replied the Irishman, 'but I was afraid ye'd go off and lave me while I was down there in the cellar.'" In *Punch*, not long since, a somewhat similar story was told. An Irish emigrant, on board a transatlantic steamer, inquired, " Where's the sails that drives the vessel?" "This is a steamship—14,000 horse-power," he was told. "Fourteen thousand horses!" he exclaimed; "then where's the stabling?" Here is another manufactured anecdote:—" Two friends, an Englishman and an Irishman, travelling, had a double-bedded room at an inn. Being awoke by noise in the night, the Englishman called his companion to light the candle. "Where is it?" asked Pat. 'At your right hand, on the table," said the other. "Are you crazy?" cried Pat. "How can I see which is my right hand in the dark?"

Stories like these, which humorously exaggerated the traditional Irishman's proneness to blunder, are very common. They are funny, and they do credit to the inventiveness and imagination of those who make them. But the latter-day writers of Irish anecdotes can hardly improve on their predecessors. I have come across these two capital manufactured stories in a rare jestbook published in London over a century ago :—" Two soldiers, one a Scotsman and the other an Irishman, on going into battle, agreed that if one was wounded the other was to help him to the doctor. It so happened that the Scotsman was wounded, and he cried out to the Irishman, 'I'm hit in the thigh ; take me to the doctor.' Pat lifted him on to his shoulders, and was carrying him to an ambulance when a cannon ball carried off his head, unknown to Pat, who, feeling the 'whiz' of the projectile, said, 'That was a close one too.' A surgeon, noticing him carrying his headless burden, asked him where he was going with it. 'Where should I be going but to the doctor to have him doctored?' said Paddy. 'But don't you see that he has had his head knocked off by a shot?' 'Oh, bedad, so he has,' cried Paddy, when he lowered the corpse of his friend. 'What a thundering liar the fellow must be! He tould me it was only a bullet wound in his leg!'" The other story is the following :—" During the progress of a battle a certain regiment was directed to wait for orders behind some weak defences. Being exposed to the fire, some of the men were killed and some were wounded. One man who had his arm shot off lay moaning and groaning. 'Stop your noise!' cried an Irish soldier. 'Do you think no one is kilt but yourself? You're making more row than the poor fellow near you who had his head shot off.'"

Of course it was an Irishman (according to the traditions of the Anglo-Saxon race), who, staying at a hotel, was called early in the morning, and, his face having been blackened during his sleep by practical jokers, exclaimed on seeing himself in a mirror, "Oh, bedad, they've called the wrong man!" It was also an Irishman who said "Arrah, Jim Dwyer, when I seen you at a distance I saw it was yourself; when I came nearer, I saw it was your brother Jack; but, be jabers, I now see it's nayther one nor the other"; and who wrote, "If you do not receive this letter in due course, it must have miscarried, so I beg you will immediately write to let me know." No one can deny that Irishmen make "bulls," but as a matter of fact many of these stories of ludicrous and impossible blunders, which are commonly "fathered" on Pat, were in circulation among the Ancients before Ireland had a historical existence. The Irishman who carried round a brick as a specimen of the house he had to sell; the Irishman who shut his eyes and looked into the mirror to see how he would appear when he was dead; and the Irishman who, hearing that crows were reported to live two hundred years, bought one to test the accuracy of the statement, were really ancient Greeks! There is also a well-known story of an Irishman who, engaged in writing a letter and discovering another Irishman looking over his shoulder, added as a postscript, "I should tell you more if there was not an impudent fellow looking over my shoulder, and reading every word," whereupon the other exclaimed, "You lie, sir; I have not read a word you have written." The root idea of that joke comes from Egypt, and is two hundred and fifty years older than the New Testament!

These anecdotes show the traditional Saxon conception of the Irishman. He is the Merry Andrew of the English-speaking world — a mightily entertaining, wild, ragged, and roguish clown, who never opens his lips but to utter a jest or a "bull." Charles Lever puts into the mouth of the inimitable "Mickey Free" (in "Charles O'Malley")—the best known and most popular character in Irish fiction, perhaps because he approaches so closely to the Anglo-Saxon standard of "a real Irishman"—the lines:—

"And the English—bad luck to them!—hate us,
Because we've more fun than them all!"

These lines were, of course, used in jest. Did

Mickey ever utter a sober expression in the whole course of his laughter-provoking career? I have never noticed any disposition among Anglo-Saxons or their newspapers to scoff at or depreciate the humorous side of the Irish character. On the contrary, they take a sort of proprietorial pride in it, as if the one object for which Providence created the Irishman was to make the Anglo-Saxon world laugh. They expect all Irishmen to be entertaining; and when they meet a dull Celt, they positively feel a sense of personal wrong, as if they had been deprived of something which was their due. But in the complex Irish character there are many startling contrasts and contrarieties. The Irish, taking them all in all, are one of the most laughter-loving, the wittiest, and the most jovial of people; at the same time they are also one of the gloomiest and most melancholy. Ireland is a land of sunshine and of rain; and in the people, as in the variable skies above them, there is a perpetual blending of the smile and the tear. They are at once wild and reckless, and sober and shrewd. At one moment they are gay and light-hearted, and the next they are plunged into the deepest depths of grief. They are an emotional race. They have not the equable, stolid, and self-centred temperament of the Anglo-Saxons. They are, admittedly, possessed of finer, acuter, and more sensitive feelings. They accordingly obtain more fun out of their pleasures, and more pain out of their sorrows, than their neighbours, who take their pleasures and their griefs soberly, and to whom the Irish peasants' ecstasy of joy or sorrow is strange and incomprehensible. As Moore so well says:—

"So closely our whims on our miseries tread,
  That the laugh is awaked ere the tear can be dried;
And as fast as the rain-drop of pity is shed,
  The goose-plumage of folly can turn it aside."

As a race they possess most of the elements of happiness. In better circumstances they would probably be the happiest people on the face of the earth.

The attempts of the average Anglo-Saxon to reproduce the Irish dialect in writing, and the Irish brogue in conversation, jar terribly on the nerves of Irishmen. He seems to think that all he has to do to render the Irish dialect or brogue in perfection is to turn the long "e" sounds into broad "a" —to say or write *kape* for "keep"; *praste* for "priest"; *swape* for "sweep"; *belave* for "believe"; *say* for "see." The Irish peasantry never pronounce these words in that fashion. It is another of the English delusions about Ireland. The Irish never err in the pronunciation of the "ee" and "ie" sounds in such words as "street," "indeed," "believe," and "priest." This statement will, no doubt, astonish many English people, but it is nevertheless the fact.

What the Irish peasantry stumble over in pronunciation are the "ea" and "ei" sounds—saying *lave* for "leave"; *nate and complate* for "neat and complete"; *resate* for "receipt"; and also over "e"—saying *plinty* for "plenty"; *gintlemin* for "gentlemen"; and *twinty* for "twenty." They give a double syllabic rendering to such words as "harm," "arm," "helm"; pronouncing them *harum, arum,* and *helum.* "D" and "t" are also incorrectly pronounced, sometimes, by the Irish peasantry. They sound the "d" correctly in the positive degree of such words as "proud," "loud," "broad"; but in the comparative degree of these words they thicken the "d" by an aspiration, and pronounce them as if written with a "dh"—thus, *proudher, loudher, broadher.* They also say *matther* for "matter"; *butther* for "butter"; *thrash* for "trash"; *scoundthrel* for "scoundrel." In his native Celtic the Irishman trills his "r's"; and when he has to pronounce "r" in an English word, he naturally trills it also. He says *warr* for "war," and *starr* for "star." This, then, is a full list of Irish mistakes in the pronunciation of English. It is not a long list. It should be borne in mind by any Englishman who attempts to convey the Irish dialect into print. But he must not forget that even a complete mastery of this list will not give him the Irish idiom, the Irish turn of phrase, or the Irish habit of mind, the lack of which make the Irish characters in fiction written by Anglo-Saxon writers so unconvincing to Irish readers.

Another English delusion is that the "brogue" is but another name for these peculiarities of Irish pronunciation. It is nothing of the sort. The brogue is an accent, an intonation — mellifluous saucy, leisurely—an index, in fact, of the Irish character—and to convey it in print is beyond the power of man. It has certain peculiarities of inflection and emphasis which cannot be represented by written words, even when the pen is in the hands of an Irishman. It is the softest, the mellowest and most musical thing in the way of accents outside Paradise — and perhaps inside, for all we know. No Englishman who has had the pleasure of a conversation with a pretty and educated Irish girl—a girl who has not tried (as, unhappily, some of them do try and spoil their pretty mouths) to electro-plate it with an affected English accent—will deny this assertion.

The brogue, as it is heard in all parts of Ireland, has certain broad characteristics; but it has varying delicate shades of intonation in the different provinces. A certain celebrated Irish law lord has a broad, full Connaught brogue, of which he is extravagantly proud. "No one, drunk or sober, listening to me, would take me for anything but an Irishman," he has truly said. One day, when he was sitting as Lord Chief Justice of

Ireland at the Four Courts, Dublin, a young junior barrister rose timidly to make his first motion in Court. He spoke in the brogue of the north, between which and the brogue of the south, east, and west, there is a wide distinction. "Sapel," said the Lord Chief Justice, leaning over the bench, to the Clerk of the Court, "who is this young fellah?" "His name is Hammond, my lord," replied the clerk. After a pause, the judge said, "Whaat parrt of the coonthry does he kum from?" "From County Antrim, my lord," was the reply. Then, after another pause, "Did yes iver kum acrosh sich a frightful accint in the whool coorse of yer loife?"

Here is a story of an Irishman who was *not* proud of his brogue, as he ought to have been, and of the just treatment he received. He was a well-known Protestant clergyman in Cork, and he was the possessor of a pronounced specimen of the sing-song brogue of that city. It came to his ears that some of his parishioners were making fun of the intonation of his voice, which greatly angered him. He immediately called upon one of his leading parishioners, and, after complaining of the injustice (!) done him, asked his friend whether, in his opinion, a single trace of the brogue was to be observed in his speech. "Well," his friend answered, "if you wish to deny that you have a brogue, I should advise you to do so in writing."

Every Irishman should be proud of his brogue. Without it he is like a potato without flavour.

I have seen it occasionally asserted that a large part of the reputation of the Irish people for wit and humour is due, not so much to what they say, as to the way they say it—in a word, to their brogue. Undoubtedly, the cadences of the brogue give a decided flavour to the most commonplace sayings; but it needs only a slight and brief acquaintance with the people to show that they are the fortunate possessors also of a genuine spirit of fun and drollery.

Chapter V

"BULLS" FROM IRISH PASTURES

"Has the traditional capacity of the Irish for making 'bulls' become impaired?" This was one of the questions to which I set myself to find an answer during a recent visit to Ireland. The Irish people, in spite of their distresses, have probably done more than all the other English-speaking races to keep the great Anglo-Saxon world merry; and it might well be regarded as an international misfortune indeed were the native wit and humour of Ireland, and, above all, that laughable confusion of thought, that delightful contradiction of meaning—commonly called a "bull"—to show any signs of decay. But I was not two hours in Ireland when I found, to my delight, that that droll mental characteristic of the Irish people, which has contributed so much to the gaiety of nations, still flourishes in undiminished vigour and freshness. I visited a hairdresser's shop in Kingstown, to have a shampoo after the night's run from London. As I was leaving the man tried to induce me to buy a bottle of hair-wash. "What sort of stuff is it?" I asked. "Oh, it's grand stuff," he replied. "It's a sort of *multum in parvo*—the less you take of it the better"! Of course, what the hairdresser meant to convey was that the use of a little of the stuff was as efficacious as a large quantity.

"Bulls" of this species are mainly due to the fact that the people are in such a hurry to express themselves that they do not give themselves time to weigh the meaning of the words they use. Two farmers were sitting on the promenade at Bray, the well-known Wicklow seaside resort. A lady of meagre proportions passed by. "Did you ever see so thin a woman as that before?" remarked one of the farmers. "Thin!" said the other; "I seen a woman down in Wexford as thin as two of her put together!" As a friend and I were walking one day over the Wicklow Mountains we met a "character," or a person well known for some reason—fondness for drink, for instance —in the district. "Well, Mick," said my friend, "I've heard some queer stories about your doings lately." "Och, don't believe thim, surr," replied Mick. "Sure half the lies tould about me by the naybours isn't thrue!"

Celtic fancy has been well described as a "reaction against the despotism of fact." The definition was recalled to my mind by several stories

I heard, and particularly by this one of an amusing miscalculation by a tramp. Two labourers set out from Wexford to walk to Dublin. By the time they reached Bray they were very much tired with their journey, and the more so when they were told they were still twelve miles from Dublin. "Be me sowl," said one, after a little thought, "sure it's but six miles apiece; let us walk on!" During a discussion at a meeting of the Trinity College Historical Society upon the slight consideration attached to life by uncivilized nations, a speaker mentioned the extraordinary circumstance that in China if a man were condemned to death he could easily hire another to die for him; "and," the debater went on, "I believe many poor fellows get their living by acting as substitutes in that way"!

A curious peculiarity of the Irish nature is the wide limits to which relationship is extended. "Do you know Pat Meehan?" a peasant was asked. "Of course I do," was the answer. "Why, he's a near relation of mine. He wance proposed for me sisther Kate." When faction-fighting was rife in Ireland it was a man's interest to "incrase his followin'" by extending the number of his relations by every possible device. Happily faction-fighting is dead in Ireland, and a man has no need now to have behind him a long line, not of "ancestors," as Sir Boyle Roche would say, but of "relations," as was imperatively necessary when the "bhoys" were accustomed to "hould dishcussions with sticks" at every fair. It is after he is dead that his relations "come in handy" to the Irishman. They give him a "grand buryin'." "Well, Mary," said a friend of mine to a domestic who had been attending a "buryin'," "had Mat Maloney a good funeral?" "Oh, he had a grate wan, sir," said Mary. "An' why wouldn't he? Wasn't he related to the whole barony? Faith, it reminded me of a Land Lague meetin'." A child went crying to its mother, and reported that it had swallowed a button. "Well, well, look at that now," cried the woman. "Begor! I suppose the next thing you'll do is to swallow a buttonhole"! This story reminds me of the graphic description given by a beggarman of his tattered coat. "Faith, yer honner, it's nothin' but a parcel of holes sewn together."

It often seems in Ireland as if words are not quick enough, or that they form too cumbersome a vehicle, for the rapid and rushing thoughts of these active-minded peasantry. A laughable instance of this occurred during a recent visitation by Dr. Walsh, the Roman Catholic Archbishop of Dublin, to a remote parish in his archdiocese, the story of which I was told by a priest. An old woman hobbled up to his Grace as he was passing through the village, and exclaimed: "Wisha, now that I've seen your Lordship, ye may die, and the Lord be praised!" It was, needless to say, her own death the old lady desired, after the great privilege of having seen a live Archbishop. The same clergyman told me that he has a parishioner who is very addicted to drink. Meeting the man one day when, as the people say, "he had a drop in," the priest insisted that he should take the pledge, for it was the only protection against the temptations of the public-house. "You've never seen a teetotaler drunk, Tom," said the priest. "Ah, your riverence," replied Tom, "I've seen many a man drunk, but I couldn't tell for the life o' me whether they wor teetotalers or not"! Dr. Murray, who was professor of moral theology in Maynooth College, was preaching one Sunday to a crowded congregation in Marlborough Street Church, Dublin. Approaching the end of his discourse, he said, "One word more and I have done." "Oh, me darlint pracher!" exclaimed an old woman, throwing up her hands, "that you may niver be done."

An Irishman got out of a train at a railway station for refreshments, but unfortunately the bell rang and the train went off before he had finished his drink. Running along the platform after the train, he shouted, "Hould on, there;

hould on. You've got a passenger aboord that's left behind!" A poor woman who had a son of whom she was very proud unintentionally paid him a very bad compliment. Speaking of the boy to the priest, she said, "There isn't in the barony, yer riverence, a cleverer lad nor Tom. Look at thim, yer riverence," pointing to two small chairs in the cabin; "he made thim out of his own head; and faix he has enough of wood left to make me a big arm-chair"! But despite the many examples of "things which should have been otherwise expressed" that one meets with in Ireland, like the foregoing, the people have often an apparently blundering way of saying things which really cannot be so forcibly or so clearly expressed as by a "bull." A poor woman was advised by a charitable lady to avail herself of a free distribution of soup. "Do you call that stuff soup?" she cried. "Why, ye only get a quart of wather and boil it down to a pint to make it sthrong"! A more contemptuous description of the stuff could hardly be imagined. Here is another amusing "bull." A restive pony which was being ridden by a peasant along a country road got into a wayside ditch. The animal, in attempting to scramble out again, had its leg entangled in the stirrup. "What are yez up to now, ye ould devil?" exclaimed the peasant. "Faith if ye're thinking of getting up here it's time for me to get down"!

I picked up two delicious literary curiosities during my stay in Ireland. The following notice was posted in a pleasure-boat belonging to a steamship company on the Suir: "The chairs in the cabin are for the ladies. Gentlemen are requested not to make use of them till the ladies are seated." The time I was in the country was just after the visit of the Duke and Duchess of York. I clipped the following delicious advertisement from a Kingstown paper: "James O'Mahony, Wine and Spirit Merchant, Kingstown, has still on hands a small quantity of the whiskey which was drunk by the Duke of York while in Dublin."

The origin of the word "bull," as the definition of a confused utterance, or an unconscious expression of an incongruity of ideas, is doubtful. Some philologists say it comes from the French *boule*—"fraud"; and others that it is derived from the Icelandic *bull*—"nonsense." But a more interesting point is when the Irish people first became noted for the making of "bulls." The idea that there exists among the people of Ireland an innate and irresistible propensity to blunder in speech and in action certainly prevailed in "the spacious days of Elizabeth," for in some of the comedies and dramas of that age are to be found specimens of that particular Irishman of whom it has been said, "He never opens his mouth without putting his foot in it"!

Joe Miller's Jest Book is a work widely known by repute, but few, I think, are informed of its contents. I looked up the first edition of the book, which was published in London so far back as 1739, in order to see how Ireland was represented in this, the first book of British jokes and witticisms. The full title of the original edition runs, *Joe Miller's Jests; or, the Wit's "Vade-Mecum," being a collection of the most brilliant Jests, the politest Repartees, the most elegant "Bons Mots," and the most pleasant Short Stories in the English Language.* The jokes and anecdotes, 247 in number, were those current in the coffee-houses and taverns of London early in the eighteenth century. They were collected by Mottley, a dramatist, and fathered upon Joe Miller, a popular comic actor of the day.

In the collection are about six Irish stories. Here is one: "An Irish lawyer of the Temple having occasion to go out to dinner left these directions written and put in the key-hole of his chamber door: 'I am gone to the Elephant and Castle, where you shall find me, and if you can't read this note carry it down to the stationer's. He will read it for you.'" This story may be met with in newspapers and journals even now, at the end of the nineteenth century, as a fresh example of an Irish bull. A better anecdote, and one with a greater air of probability, is the following, which is given as a specimen of ready Irish wit: "A lieutenant-colonel to one of the Irish regiments in the French service being despatched by the Duke of Berwick from Fort Kehl to the King of France with a complaint relating to some irregularities that had happened to the regiment, His Majesty with some emotion of mind told him, 'that the Irish troops gave him more uneasiness than all his Forces besides.' 'Sir,' says the officer, 'all your enemies make the same complaint.'"

Ten years after the appearance of *Joe Miller's Jests*, when the book, which was an undoubted success, had run through several editions, there appeared in London a work devoted exclusively to Irish anecdotes. Its title is *The Irish Miscellany; or, Teagueland Jests: being a compleat collection of the most Profound Puns, Learned Bulls, Elaborate Quibbles, Amorous Letters, Sublime Poetry, and wise sayings of the Natives of Teagueland. Collected by Mac O Bonniclabbers of Drogheda, Knight of the Mendicant Order*. The attempts in the book to render the Irish dialect are execrable; but no doubt they represent the notions which prevailed in regard to it in London at that time. The author—the supposed " Mac O Bonniclabbers "—says that he left Ireland for London in search of employment. He could find no work, and in despair was about to hang himself, when he met a man who said to him :—

"If thou canst furnish me with some good current Bulls, thou shalt have ready money for them." "Noow, de Dee'l tauke dee, dear Joy," I did shay to him, "dou hasht mauke me dede agen, be me shoul, for de Armish did mauke Plundar upon mine Fader; and did tauke avay all hish Bullsh, Cowesh, and Horshes, too, before dat I vash born indede. And noow, if dat be aull I vill onsh moure tauke hanging into me Conshideration, indede, and sho fare dee vell, dear Joy." "But stay," he did shay to me agen, "I do not mean Horn'd Beasts, my friend, we Citizens have enou of this sort of Cattle; I say, I mean a sort of comical Jokes, called Bulls, that are a preposterous kind of speaking, when you return my meaning as by mistake. In short I do not mean the Bull *for* the mouth, but the Bull *of* the mouth; and such as these and any other pleasant stories for diversion are the market I would be at." "Enoow! enoow! dear Joy," I did shay, "I doe undershtand dee indade, it ish shome shtories consharning me shelfe, and Bryan, and haf a doshen more of ush. Be me shoul, I can tall dee abondaush indede. And if dee vilt be sho shivil to mauke paymensh of shom monysh I vill tall dee sho many ash a vhole drove at dish time indede. And vhen vee doo meet agen, vee vill hauve de toddar Bout, be me Broguesh, in fait now."

All the stories in the book are palpable inventions; and there is very little humour to relieve their senile buffoonery. Here is one of the few anecdotes with a faint glimmer of humour in them :—

"Bryan having hurted one of his Legs, that it was much swollen, and his Master having occasion to send him a considerable Journey into the Country, Bryan went to the Shoemaker, directing him to make one of his Boots larger than the other. When the Boots were brought home, and to be put on, Bryan fell into a great passion with the Shoemaker, swearing at him—' Be de shoul of mine Fader aund me Graundfader, let a toushand Deevilsh pull me to Peeshes, if dou beesht not de greatesht Fool hat ever wash borne. Vaat de Deevil, cansh dee not undershtan vaat ish sho plain shaid to dee? I did bad dee mauke one of me Botosh biggar dan de toddar; and de shimpleton have mauke one lesher dan de toddar. Preddee, dear Joy, dee maisht tauke dem home vid dy none shelfe again indede, day vill not be upon Sharvish for me, la!'"

The popular notion that the Irish people

habitually blunder in their speech is, therefore, of a very ancient date. Of course there is a good deal of foundation, as I have already shown, for an opinion so old and so wide-spread; but, unfortunately, this racy and amusing national characteristic has suffered through having every stupid and confused utterance—the dull inventions of clumsy wits—ascribed to an Irishman. The manufactured "bull" is easily detected by its silliness and its vile caricature of the Irish dialect. But why is it that of all the English-speaking peoples the Irish are undoubtedly most prone to the making of "bulls"? What is the secret of that curious national characteristic? Maria Edgeworth, in the *Essay on Irish Bulls*, published in 1803, advances this explanation: "English is not the mother tongue of the natives of Ireland; to them it is a foreign language: and consequently it is scarcely within the limits of probability that they should avoid making blunders both in speaking and writing." The force of this argument has, perhaps, been weakened by the spread of education and a knowledge of the English language in Ireland since the days of Maria Edgeworth, when Irish was almost universally spoken by the peasantry, and was the vehicle of their every-day communication with each other. But even to-day the Irish peasant, though he may have little or no Irish, uses many Celtic idioms in an English dress, and moulds his thoughts in a Celtic form. A "bull" is not evidence of stupidity; quite the contrary. Mental confusion is, of course, in every case the source of its origin, but that mental confusion often arises from rapidity of thought—from a plethora of ideas which, in the course of expression, get mixed up and confused in an odd and ludicrous fashion, like objects in a dissolving view. "Bulls," to put it briefly, more often spring from mental quickness than from mental sluggishness.

An Irish peasant was once asked whether he knew what an Irish "bull" was. "To be shure I do," he replied. "If you was dhrivin' along a high road and you seen three cows lyin' down in a field and wan ov thim's standin' up—that wan is an Irish bull." The Yorkshire and Lancashire Agricultural Society fell into a somewhat similar error on the appearance of Miss Edgeworth's essay on Irish "Bulls." Several copies of the work were ordered for the use of members of the society, who were mortified to find that the bulls were mere creatures of the brain, and not, as they had expected, robust animals pastured on the rich grazing lands of Meath and Limerick. But what is a "bull"? Many definitions have been attempted, but the best, probably, is that of Sydney Smith. Writing of the difference between wit and "bulls," he says: "Wit discovers real relations that are not apparent; 'bulls' admit apparent relations that are not real. The pleasure arising from wit proceeds from our surprise at suddenly discovering two things to be similar in which we suspected no similarity. The pleasure arising from 'bulls' proceeds from our discovering two things to be dissimilar in which a resemblance might have been suspected." That a "bull" and nonsense are not the same thing he clearly establishes. "If," he writes, "a man were to say he would ride to London upon a cocked hat, it would not be a 'bull'—it would be nonsense." Again he writes: "The stronger the apparent connection and the more complete the real disconnection of the ideas, the greater the surprise and the better the 'bull.' The less apparent and the more complete the relations established by wit, the higher gratification does it afford."

The propensity of the Irish people to make "bulls" is admittedly a deep-rooted national characteristic, and it will probably be one of their mental attributes to the end of time, or until the race is radically transformed,—a consummation *not* to be wished for, indeed. This gift—for there is really something to be proud of in its possession—is not, as is commonly supposed in England, confined to the lower, or perhaps it would be better to say the uneducated, classes.

Even learned and astute persons often inadvertently tumble into these colloquial pitfalls. When Sir Richard Steele, who was born in Ireland, was asked by an English friend how it was that his countrymen were so addicted to the making of "bulls," he replied: "It must be something in the atmosphere of the country. Probably if an Englishman were a native of Ireland he would do the same." This explanation is not altogether free from the fine flavour of Hibernianism. But at any rate, educated Irishmen and Irishmen who have lived most of their lives outside their native land make "bulls" just as readily as illiterate Irishmen who have never gone outside the four corners of their island. There was recently published in an Irish newspaper an extract from a letter written by an old Indian official of Irish birth, defending India against the charge of general unhealthiness. "The way it is," he wrote, "is that a lot of young officials and military officers come out here, and they eat and they drink, and they drink and they eat, and they die; and then they write home to their friends saying it was the climate that did it." The unhealthiness of India was also the subject of discussion at a Dublin dinner-table. "I think this will be admitted—that vast numbers die there," said one. "Very true," said another; "but if you tell me of any country where the people don't die, I will go and end my days there." A gentleman, speaking of a friend's wife, regretted that she had no children. "Ah," said an Irish doctor who was in the company, "to have no children is a great misfortune; but I have noticed that it is hereditary in some families." An Irish landlord, passing through a village, said to the local butcher, "Well, Jim, how's trade?" "Bad, yer honner," said Jim. "The people are so few and so poor here that it's hard pushed I am to dispose of a carcase before it gets tainted." "Why not kill half a cow at a time?" suggested the squire.

In a description of an abnormal shower of rain which appeared in an Irish newspaper, the following rare specimen occurred: "The heavy drops of rain varied in size from a shilling to eighteenpence." At the Limerick Police Court recently, a man who was known to the police as an habitual drunkard was brought up on the old charge. "Ten shillings, or a fortnight," said the magistrate. "Shure, yer honner, I've only two shillings in the world," pleaded the man in the dock. "Well, sir," said the magistrate, "you must go to gaol. If you hadn't got drunk with your money you'd be able to pay the fine." An Irish clergyman, at the end of a sermon on Grace, said: "Ah, my brethren, if there remains one spark of grace, water it, water it." Having been in the habit of comparing grace to a tender plant, he had got his illustrations "mixed." Thus, very often, amusing examples of "bulls" come tripping from the hasty tongues, and even from the leisurely pens, of educated people. In a recent annual report of a benevolent society having its headquarters in Dublin, the following delightful sentence occurs: "Notwithstanding the large amount paid by the Society for medical attendance and medicine, very few deaths occurred during the year." A Cork newspaper published a report of an open-air political meeting, in which this paragraph appeared: "Mr. M. A. Brennan next spoke at much length in his usual happy style, but from the distance we were wholly unable to catch the purport of his remarks." Even the Commissioners of National Education in Ireland are occasionally subject to this strange, but laughable, confusion of thought and utterance In a Parliamentary Blue-book, containing the annual report of the Commissioners of National Education, and signed by these august personages, the following tit-bit may be read: "The female teachers were instructed in plain cooking. They had, in fact, to go through the process of cooking themselves in turn." At a meeting of a company in Cork dissatisfaction was expressed with the management of affairs by the board. The chairman, in reply, said: "Perhaps you think that in our board half do the work and the other half do nothing. As a matter of fact, gentlemen, the reverse is the case."

But it is, as I have said, amongst the simple and unlettered peasantry, as a class, that the making of "bulls" more widely prevails. A country-woman walking through the streets of Limerick caught sight of a small coffin displayed as a gruesome trade sign in an undertaker's shop window. "Oh, glory be to God!" she exclaimed, "is it possible that coffin can be intinded for any livin' crature?" The owner of a valuable horse was very indignant with his stable-boy for having allowed the animal, which he had taken out for a morning trot, to take head. "The divil a bit o' me could sthop him, sir, for I had no spurs," was the boy's strange excuse. An amusing story was told me by a friend who is a dispensary doctor in a union in the South of Ireland. One night he was awakened by a rapping at the front door of his residence, and going to the window, saw a labouring man below. "What's the matter, my good fellow?" he said. "'Tis me ould mother that's tuck bad, docther," replied the man. "Have you been long here?" asked the doctor. "I have thin, yer honner." "And why on earth didn't you ring the night bell?" "Sure, I was afraid I'd disthurb yer honner," was the man's perfectly sincere reply. No doubt, with the Irish peasant's desire to make himself as little troublesome as possible to his betters, from whom he has to ask a service, the man had a confused idea that rapping at the door would disturb the doctor less than ringing the night-bell.

A person has only to mix with an Irish crowd to have his ears tickled with many laughable examples of confusion of thought or expression. As the Duke and Duchess of York were leaving Dublin, August, 1897, amid the cheers of an enthusiastic crowd, an old woman was heard to remark, "Glory be to God! isn't it the fine reception they are gettin' goin' away." The celebration of the Tercentenary of Dublin University in 1892 attracted a large number of graduates of the University and other visitors to Dublin. Two labourers, who were among the spectators of the rejoicings in the grounds of Trinity College, expressed their feelings as follows: "Well, Tim," said one, "thim tarcintinaries does a dale for the thrade of Dublin, and no misthake." "Oh, faix they do," replied the other, "and whin, with the blessin' of God, we get Home Rule, shure we can have as many of thim as we plase." "Mick," a huntsman, well known on the fields of Kildare, rode a young, restive horse at a meet. On returning he was asked by the Master how he had fared. "Faith," he replied, "be the time we wor on the crest of the ridge the baste was quite paceable, and at the end of the run a child might have milked him." An old woman, who was hurt by the spectacle of a man pulling a young calf roughly along the road, exclaimed: "Oh, you bla'guard, that's no way to thrate a fellow-crather!" A young lady of my acquaintance who was urging the wife of an agricultural labourer to send her children to school, received the following reply: "Shure, I'd do anythin' for such a sweet, gintlemanly lady as yourself." "Have you any near relatives, Norah?" asked a mistress in the South of Ireland of her servant. "Only an aunt, ma'am," was the reply, "and she isn't what you would call near, for it's in Ulshter she lives, ma'am."

On a certain large estate in county Waterford it was the custom to pay the labourers fortnightly, but the labourers, thinking that weekly payments would be more convenient, decided to send a delegate to headquarters to state their case. Tom Blake, the man selected, having obtained an audience with the land agent at the office, the following conversation took place: "Well, Tom, what can we do for you this morning?" "If you plase, sur," said Tom, "it's me desire, and it is also ivery other man's desire, that we resave our fortnight's pay ivery week." A sergeant was drilling at Limerick a squad of Militia recruits whose mode of marching in line was decidedly eccentric. At length, utterly exasperated by their irregularity of step, the sergeant bawled out: "Halt! Jist come over here, all of ye, and look at yerselves. It's a fine line ye're keepin', isn't it?" During the absence in London of an Irish peer, whose family estates are in county Clare, the steward received an ostrich's egg from one of his master's friends abroad. The steward wrote at once to the peer informing him of the safe arrival of this valuable present, and thus concluded the letter: "My lord, as your lordship is out of the country, I have got the biggest goose I could find to sit on the egg." A fishing smack sailing in Dublin Bay in the teeth of the wind tacked so frequently that an observer remarked: "Begor, for ivery mile that man travels, he travels three!" The Irish peasants are very proud of the fact that Irish miles are superior in length to English miles, for it takes fourteen of the latter to make eleven of the former, and should a visitor grumble about the condition of the highways he will be told that, after all, he has nothing to complain about; and that what he loses in one way is made up for him in another. "That's all very well," said a native to a stranger, who expressed an adverse opinion on the roads, "but if the quality is infarior, we give a good measure of it anyhow." Another visitor complained of the narrowness of the roads "Well, what ye lose in the breadth you gain in the length," replied his driver. When it was proposed some years ago to adopt the English measure of miles, a great outcry was raised against it. One reason humorously suggested against it was that it would increase the distance between places from five and a half miles to seven miles, or from eleven miles to fourteen miles, so that travellers would have to rise earlier in the morning to perform their journeys!

"Bulls" often originate in a misunderstanding of the meaning of words or terms. A lady asked a widow whether her son was still in the orphanage in Dublin. "Och no, me lady," was the reply. "Shure he's an orphan no longer. He's now workin' at a thrade outside." At an inquest held recently in Galway concerning the death of a child under rather suspicious circumstances, a quack doctor, who attended the child, stated in the course of his evidence that he had given him ipecacuanha. "You might as well have given the Aurora Borealis," said the coroner. Now, there is one thing an Irish peasant will not do, and that is, acknowledge his ignorance of any subject; so the quack doctor returned the prompt reply, "And shure, yer honner, that was the very thing I was goin' to give him next if he hadn't died just thin"! A proposal was once made in the Limerick Corporation to introduce gondolas on the river Shannon, in the expectation that they would prove attractive to tourists. One of the good "City fathers" deprecated, on the ground of expense, the idea of ordering a dozen. "It would be enough," he said, "to get a pair of thim, and let thim breed." A very quaint reason was advanced by a domestic servant for thinking that the house she worked in was in every way desirable. "Are yez in a good place, Mary?" asked one of her friends. "Oh, a mighty foine place, entirely," she replied. "Shure me mistress is so rich that all her flannel petticoats is made of silk"! "Look at that, now!" exclaimed the other in amazement. Here is a "bull" from the nursery. "That's a terrible noise in the nursery, Molly," said the mistress. "What's the matter? Can't you keep the baby quiet?" "Shure, ma'am," replied Molly, "I can't keep him quiet unless I let him make a noise." And, after all, knowing, as we do, the contrariness of babies, Molly was right. Another Irish domestic was told that her master, a clergyman, was going to Larne to preach. "Goin' to larn to prache?" she exclaimed, her knowledge of the geography of her native land being limited. "Faix, he larned to prache long ago." The incapacity of the average Irish mind to rapidly grasp the import of numbers is also the fruitful source of "bulls." A stevedore unloading a ship went to the hatchway and shouted down to the men in the hold, "Now thin, how many of yes is down there?" "Five of us," was the reply. "Thin, half of yes kum up directly," cried the stevedore.

An old officer, walking to his club in Pall Mall, London, stopped to talk to a crossing-sweeper who gave him a military salute as he approached. "You have been in the Service, my man," said the officer. "I have thin, yer honner," replied the sweeper, in a broad Irish brogue. "Have you been in any engagements?" "Shure I was all through the Crimaya War." "Did you get any wounds?" asked the officer. "I was shot through me heart," replied the crossing-sweeper, without the slightest hesitation. "Get along, fellow!" said the officer indignantly, assuming that the sweeper was an impostor. "If you had been shot through the heart you would have been as dead as a doornail." "But shure, sur," said the man, "me heart was in me throat at the time."

An English gentleman travelling through County Wexford came to a ford and hired a boat to take him across. The water being rather more agitated than was agreeable to him, he asked the boatman if any person was ever lost on the passage. "Niver," replied the boatman. "My brother was drownded here last week, but we found him next day." I heard another amusing instance of literal accuracy at the Parnell Commission in 1889. A peasant who was examined in regard to a certain boycotted farm was asked by counsel, "Is the farm vacant now?" "No; it's stocked with a caretaker and two policemin," was the reply. But the most amusing "bull" for which we are indebted to that Commission is the philosophic axiom of the witness who admitted that he ran away on one occasion when a revolver was presented at him. "Better," said he, "to be a coward for five minutes than dead all your lifetime!" At a meeting of a branch of the Agricultural Organization Society, held recently in Tipperary, a speaker said, "I'm a poor workin' farmer, and 'tis with the greatest difficulty I can make the two ends of the candle meet." A delightfully mixed metaphor, truly! The wife of a well-known landlord in Cavan directed the steward of the estate to purchase a sow of a particular size and description at a local fair. On his return he burst into the drawing-room, where the lady was entertaining some guests, proclaiming with a satisfaction he could not suppress, "I've been to the fair, me lady, and I've got a sow exactly of your ladyship's size and description."

The light in which domestic service is regarded by some servants in Ireland is illustrated by an amusing anecdote which was told by a lady in a letter written to a Dublin newspaper some time ago. A young country girl called on her in answer to an advertisement for a general servant. "Have you a reference?" asked the lady. "A riference!" exclaimed the girl, in injured tones. "What do I want that for? Shure, 'tis I've got to live with you, and not you with me"! That letter led to the relation by a second mistress of the story of another laughable "bull." One day her servant answered a knock at the hall door. "Who was it that called?" she asked the maid subsequently. "It was a gintleman, ma'am, lookin' for the wrong house," was the reply. There is a story told in journalistic circles in Dublin of a delightful display of 'cuteness by a farmer who called at one of the newspaper offices to have an advertisement inserted. He was informed that the charges were 6s. for the first insertion, and 2s. 6d. for the second. "Faith, thin," said he, "I'll have it in the second toime." Here are two comical "bulls," due to the Celt's lightning rapidity of thought: "Is it a son or a daughter your sister, Mrs. Healy, has got?" asked a gentleman of one of his tenants whom he met on the road. "The curse of the crows on me, but I don't know whether I'm an uncle or an aunt," was the immediate reply. I was once present at a review of a Militia regiment in the South of Ireland, when the sergeant-major came up and reported to the colonel that all the ammunition was exhausted. "Then sound 'Cease firing'!" roared the commanding officer. At Killarney every visitor hears some laughable stories. Here is one

—new and fresh, I think—which I picked up during my last visit to the glorious lakes. A number of boatmen who were quarrelling about the division of "tips," indulged at the top of their voices in a good deal of profane language, which the marvellous echo repeated verbatim. "Arrah, look at that now for a schandal," said one of the party who was of a pious turn. "Tachin' the poor, harmless echo to curse and sware."

There are "bulls" in action as well as "bulls" in expression. These blunders are really due to mental sluggishness; they are committed by hare-brained individuals, but they have often the saving grace of humour. I remember reading in a speech delivered by Lord Dufferin many years ago a very laughable story of a blunder of this character. On his estate in County Down there was an old historic ruin, formerly a stronghold of the O'Neills, who ruled over that part of Ulster. Anxious that this interesting survival of an historic past should be preserved, on the eve of his departure for India as Viceroy, he summoned his steward, and gave him directions to build a wall around the ruin at a certain distance, in order to keep out trespassers, for the local peasantry if they wanted a stone to repair a gap in a pig-stye or a wall were accustomed to resort to the old castle for the material. That being done, Lord Dufferin set off on his mission to India, feeling secure of the preservation of this ancient monument. On his return home, several years after, he found to his amazement that the old castle had disappeared, and in its place was a circular wall enclosing nothing. Sending for the steward, he demanded to know why his orders had not been carried out. The steward insisted that what he had ordered had been done. "But where is the castle?" asked the Marquis. "The casthle, me lord?" repeated the steward. "That ould thing. Shure, I pulled it down to build the wall wid! Did ye want me to be goin' miles for matherials with the finest stones in Ireland beside me?" In telling the man to build the wall, his lordship had said nothing about the preservation of the castle. The neglect of that little detail made all the difference in the world. At a fire in the town of Longford, a man who had been aroused from sleep by the alarm had only time to slip on his trousers and jump from the window. In his flight and hurry he had unconsciously pulled on the garment wrong side foremost, with an effect which, when he recovered his equilibrium after the jump, excited his profound consternation. "Are you hurt?" asked a bystander. "No," he replied, with a quiver in his voice, "but I'm afraid I'm fatally twisted."

A Dublin optician advertised a pair of spectacles, by the aid of which any person could easily read the finest print. A countryman called at the shop one day to be fitted with a pair. After he had looked hard through the spectacles at the open book which had been set before him he declared that he could not make out the printed page. Another pair of spectacles of a stronger power was placed upon his nose, but the effect was as unsuccessful as before. Further trials with other glasses yielded no better result, until at length the almost distracted shopman passed him a pair with the most powerful lenses he had in his shop. The countryman, quite as impatient as the shopman at having to try so many different pairs of glasses, now glowered at the printed page with all his might. "Can you read the printing now?" inquired the shopman, pretty certain that he had the right pair this time. "Shure not wan bit," was the reply. "Can you read at all?" said the shopman, unable to conceal his vexation any longer. "Read at all, is it?" cried the countryman. "There's not a single word among thim that I can identify the faytures of." "Do you know how to read?" demanded the shopman impatiently. "Out wid ye," exclaimed the countryman, throwing down the spectacles in anger. "If I cud read, what would I be after buyin' a pair o' spectacles for? You chate the people by sayin' that yer glasses wud help thim to read aisily; but it's a big lie! Ah, ye bla'guard;

ye thought I'd buy thim widout tryin' thim on!"

"I've got the betther of that murdherin' railway company now, at any rate," said a farmer who had a grievance against the local railway to a friend. "How is that, Denis?" asked the friend. "Shure, I've taken a return ticket, and I'm not goin' back at all, at all," was the reply. A country gentleman observed his Irish man-servant at the top of a ladder, doing something to the weathercock on the stable turret. "Hallo, Pat!" cried he, "what are you up to now?" "The misthress wants to go for a dhrive," replied Pat, "an' she towld me to put the pony in the dogcart. But, faix, it's blowin' so nasthy an' cowld from the aste, an' she is so purty and delicate, that I thought I'd be after tyin' the bla'guard of a wind round to the so'west with a bit of string, an' keep it there till she had her dhrive and cum home agin." An Irishman, fishing with a rod, in a shower of rain, was observed to keep his line under the arch of a bridge. On being asked the reason, he said: "Och, shure, the fishes will be after crowdin' in there to get out of the wet." A workman, who was repairing the roof of one of the highest buildings in Dublin, lost his footing and fell, but, striking a telegraph line, he managed to grasp it. "Hang on for your life!" shouted a fellow-workman, whilst some of the spectators rushed off to procure a mattress, on which he could drop. He held on for a few seconds, when suddenly, with a cry, " Sthand from undher! " he dropped, and lay senseless in the street. He was brought to an hospital, and on his recovery was asked why he did not hang on longer. " Shure, I was afraid the wire wud brake," he feebly replied.

Chapter VI

IN THE IRISH LAW COURTS

IT is said that an eminent English *litterateur*, who attended the celebrations of the Tercentenary of Trinity College, Dublin, when asked what was the pleasantest and most vivid impression of the Irish capital which he brought away with him, replied, " The good stories I heard from its lawyers at its dinner tables." It is, perhaps, in the Law Courts that the varied phases of the many-sided Irish character are best exhibited ; and what with the traditionary wit, the legal acumen and subtlety of the Bar, and the no less renowned humour of the Bench, small wonder that the Irish lawyers should have an entertaining stock of anecdotes.

The most famous of the Irish judges of the century is Lord Norbury. As John Toler he was Attorney-General in 1798—the year of the Great Rebellion—and for his services in sending to the gallows or transportation the leaders of the United Irishmen, and in abusing and shooting—for, as we have already seen, he was a noted duellist—

the opponents of the Union in Parliament, he was rewarded in 1800 with the Chief Justiceship of the Common Pleas and a peerage as Baron Norbury. On the Bench, as at the Bar and in the Senate, he was noisy, blustering, and bellicose. But he was also a man of a vivacious temperament and a keen sense of humour. "Lord Norbury's Latest Joke" was a standing headline in the Dublin newspapers of the time; and in the Hall of the Four Courts the Court of Common Pleas was easily distinguished by the shouts of laughter which issued through its doors. He bears an evil name as "a hanging judge" even to this day among the peasantry, and so overmastering was his desire to be funny on all occasions that he could not refrain from indulging in a witticism or an epigram even at the expense of the trembling wretch in the dock whom he was consigning, within forty-eight hours, to an ignominious and horrible death.

"I am reminded, my lord," said Harry Dean Grady, a barrister in a trial for murder before Lord Norbury, "of a judge I once heard of who never wept but once, and that was at a theatre." "Some high tragedy, I suppose?" interjected the judge. "Not at all, my lord," continued the barrister; "it was at *The Beggar's Opera*, when they reprieved Macheath." Dining once in the company of John Philpot Curran, he said, "That beef appears tough. Has it been hung?" "No, my lord ; you have not tried it," was Curran's ready and apt reply.

Many stories are in circulation about Lord Norbury. I select three, which are authentic, characteristic, and fresh. A breach of the game laws was in his opinion a very grave crime, and the common juries, who had a natural sympathy with poaching—indeed, it was only quite recently that I heard a distinguished Nationalist member say in the House of Commons, " My sympathies are always with the poachers "—were, besides, so appalled by the severity of his sentences that, as a rule, they declined to convict for such an offence. In one case, in which the charge was clearly proved against the accused, the jury, instead of at once returning a verdict of " Not guilty," made a show of putting their heads together in the box and arriving at some plausible pretext for their verdict. The old judge craftily leaned his head upon his hand, and, as if talking to himself, mumbled aloud in broken sentences, " A poor man with a large family—great temptation—after all, a slight offence —a very slight offence." The jury overheard the ruminations of the judge—as of course Toler intended—and thinking he was relenting in his views in regard to poaching, they came to the conclusion that they might safely venture on a conviction without any very great harm to the prisoner. "Guilty, my lord," said the foreman. " Ten years' transportation!" shouted the judge. It was the last time a poacher was convicted on that circuit.

On another occasion he ordered a man who had been found guilty of an assault on a police constable in Dublin to be whipped on three successive days from Newgate jail to the Tholsel. When the judge had pronounced the sentence the prisoner, with Irish impetuosity, exclaimed, "The divil thank ye, you ould bla'guard! that's all ye can do!" "Hould your tongue, sir!" roared Norbury. "How dare you interrupt the judgment of the Court!" Then he added, "*And back again*"!

Norbury was "fat and scant of breath," and in Court was perpetually puffing and panting. On one occasion he sentenced five prisoners together to death. As he was about to leave the Bench he was reminded by the clerk of the Court that one of the party, a man named Darbey Molony, had not been included in the sentence. The convict was put forward. "My good man," said Norbury, as usual swelling out his pursy cheeks with wind, "I made a mistake about you, and I really must beg your pardon (puff). I should have sentenced you with the others (puff), but in a moment of forgetfulness I omitted your name (puff). Pray excuse me. The sentence of the law is that you, Darbey Molony (puff), be taken hence to prison, and from the prison to the place of execution in forty-eight hours (puff), and there hanged by the neck until you are dead (puff). May the Lord have mercy on your soul, Darbey (puff). That's all, my good man (puff). Turnkey, remove Darbey Molony (puff)." The convict coolly turned round as he was leaving the dock and exclaimed, "Faix, me lord, I can't thank ye for your prayers, for I niver heard of any one that throve after ye prayed for thim." Norbury, who relished a good retort, granted Darbey a reprieve, and on returning to Dublin successfully recommended him for a commutation of punishment.

Lord Norbury remained on the Bench until he was eighty-seven years old. For many years previously, he had been mentally and physically incapable of discharging the duties of a judge, but he scouted every friendly suggestion that he ought to resign. At last a petition for his removal was presented to Parliament. It was proved that on one occasion, when six men were being tried before him for murder, he fell asleep, and counsel for the prosecution requested the foreman of the jury to take notes of the evidence, so that he might inform the judge when he awoke of what had happened during his slumbers. Brougham supported the petition in a powerful speech in the House of Commons, which so incensed Norbury that he swore the only thing which would induce him to resign was that he might be able "to show that Scotch *broom* that what he wanted was an Irish *stick*." Representations were made to him on behalf of the Government that it would be well if he retired from the Bench. He pleaded for time to consult his friends. A month afterwards the Chief Secretary called on him to learn his decision. But if Norbury was a dotard, a good deal of his humour and animal spirits still survived in him. He told the Chief Secretary that Lord Combermere was his most particular friend, and that he had written to him at Calcutta; and also that he had asked the advice of Sir E. Parry, the explorer, who was then upon one of his expeditions to the Polar regions. Another year was thus gained! In 1827 he marched out with the honours of an Earldom. He died in 1831, at the great age of ninety-one years.

The following punning doggerel, attributed to himself, was circulated as his epitaph. It certainly is characteristic of the man :—

> "Oh, he is gone—facetious punster,
> Who with keen jests made wigs with fun stir!
> From Heaven's High Court, a tipstaff sent,
> Calls him to hear his punishment.
> Stand to your bells, ye sextons—ring
> With all your clappers, ding, dong, ding;
> NOR BURY him without honours due,
> For he was himself a *Toler* too!"

Another famous judge of the early years of the century was Chief Baron O'Grady, afterwards Lord

Guillamore. On the last day of the Assizes at Kilkenny a man was tried before him for highway robbery. To the surprise of the Chief Baron, who thought the case clearly proved, the verdict was "Not guilty." The judge turned to the Crown solicitor and said, "Is there any other indictment against this innocent man?" "No, my lord," was the reply. "Then," said the judge, "tell the jailor not to let him loose till I get half an hour's start of him, for I'd rather not meet him on the road."

Mr. Justice Ball, an Irish judge of the middle of the century, was noted for his amusing manifestations of ignorance; but whether they were real or pretended has never been clearly established. I think, though, we may take it for granted that the judge was a rare jokist. He tried a case in which a man was indicted for robbery at the house of a poor widow. The first witness was the young daughter of the widow, who identified the prisoner as the man who had entered the house and smashed her mother's chest. "Do you say that the prisoner at the bar broke your mother's chest?" said the judge, in astonishment. "He did, my lord," answered the girl; "he jumped on it till he smashed it entirely." The judge turned to the Crown counsel and said: "How is this? Why is not the prisoner indicted for murder? If he smashed this poor woman's chest in the way the witness has described, he must surely have killed her." "But, my lord," said the counsel, "it was a wooden chest." Some men were indicted at the Cork Assizes for riot and assault before the same judge. The prisoners had beaten labourers who were drawing turf from a bog belonging to an obnoxious landlord. One of the witnesses said, in the course of his evidence, " As we came near the bog we saw the prisoners fencing along the road." " Eh, what do you say the prisoners were doing ? " asked Mr. Justice Ball. "Fencing, my lord." " With what ? " " Spades and shovels, my lord." The judge, looking amazed, said to the Crown counsel, "Can this be true ? Am I to understand that peasants in this part of the country fence along the roads, using spades and shovels for foils ? " " I can explain it, my lord," said the counsel. " The prisoners were making a ditch, which we call a fence in this part of the country, my lord."

At the Castlebar Assizes in 1858, an action for excessive seizure of goods and chattels under a distress warrant, at the suit of a farmer against the Rev. Theophilus Sumner, D.D., was tried before Mr. Justice Ball. The junior counsel for the plaintiff, in the course of opening the pleadings, said, "There are several counts, my lord, in the summons and plaint, the last of which is for the wrongful conversion of the plaintiff's cow." " Do I hear aright ? " said the judge ; " conversion of the plaintiff's cow ! did you say ? Who effected this marvellous conversion?" "The reverend defendant, my lord," replied the junior counsel. "Wonderful! wonderful!" exclaimed the judge. "Truly has it been said, 'Miracles will never cease.' Will counsel kindly read the count describing how the cow was induced to adopt the Christian faith?" "It isn't that, my lord," said counsel, amid roars of laughter; and from his brief he read, "And also that the defendant converted the plaintiff's cow *to his own use*."

In a case of assault tried before Mr. Justice Ball at Roscommon Assizes, counsel for the prisoner said, "The whole affair rose out of a scrimmage at a wake, me lord." "A scrimmage!" said the judge, as if in profound thought. "I don't remember having seen that word in the books." "A fight, me lord; it all arose out of a general *mêlée* at the wake," explained counsel; but, being weak in his pronunciation of French, he said, "general maley." "What?" again queried the judge. "A general maley, me lord," said counsel. "What!" cried the judge, in astonishment; "do you mean to say that my old friend, General Maley, the foreman of the County Grand Jury, was at this wake kicking up a row?" "Oh, no, me lord," explained counsel; "I meant the French general maley." "What! a French General, a soldier of a neighbouring sovereign in amity with our Queen, committing breaches of the peace, amounting to a felony at a wake? Monstrous! monstrous!" And so the judge would go on, keeping the Court, we may presume, in roars of laughter. But the judge found his match in the late Baron Dowse. In a case tried at Belfast before Mr. Justice Ball, Dowse, who was then at the Bar, appeared for one of the parties. He spoke with a broad northern accent, and therefore "a mill," to which he had to make several references, was pronounced "a mull." "Excuse me," said the judge, "but pray what is 'a mull'?" "What you generally make of a case, my lord," was the ready reply of the irate counsel.

Some years ago there was a Recorder of Dublin named Walker, who was also an amateur farmer, and who prided himself on the abundant crops of early hay which he produced from his acres at Harold's Cross. On entering court one day, late in summer, to discharge his judicial duties at an adjourned sessions, he was greatly annoyed to find that there were upwards of twenty criminal cases to be tried. He wanted to get back to his haymaking; but here was judicial work enough to occupy a week. The first prisoner indicted was an old offender named Branagan, who was charged with stealing the leads from roofs of houses. The recorder had an intimation conveyed to him that if he pleaded guilty his sentence would be light. He accordingly did plead guilty, and was sent to jail for three months. Branagan retired from the dock delighted with having escaped the transportation which he had expected, and as he passed through the room below the dock he told the other prisoners of his good luck. "Only three months!" they exclaimed. "That's gran' news! Faix, the recorder is as mild as milk this mornin'!" They all decided to follow Branagan's example; and as they were rapidly arraigned in turn the same plea of "guilty" was recorded in each case. When the calendar was thus exhausted, the recorder had all the prisoners arranged in the front of the dock, and he thus addressed them: "The sentence of the Court is that you and each of you be transported for seven years. Crier," he added, "adjourn the Court!"

Not even the occupants of the Bench in Ireland are free from that proneness to make "bulls" which is one of the curious mental characteristics of the Irish people. "Are you married?" asked a magistrate in the Dublin police-court of a prisoner who was charged with having committed an unprovoked assault on another man. "No, your worship," replied the man in the dock. "That's a good thing for your wife," said the magistrate. A witness giving evidence in a case tried at the Limerick Assizes used the expression, very common in Ireland, "I said to meself," so frequently that the judge interposed with the remark, "You must not tell us what you said to yourself, unless the prisoner was by. It is not evidence." I heard a judge say to a noisy, voluble witness, "Hold your tongue, sir, and give your evidence quietly and clearly"! In a case of an assault by a husband on a wife, the injured woman was reluctant to prosecute and give her evidence. "I'll lave him to God, me lord," she cried. "Oh, dear, no," said the judge; "it's far too serious a matter for that"! Dublin once boasted of a police magistrate named O'Malley, whose eloquence made him the pride of the *habitués* of his court. "So, me man," he thundered at an old offender, who had often escaped what the magistrate always spoke of as "the butt end of the law," "so you're about to incur the just pinalty of yer manifold malifactions. Justice may purshue the evildoer wid a leaden heel; but she smites"—here the quotation eluded him—"she smites"—then triumphantly—"she smites wid a cast-iron toe"!

Members of the Bar, in all countries, have not infrequently to suffer snubs, rebukes, and sarcasms from the Bench, but in Ireland—as we have seen in the case of Mr. Justice Ball and Mr. Dowse—the judge often comes off only second best. At the close of the last century there was an Irish judge named Robinson, who, in the words of Lord Brougham, was "the author of many stupid, knavish, and scurrilous political pamphlets," for which he had been raised to the Bench. Soon after John Philpot Curran was called to the Bar, he appeared in a case heard before this judge, and, in combating some opinion of counsel on the other side, remarked that he could not find in his law books a single instance in which the principle contended for was established. "That may be, sir," said the judge, "but I suspect your library is very limited." "It is very true, my lord, that, owing to circumstances, my library is rather small," said Curran, in a scathing retort, "but I have prepared myself for this high profession rather by the study of a few good books than by the composition of a great many bad ones"! On another occasion Lord Chancellor Clare, who had a discussion with Curran in court on some legal point, exclaimed sharply, "Oh, if that be law, Mr. Curran, I may burn my law-books." "You had better read them, my lord," was Curran's happy rejoinder. A more good-humoured encounter was that between Chief Baron O'Grady and Charles Kendal Bushe, the eminent lawyer, and subsequently Chief Justice of the King's Bench, at the Kilkenny Assize, which was held in a courthouse abutting on the fair green. While Bushe was addressing the jury a donkey on the green began to bray. "Wait a minute, Mr. Bushe, please," said the judge; "I can't hear two at a time"! Presently, as the judge was summing up, the animal commenced crying again. "Will your lordship speak a little louder," said Bushe; "there is such an echo in the court"!

Lord Morris, the well-known Irish law lord, who, as I have already pointed out, has a racy Irish brogue, was conducting a trial in Coleraine, in which a gentleman sought damages from a veterinary surgeon for having poisoned a valuable horse. The issue depended upon the question how many grains of a certain drug could be safely administered. The dispensary doctor proved that he had often given eight grains to a man, from which it was to be inferred that twelve for a horse was not excessive. "Docthor dear, niver mind yer eight grains, in this matter o' twelve," said the judge. "Becaws we all know that some poisons are accumulative in effect; an' ye may go to the edge o' ruin with impunity. But tell me this: the twelve grains, the twelve, wouldn't they kill the divil himself if he swallowed them?" "I don't know, my lord," said the doctor, pompously drawing himself up. "I never had the honour of prescribing for that patient." "Ah, no, docthor dear, ye niver had; more's the pity. The ould bhoy's alive still."

The great powers of judgment and penetration of Daniel O'Connell were strikingly and dramatically shown in the course of a trial in Dublin as to the validity of an important will. The action was to set aside the will, on the ground that the testator was dead at the time he was said to have put his signature to the document. One of the witnesses to the will asserted over and over again, in cross-examination, when asked by Daniel O'Connell whether the testator was really alive when he was alleged to have written his name, " Yes, there was life in him, sure enough ; oh, I'm sartin sure he had life in him when signing the will." Struck by a sudden inspiration, the lawyer cried out, " Now, sir, by the solemn oath you have taken, and as you shall one day have to answer before God for the truth, the whole truth, and nothing but the truth of your evidence, was not the life you speak of nothing more than a live fly, which was put into the dead man's mouth while his name was being put to the will?" The witness, now scared and trembling, confessed that so it was !

A landlord in the county of Cork diverted so much of the water of a stream from its original channel as to cause loss and inconvenience to a neighbouring farmer, who accordingly brought an action against him for damages. The landlord engaged for his defence an attorney named Fogarty, who had the roseate, purple face of a toper, and was well known for his love for whisky, though, indeed, he could not love it to the extent for which his countenance gave him credit. Daniel O'Connell, who appeared for the injured party, dwelt on the harm which had been done his client through his farm having been deprived of the benefits of the stream. "The stream is running dry," he continued; "so low is it, and so little of it is there, that"—turning to the rubicund attorney—"there is not enough of it to make grog for Fogarty"!

As this story shows, Irish lawyers of days gone by indulged extravagantly in personalities. And they were often made to suffer for it from the pistol or the horsewhip of the man assailed. At the Tipperary Assizes Curran referred in scathing terms to a local land-agent. Two days after, as the lawyer was lying in bed in his house in Dublin, his servant told him that a gentleman was waiting downstairs to see him; but before he could reply the gentleman—travel-stained, highly irate, and of herculean proportions—rushed into the bedroom and cried, "Sir, I'm the gintleman you insulted in the courthouse at Clonmel in the presence of the whole county; and I'm here to thrash you soundly!" as he excitedly waved a horsewhip over the recumbent lawyer. "What!" said Curran, "you call yourself a gentleman, and yet you mean to strike a man when he is lying down?" "No, bedad," said the visitor, "I'll just wait till ye get out of bed, and thin I'll give it to ye, hot and heavy." "If that's the case," said the lawyer, quite coolly, "I'll lie here all day;" and he turned over on his other side. The visitor was so tickled by this humorous announcement that he dropped his horsewhip and dismissed his anger in a roar of laughter, in which Curran heartily joined. And he who had come to horsewhip remained to dine.

The members of the Irish Bar have also a well-deserved reputation for wit. Baron Dowse, when a counsel, was asked by a judge, "For whom are you concerned in this action, Mr. Dowse?" "I am *concerned*, my lord, for the plaintiff; but I am *engaged* for the defendant," was the ready reply of counsel. The "cocksuredness" with which experts in handwriting give their evidence was the subject of a striking rebuff in an Irish court some years ago. An expert having emphatically sworn that a document was a forgery, Mr. Sergeant Armstrong, a celebrated leader of the Irish Bar in the Seventies, rose to cross-examine. He looked at the witness for a second or two, and then asked this question, "What about the dog?" The witness seemed at a loss to understand the query, which was repeated three times by the lawyer, with ever-increasing loudness of tone. At last the witness said, "I do not understand you, sir. Pray be more explicit. What dog?" "What dog!" rejoined the sergeant; "of course I refer to the dog that Baron Dowse told a jury he would not hang on your evidence!"

Some years ago the assistant-barrister of the county of Clare was a Mr. William Major, between whom and a solicitor practising in his courts there was no love lost. A farmer processed a neighbour for the loss of a sheep which had been killed by the defendant's dog. The solicitor, who appeared for the plaintiff, thus examined his client—" What sort is the dog that killed your sheep—is he a bulldog or a terrier?" "He's a brown terrier, sur." "Is he wicked?" "Troth, he is, sur, wicked and bad enough." "He is a snarling cur, I suppose, and shows his teeth where he cannot bite?" "You may say that, sur." "What is the dog's name?" the solicitor then asked; but the witness scratched his head and hesitated to reply. "Don't be delaying the Court, sir," said the assistant-barrister, "or I protest I'll dismiss your case." "Oh, thin, as I must tell it," said the witness, "shure he's a namesake of yer own, yer honner, for his name is Major!" This palpable hit convulsed the Court—save the judge, of course—with laughter.

Occasionally there are most amusing mixtures of metaphors by counsel in their addresses to juries. In one case where a small farmer brought an action against a neighbour for alleged malversation of three bullocks, counsel for the plaintiff concluded his speech by saying, "Gentlemen of the jury, it will be for you to say whether the defendant shall be allowed to come into court with unblushing footsteps, with the cloak of hypocrisy in his mouth, and draw three bullocks out of my client's pockets with impunity"! In another case counsel said, "My client acted boldly. He saw the storm brewing in the distance; but he was not dismayed. He took the bull by the horns, and he had him indicted for perjury"!

Sometimes very funny incidents occur in court. A man who was being tried for murder at the Clare Assizes many years ago was defended by Peter Burrowes, who was noted for his absent-mindedness. He it was who was found one morning standing by the fire with an egg in his hand and his watch in the saucepan! Burrowes, on the occasion of this trial, happened to have a bad cough, which he sought to soften by the occasional use of a lozenge. The bullet which killed the murdered man was produced, and was given to the barrister, who urged that it could not fit the bore of the gun belonging to the prisoner, with which the Crown contended the fatal shot had been fired. Counsel held the bullet in one hand and a lozenge in the other; but in the ardour of his cross-examination of a police officer he forgot which was which, and, instead of the lozenge, swallowed the bullet! The inveterate tendency of an Irishman to make a joke on all occasions got the better even of the solemn judge, for, with a merry twinkle in his eye, his lordship remarked, "The only thing that can be done, in the circumstances, is to administer a charge of powder to counsel!"

Chapter VII

FROM THE WITNESS TABLE AND THE DOCK

THE simplicity of the Irish peasant—with all his natural shrewdness and brightness he is often, indeed, a very simple being—is the source of many quaint and whimsical replies to questions or sayings from the witness table and the dock in the Irish Law Courts. In Ireland witnesses stand, not in a box (as in England), but on a table beneath the Bench. There was recently tried at Cork a case of assault, in which a man had been beaten while he lay asleep. His evidence was that he had been suddenly aroused by a blow on the head. "And how did you find yourself then?" asked the counsel. "Fasht asleep, sur," was the reply. "Take the book in your right hand," said the clerk of the Court, in the usual phrase, to a man on his appearance on the witness table. The witness, however, put forth his left hand. "I said your right hand," said the clerk testily. "Plase, yer honner," said the witness, still proffering his left hand, "shure I'm left-handed." "Where did you receive the blow?" asked counsel of the prosecutor in an assault case. "Just close to me own door, sur," was the reply. That answer may be classed as a "bull." The following instance, certainly, is an undoubted example of confusion of thought and expression. In the case of a quarrel between husband and wife which I heard tried in one of the Dublin police-courts the husband said, "I couldn't get home, yer honner, for she locked me in." "In?" said the magistrate; "out, you mean." "No, yer honner; *in* the street, I mane. I couldn't get *out*"! said the husband.

The misunderstanding of words and terms is also fruitful of incidents of an amusing character. "He also called me out of me name," said the prosecuting witness in a case of assault by a man on a woman. "That's a civil action, ma'am," said the magistrate, trying to preserve the relevancy of the witness's evidence. "Musha, thin, if you call that a civil action 'tis you must be the bad bla'guard yerself!" cried the witness indignantly. To be "killed" in Ireland does not always mean to be deprived of life. If a peasant gets a beating he describes it as being "kilt entirely." An old man who had been assaulted was being examined at a recent trial at Sligo. "And were you stunned when you were knocked down?" asked a young and inexperienced barrister who was conducting the prosecution. "Was I what, yer honner?" asked the witness. "Stunned," repeated the barrister. "Shure, I don't know what yez mane, sur," said the witness. "Were you rendered insensible?" explained the barrister. "Shure, what's insinsible, at all, at all?" asked the perplexed witness, in bewildered tones. "I'm afraid I can't get any good of this stupid witness, my lord," said counsel. 'Let me try him," said the judge. "Come, my good man, did they kill you now?" The face of the witness brightened up, and he exclaimed, "Faix, that they did entirely, me lord." Patrick Flanigan was a witness in a case tried at the Galway Assizes. As the perverseness of fate compelled him to give evidence against his particular friend, the prisoner, he was, no doubt intentionally, not very clear in his statements; and his thickness of utterance, caused by the recent loss of some of his front teeth, increased his unintelligibility. He was frequently called upon to repeat his answers, which were manifestly made reluctantly; and between these constant requests, his concern for his friend in the dock, and the long, bewildering words with which the air of the court seemed to Pat to be filled, his anger rose, and his confusion and incoherency steadily increased. "Don't prevaricate, sir," cried the judge, as the witness returned an amazingly unintelligible answer to a question addressed to him by counsel. "Prewaricate is it!" exclaimed Pat. "I'm thinkin', me lord, it's yourself wouldn't be able to help prewaricatin', if three or four of yer lordship's front teeth wor knocked out of yer head"!

A novel term of reproach was discovered on the hearing of a summons for abusive language in one of the Dublin police-courts. The complainant, a fish woman from the neighbouring classic district of Pill Lane, deposed, "The difindant went down forenenst the whole world at the corner of Capel Street and called me 'a . . . ould excommunicated gasometer'"! In a case of assault by a husband on a wife, the solicitor for the complainant said to her, "And now, Mrs. Sullivan will you be kind enough to tell the Court whether your husband was in the habit of striking you with impunity?" "With what, sur?" "With impunity." "Faith he was, sur, now and thin," replied the witness, "but he struck me oftener with his fisht."

As an example of "a remark that should be put differently," the following anecdote is amusing: A labourer was summoned to Tramore Petty Sessions for the nonpayment of the rent of his cottage. Said he, "Yer worship, sixpince a week is too much rint entirely for the little cabin. Come down, yer honner, and go into it yerself, and if an ass can turn in it I'll be contint to pay the full sixpince a week." The politeness of the Irish peasant is proverbial. Here is a curious illustration of it. At the Roscommon Assizes a man was indicted for robbery. An old peasant woman was the prosecutrix. On being asked the usual question, whether she saw in court the man who entered her cabin and stole her things, she turned round, and, pointing to the prisoner in the dock, said politely, "There's the very gintleman."

The exaggeration to which the peasant is prone is illustrated by the following story: Peter Meehan, of Newcastle West, County Limerick, was summoned for allowing his pig to stray on the public road. His defence was that the perverse animal could not be kept in confinement. "Have you a gate to your haggard?" asked the magistrate. "I have, of coorse, sur; but the pig aisly opens it," replied Peter. "Have you a latch to the gate?" "To be shure I have, sur; but he opens that, too." "I suppose," said the magistrate, "he also closes the gate after him;" and Peter, who did not detect the sarcastic note in his worship's voice, answered readily, "Shure, that's the worst of the desaver. He always closes the gate after him, so that we niver can tell whin he's out." And Peter, who was congratulating himself on having made out so splendid a case, was amazed on hearing the magistrate say, "I fine you five shillings."

Here is not a bad illustration of the fancy of the Irish peasantry. A debtor who was sued at Quarter Sessions in Kerry acknowledged that he had borrowed the money in dispute, but declared the plaintiff knew at the time that it was "a Kathleen Mavourneen loan." "'A Kathleen Mavourneen loan'?" questioned the judge, with a puzzled look. "What in the world is that?" "That's what we call some loans down in our parts, yer honner—the 'It may be for years, and it may be for ever' sort," quoting a line from the well-known song "Kathleen Mavourneen."

One also hears in the Irish law courts many quaint, humorous, and shrewd answers by witnesses to questions from counsel, and many a witty paying-back of incivility, unreasonableness, or weak logic from those "gentlemen learned in the law." A man was indicted at the Cork Quarter Sessions for stealing ducks from a farm. The farmer swore he should know his fowls anywhere, as they had certain peculiarities, which he went on to describe. "Why," said the counsel for the prisoner, "they can't be so very rare. I have some like them in my own yard." "Faix, I shouldn't wonder," said the farmer; "I've had some of them stolen before this time." I attended the first sittings, at Kilmallock, of the County Limerick Sub-Commission Court under the Land Act of 1881. In one case the tenant who applied to have a fair rent fixed told the usual story of his difficulty to make the rent out of the farm. "Come, now,' said the counsel for the landlord, "isn't it the fact that your father paid this rent for thirty years before you without ever grumbling?" "Well," replied the witness, "if me father told you that, I wonder did he ever tell you that I had to borrow the money to buy him a coffin, and that I haven't paid it yet?"

In a case tried at the Letterkenny Assizes, an old pedagogue named Paddy Doherty, of considerable local celebrity, was examined as a witness. "Where were you, sir, this night?" asked the cross-examining counsel. "This night!" exclaimed Paddy. "Och! but 'tis you're the larned man entirely! Shure *this night* isn't kum yit, man. I suppose you mane *that night*?" "Well, let it be 'that night' to please you," said the counsel good-humouredly. "I suppose the schoolmaster was abroad that night, doing nothing?" "Before I answer you, will you tell me what's nothing?" returned Paddy. "What is it yourself?" said counsel. "It's a footless stockin' without a leg," cried Paddy triumphantly, without a moment's hesitation. In a case which was tried at Wexford before Chief Baron O'Grady, a wild, refractory peasant refused to answer a question as to character put to him by counsel, and said, "If ye ax me that ag'in I'll give ye a kick in the gob!" "Does your lordship hear that language?" said counsel, appealing to the judge. "An answer to my question is essential to my client's case. What does your lordship advise me to do?" "If you are resolved to repeat the question," said the judge, "I'd advise you to move a little from the witness." In a recent murder trial at the Galway Assizes, a witness for the defence was severely cross-examined by the counsel for the Crown, with a view to discrediting his evidence. A pistol was found in his possession, but he denied that he had it for any felonious intent. "Come, sir," said the lawyer; "on the virtue of your solemn oath, what did you get the weapon for?" "On the vartue of my solemn oath," replied the witness, quite innocently, and without the remotest intention of making a joke, "I got it for three and ninepence in Mr. Richardson's pawn-office"!

Lord Avonmore, better known as Barry Yelverton — a distinguished Irish lawyer, orator, and judge—had a strong antipathy to Kerry people. In his junior days he went down to the Kerry Assizes, held at Tralee, for the fee of a guinea. He failed in the case; and a day or two after, as he was travelling alone on the road to Cork, his client, with a big following of "shillelagh boys," waylaid him, reproached him for his want of skill, and compelled him to refund the fee! But the successful lawyer may command any service of his clients. O'Connell, having freed from the meshes of the law a rascal who had stolen and killed a fat sheep belonging to a neighbour, got this useful piece of professional advice from his client:

"Whin ye're for to steal a cow, yer honner, mind and take the wan that's farthest from the ditch. The poor, thin craythurs always goes to the ditch for shelter, while the fat bastes keeps outside." Another evil-doer, who for the second time was indebted to the great advocate for his liberty, cried out, as he was leaving the dock—with his eyes fervently cast heavenwards—"Oh, may the Lord spare you to me, Counsellor O'Connell!" The trust which the people had in the great lawyer, advocate, and demagogue was, indeed, profound. A man once applied to him to get him into the police. O'Connell said he could not do it, as he had no influence in Government quarters. "Shure 'tis yer honner that cud aisly do it," rejoined the applicant. "Troth, if I happened to kill some bla'guard of a prosecuthor of the people, 'tis you that cud bring me back from the gallows, let alone to git me into the police"! William Conyngham Plunket, who subsequently became Lord Chancellor of Ireland, was paid a similar compliment. At the Enniskillen Assizes he defended with such skill and success a horse-stealer—a member of a notorious gang — that one of the fraternity, frantic with delight, exclaimed, on meeting the barrister in the street, "Long life to yer honner! The next horse I'm up for staling, be jabers, I'll have Plunket"!

A quaint answer from a child, called as a witness, to the usual question whether it knew the nature of an oath is a familiar incident in all courts. Here are three amusing Irish examples. A little boy appeared as a witness in a case tried at Belfast, in which an Orangeman was charged with party-rioting. The judge, anxious to discover whether he knew the nature of an oath, said to him, " If you do not tell the truth, where will you go when you die?" The lad, who was brought up in a hot Orange environment, promptly replied, "Where the Papists go, sir." In another case, tried at Waterford, a little girl was asked what would happen to her if she did not tell the truth when giving her evidence. " I suppose, sir," she replied, " I wouldn't get me expinses." Another little girl was asked, in one of the Dublin courts, if she knew what an oath was? " Yis, sur," she replied. "Well, what is it?" The child seemed reluctant to reply. " Come now, my little girl, tell me, what is an oath?" said the judge. "You be damned, sur!" said the girl. There are two large cemeteries in Dublin, and the interments in one and the other are almost entirely a matter of religion — the Catholics going to Glasnevin and the Protestants to Mount Jerome. The present Recorder tried a case in which a nice little child would have been an important witness, but was objected to as being too young. " My dear girl," said the judge, "do you know the meaning of an oath?" "Oh, yes, sir, I know very well," said she. " Well, try her, your honour; ask a question or two," said the objecting barrister. The Recorder, embarrassed by the need of avoiding controversy, said, " Well, do you know where people go when they die?" "Yes, sir," said she; "the good people go to Glasnevin, and the bad people to Mount Jerome."

The "voices from the dock" one hears in the Irish courts are also extremely entertaining. I was sitting one day in the reporters' box in Green Street courthouse, Dublin, listening to the trial of a man for burglary. The prisoner carried off a small sum, a few loose shillings, I think it was, from the till of the shop into which he had broken. The evidence showed that the till also contained, in a small drawer, twenty pounds in gold, which was not touched. Counsel for the accused, in his address to the jury, made the excellent point that his client was a poor man out of work and in distressed circumstances, who wanted a few shillings to buy bread for his starving children. " Remember, gentlemen of the jury, that there were twenty pounds in this till, and the prisoner never touched it." But, unhappily, the prisoner looked upon this as a reflection on his capacity as a burglar. "Ah, thin, shure," said he, with tears in his voice, "the divil a wan of me clapt eyes on that same twinty pounds"! A somewhat similar incident occurred in a case tried before the Recorder of Dublin. A man was charged with stealing the contents of the till of a little sweet-shop kept by a poor woman. The prisoner looked so dejected that the recorder (Sir Frederick Falkiner), a kindly and most humane gentleman, thought he was penitent. "It's a sad thing," said the recorder, "to see a young man of your age fall into evil ways. See how you have lost character, prospects, everything—and all for sevenpence-halfpenny." "Shure now, me lord, that was not my fault at all," said the unhappy victim of circumstances. "It wasn't?" queried the recorder, who was hoping to hear of something which would justify him in imposing a light sentence. "No, me lordship," replied the prisoner. "How was I to consave that there'd be only a dhirty sivenpence-ha'penny in the d——d till? Didn't I clane out ivery blessed farthin' I could find?"

A peasant was indicted at the Kerry Assizes for the robbery of a sheep, the property of a well-known county landlord, Sir Garrett Fitz-Maurice. He pleaded that he found the sheep straying on the high road, and was simply driving it home. "Can you read?" asked the judge. "A little, me lord," replied the prisoner. "You could not have been ignorant then that the sheep belonged to your landlord, Sir Garrett Fitz-Maurice, as his brand, '*G. F. M.*,' was on the animal," said the judge. "Thrue for ye, me lord," replied the prisoner, "but shure I thought the letters meant 'Good Fat Mutton.'"

Some years ago there was a well-known magistrate named Thorpe Porter, in Dublin. A woman was repeatedly brought before him for being drunk. He had let her off on several occasions with a week's imprisonment, but as these light sentences had evidently no effect in reforming her habits, he determined to try the efficacy of a much longer term in jail. "You must go to prison for two months," said he. "That will give you time to reflect on the past; to reform your habits, and to curse whiskey, the cause of all your misfortunes." "Faix, I've no fault to find with whiskey, and I'll not curse it," said the woman in the dock, "but from the bottom of me heart I say, 'Bad luck to Porter.'" Another notorious Dublin virago and drunkard was brought before the same magistrate. He called her a pest and a disgrace to the city, and sent her to prison for a month. "Look at that now for ingratitude!" shouted the woman, as she was being taken from the dock. "If it wasn't for me and the likes o' me, that gets a bit disorderly whin we have a drop taken, and kicks up ructions now and thin, there 'ud be little call for police magisthrates, and policemen, and sich varmint! It's crathurs like me that's yer best frinds and keeps the bit and sup in yer mouths, and all we get for it is jailin' and impudence!"

The Irish peasant's powers of apology, explanation, and excuse are extensive and ingenious. A Limerick man, who was charged at petty sessions with being drunk and disorderly, said: "Let me go, yer honners, this time. It wasn't the drop I took that did the harm, but I had a blast out of a neighbour's pipe, and that leant upon me." The Limerick magistrates, who were noted for their leniency, discharged the poor man. I was in the Northern Police Court, Dublin, one morning, when a cattle-dealer from Limerick was fined £4 for an assault on another cattle-dealer from the same city. The man paid the money with considerable reluctance, and as he passed out of the court I heard him say, "Wait till I get the fellow in Limerick, where beating is chape, and I'll take the change out of him!" A Galway magistrate, who was a major in the county militia, sentenced an old woman to six weeks' imprisonment for shoplifting. "Well, thanks be to the Lord," exclaimed the prisoner fervently, "low as I am, there's wan thing I'm thankful for—not wan of me kith or kin ever had anythin' to do with the milishy."

At the Kilkenny Assizes a policeman gave evidence against a prisoner, when the latter, affecting to be horrified at the constable's statements, cried out, "It's no wondher for the pitaties to be black, when the likes of you is in the country." A man was convicted at the Londonderry Assizes of a violent assault. The judge in passing sentence said: "You have committed a brutal and a cowardly act. I shall not waste words on you—eighteen months' hard labour." "I beg your pardon, me lord," cried the prisoner sarcastically, "but, if it's all the same to ye, I'll take a little more of the words and a little less of the months." A stammering prisoner was brought up at a Dublin police court. Upon being asked his name, he began something like this, "S-s—s-s-s—sp—s-sp——" "Don't get flurried," said the magistrate kindly, "take your time." The man began again, "S-s-sp-s—sp—s-s-sp-s-s—s-spw-s-s-s-w-s." "Oh, this will never do!" cried the magistrate, getting impatient, and turning to the policeman. "What is he *charged* with?" "Please sir, I think it must be soda water," was the grave reply.

Chapter VIII

"AGIN THE GOVERNMINT"

ABSTRACT principles do not appeal to the average Irish peasant. Loyalty to an institution he is, generally speaking, unable to understand, but his fidelity to his leader, to his neighbour, to his community or his *caste*, is unequalled for its strength and endurance. Years ago the peasantry regarded the Government, in a dim and hazy fashion, as some mysterious agency of oppression. The only clear conception they had of it was that the police, the sheriffs, the tithe-proctors, the magistrates and the judges were its agents; and these officials were associated in their minds with raids on their farm stock or crops, evictions, arrests of " poor bhoys," fines, imprisonments, transportations and hangings. Hence the by no means improbable story of the Irishman who, on landing in New York, after the Great Famine of 1847, was asked by a political agent what were his opinions, and replied, " I'm agin the Governmint."

Hence, too, the intense sympathy which the

peasantry entertain for those in the clutches of the law. Owing, no doubt, to the circumstances of their unhappy history, they have never been able to see the justice of the law, or to recognise its equality. When the telegraph was first introduced into the county of Kerry the wires were constantly cut, despite Government proclamations threatening condign punishment to the evil-doers and offering tempting rewards for their apprehension. At last the priest of the district was appealed to, and, with a deep insight into the ways of his flock, he thus addressed them at Mass on Sunday: "The cutting of the telegraph wires must stop at once. I'm ashamed of ye! At the time ye were cutting the wires a telegram might have been on its way from Dublin Castle with a reprieve for some poor boy that was going to be hanged." A telegraph wire has never been cut in the district since. Some years ago an agrarian murder took place in the county. A few months subsequently the police received intelligence that a man who acknowledged he was the murderer was being sheltered by the people in one of the wild and mysterious valleys beyond Killarney. A force of police was sent there, and the man was captured. He turned out to be an impostor. He was an unfortunate tramp who, wishing to take things easy for a time, gave it out that he was the Castle Island murderer; and for two months he had the best of eating, and drinking, and lodging in the homes of the peasantry !

This sympathy with the wrong-doer is confined to political and agrarian crimes. It is due to the loyalty of the peasant to his *caste* and to his belief that recourse to " the wild justice of revenge " for what he conceives to be wrong and oppression is justifiable. Besides, the criminal is usually a good father or husband, a devoted son, an excellent neighbour, for in considering this phase of Irish character the strange fact must be noted that, as the criminal records of the country prove, some of the most appalling crimes, political and agrarian, have been committed by men of otherwise blameless lives. The Irish peasant will make any sacrifice to aid a criminal of this class in escaping the just vengeance of the law. The *alibi* is a popular form of defence in Irish courts of justice. A witty Dublin barrister was once asked for a definition of it. " It is *a lie by* which Irish criminals escape punishment," he replied. Undoubtedly truth is often at a discount in the making of an *alibi* on behalf of " the poor bhoy " in the dock. It would seem, indeed, as if among the peasantry the commandment "Thou shalt not bear false witness against thy neighbour " is held to include, " Thou mayst bear false witness in his favour."

That mixture of loyalty and rebellion in the

Irish peasant's nature which is so incomprehensible to the stranger is illustrated by the following anecdotes. As a boycotted landlord, accompanied by two armed policeman, passed the door of a cabin on his estate, the woman of the house ejaculated, "Long life to yer honner!" "That's a strange salutation from you, Mary," said the landlord, smiling bitterly, "when it is your husband and a few others like him who make it necessary for me to walk about with this guard." "Och, now, yer honner," remonstrated Mary, " don't be too hard on Tim. If he's for shootin' yer honner wan day, shure it's layin' his life down for ye he'd be the next." During the operations of that terrible agrarian conspiracy the Ribbon Society, in Westmeath, in the early Seventies, two men were arrested for the attempted murder of a landlord. One of the accused turned "informer," and in the course of his evidence at the trial stated that the prisoner and he lay behind a ditch with loaded blunderbusses awaiting the return of the landlord from petty sessions. Some hours passed, but the landlord did not come. "At lasht," continued the informer, "the prisoner says to me, 'Isn't the masther a mortal long time comin'?' 'Bedad he is,' says I. 'I hope no axidint happened to the poor gintleman.'"

A few months ago an action for divorce, a *mensa et thora*, at the suit of the wife, on the ground of cruelty, was tried in the Dublin courts. The parties were of the well-to-do farming class from the county of Limerick. In the course of the cross-examination of the wife—which was directed to show that she had provoked her husband by her insulting language to him and his relatives—she was asked, "Did you call your husband's uncle 'Carey, the informer'?" "No," she replied; "I didn't go so far as that. I called him Anti-Christ." This question and answer throws light on another curious phase of Irish character—the intense hatred and abhorrence with which "informers" in political and agrarian trials are held by the community. No more opprobrious term than "informer" is contained in the Irish peasants' ample vocabulary of abuse. In that word is concentrated all the malignity of which they are capable. As the women, who are extremely chaste, regard an imputation of the want of female virtue as the vilest of charges, so among the men the term "informer" is looked upon as the strongest term of abuse or reproach. The informer is boycotted as one who has been faithless to his *caste*. He is subjected to the severest ostracism by the community—an ostracism harder to bear than death in a rural district; and indeed his life would not be safe for a day were he to remain among the people to whom, as they think, he acted the traitor.

The informer is, nevertheless, a familiar figure in political and agrarian trials. But in no case that I have been able to trace has the informer been tempted to divulge his terrible secret by the reward usually offered by the Government. It is the fear of death, or the fear of penal servitude that usually induces the superstitious and home-loving peasant who is mixed up in treasonable or agrarian conspiracies to round upon his comrades. The Irish peasant is, indeed, an amazing and inscrutable bundle of opposite qualities. He is a very suspicious being, and with all his fidelity to a cause or a community, he is, when arrested with others for a crime, often seized with a fear that his comrade will betray him, and to save his neck or his liberty he will rush to the authorities with his story. It was this characteristic that led to the conviction of the Phœnix Park murderers. The authorities got to know who the perpetrators were a few weeks after the crimes were committed. They had, however, no evidence to proceed upon; but they arrested the principals as "suspects," under the Peace Preservation (Ireland) Act of 1881, and instituted under the provisions of the same Act a secret inquiry, which ultimately led to the tendering of information by panic-stricken Invincibles,—each fearful that he would be betrayed by his accomplices if he were not first to the authorities with his own story,—and resulted in the suppression of the most desperate murder conspiracy ever formed in Ireland, and the death on the scaffold of its leaders.

Charles Lever, in his novel *Harry Lorrequer*, tells a story of how the evidence of an informer which broke up a powerful agrarian conspiracy was procured. The following are the true facts of the case. About 1830 the county of Clare was greatly disturbed, owing to exactions in respect of tithes, and the loss of agricultural employment, through vast tracts of land, hitherto tilled, being used for the purposes of meadow and pasture. Several murders were committed, houses were levelled, fences and hedges thrown down, and the cattle of poor tenants driven in to graze on the meadow lands. Tomkins Brew, one of the first of the resident magistrates, then known as stipendiaries, was stationed at Ennis, the chief town of the county. It came to his knowledge that a workman named Tom Sheehan, whom he knew well, was one of the leaders in the conspiracy. He asked Sheehan to call on him at his office one day about some work he wanted done. The office looked into one of the main streets of the town, and during the interview he kept Sheehan at the open window, asking him indifferent questions about things in general, while he sat himself at his desk writing letters. It happened to be market-day, and the town was crowded. As the people passed up and down the street and saw Sheehan in the office, and the magistrate writing, they jumped to the conclusion that they were being sold. This, needless to say, was the object the magistrate had in view. On the appearance of Sheehan in the street he was violently assailed by an angry mob, amid cries of "Down with the thraithor!" and was compelled to fly for his life back again to Brew's office. The information he gave led to the break up of the conspiracy and the conviction of a large number of people, ten or twelve of whom were hung.

In past times it was the custom to hang a felon guilty of an agrarian murder on the scene of the crime, or if that were not possible, close to his residence. A rude, temporary cross-beam was fixed up on the road-side. Forty-eight hours after the sentence the culprit was brought to the scene of execution on a rough, springless cart, surrounded by a force of dragoons. Arrivin under the gallows, the condemned man was made to stand up in the cart, a rope, suspended from the cross-beam, was adjusted round his neck, and the hangman, taking hold of the horse's head, drew away the cart, thus giving the death-fall to the convict.

The object of these public executions was, of course, to impress the people who assembled in thousands to witness them; but the horrible spectacle did not always convey the lesson the authorities intended it to teach. A gentleman, named Foote, was murdered near New Ross, co. Wexford, by the son of a peasant named Murphy. It arose, as usual, out of a dispute about land. The execution was public. The father was among the crowd. He watched the proceedings with tearless eye, but his heart, no doubt, raging on fire within him; nor did he utter a word until the body ceased to move, when he turned away, exclaiming: "An' to think I lost me beautiful boy for ould Foote!" What pride there was in that exclamation! William Carleton in his *Traits and Stories of the Irish Peasantry* has a sketch, entitled "Wildgoose Lodge," in which he describes a terrible agrarian murder. A whole family, named Lynch, was exterminated. The principal of the murderers, a man named Paddy Devaun, was gibbetted near his own door. The body, enclosed in a tarred sack, was allowed to remain swinging from the cross-beams; and the old mother, as she crossed the threshold of her cabin, and the spectacle met her eyes, always exclaimed: "God be merciful to the soul of me poor marthyr."

The clannishness of the Irish people, the habit of sticking to each other, also explains the verdicts of "not guilty" returned by juries in cases in which the crime seems to be brought clearly home to the prisoner. In former years it was the custom to subject juries who failed to agree to a curious form of degradation. They were brought on the common carts (used in conveying felons to the gallows—as I have already described—in the days when executions took place on the scene of the murders) to the bounds of the county, and then discharged. In a case tried at the Roscommon Assizes many years ago, the jury, on failing to arrive at a verdict after they had been locked up all night, were informed that at three o'clock in the afternoon—unless they previously came to an agreement—the execution carts would be ready to convey them to the bounds of the county, fifteen miles distant. Four of the jury were holding out for an acquittal of the prisoner. The others, unwilling to face this humiliating journey on a wet and cheerless day, as it happened to be, insisted on the recalcitrant four giving way; and as these still refused to budge, a fight between the rival sides took place in the jury-room. The uproar reached the ears of the judge, and by his orders the jurymen were dragged, battered and bleeding, into court. After a severe reprimand by his lordship, they were led out to the execution carts, three in number; and attended by the sub-sheriff on horseback, and a troop of dragoons, these rough, springless vehicles, with the unhappy jurors, went slowly bumping their way over the rough, uneven roads. When the strange procession had got a few miles outside the town, a compromise was arrived at between the jurors It was agreed to find the prisoner guilty on a minor count. The carts were then turned back, but when they arrived in the town it was found that the judge had left, and so with enhanced misery the jurors had to set off again on their fifteen miles' journey to the bounds of the county.

A man was charged at the Nenagh Assizes, a few years ago, with cattle lifting. After the jury had been sworn, the judge, observing that the prisoner was unrepresented, said to him : " Have you no counsel ? " " I have not, me lord," he replied. " I must tell you what, perhaps, you do not know," said the judge kindly, " that you are charged with a very serious offence, and if convicted you may be sent to prison for a considerable time. Surely you have at least a solicitor to say something for you ? " " Sorra a wan, me lord," replied the prisoner ; " but," he added, with a knowing smile towards the jury-box, " I've several good frinds among the jury." But some prisoners do not know a friendly juryman when they see him. I remember a case which occurred not very long ago at the Tralee Quarter Sessions. The accused was unrepresented by counsel, and in the course of exercising his right of challenge, he told his good neighbour, James Molloney, to "stand by."

"Arrah, what are yez about, Pat, you fool!" roared James, as he stood on the steps leading to the jury box. "Shure, man, I'm for yez!" Talking on the subject of challenging with a friend who is a solicitor, he told me an amusing experience. He challenged several jurymen, on the advice of a prisoner for whom he appeared, on the ground that they were prejudiced against him. When the swearing of the jury was completed, the prisoner leaned over the dock and whispered to his solicitor, " The jury's all right, I think, sur, but I want yez to challenge the judge. I've been convicted under him several times already, and maybe he's beginnin' to have a prejudice agin me."

John Anster, a Dublin lawyer, and the author of the well-known translation of *Faust*, used to tell of a strange professional experience which once befell him. He defended a prisoner tried for the murder of a man named Kelly at the Cork Assizes, and succeeded in getting him acquitted. After court, as he was walking to his hotel, he met the man whose life he had saved, and saluted him with, "Oh, Kelly, is that you?" naming by mistake not the living man, but the dead man. " I'm not Kelly, yer honour," replied his client; "but the boy that shot him"!

But the most curious and unique incident that ever came under my notice occurred at the Kilkenny Assizes, some years ago, at a trial for an attempted murder. A man had been fired at on a country road at night. Behind the hedge the police found an old blunderbuss, which had burst in the firing, and near it a finger, evidently torn off the hand of the intended assassin by the explosion of the weapon. A peasant, who was suspected of the crime, was arrested; and a most damning fact against him was that he was minus a finger, and that manifestly, from the condition of the hand, the loss had been very recent. The prisoner was, however, found "not guilty" by the jury, and was accordingly discharged. "What shall we do with the finger, my lord?" asked the Crown prosecutor. "Why, return it to its owner, of course—the man who has just left the dock," said the judge. His lordship could not have shown his opinion of the verdict of the jury in a more striking or a more dramatic way.

Chapter IX

IRISH HUMOUR

THE Irish people enjoy a world-wide reputation for colloquial humour. It is theirs by the best of all rights—the right of having well earned it. The colloquial drollery of the Irish people has been the source from which many generations of the English-speaking peoples of the globe have drawn much wholesome and hearty laughter. What is the national characteristic of this humour of the Irish people? What is the element in it which excites us to laughter? It cannot, perhaps, be exactly and precisely defined. Indeed, the attempts which have been made by several acute literary critics to define the nature and composition of humour generally, have been to little advantage. We hear a good story, and enjoy it; but if we were asked what it was exactly in the story that excited in us the feeling of pleasure, that stirred in us the emotion of surprise, that made us shout with laughter, we would often be at a loss to explain. However, this much I may say as a generalization on the subject of

Irish humour. Everything, no matter how sober, serious, or solemn, has its comic or its ludicrous side—if we could only see it; and it seems to me that the source of Irish humour lies in the extraordinary intuition of the people in discovering this, not always obvious, side of a situation. A priest met a parishioner going by train to a race meeting. "Where are ye off to now, Mick?" he asked. "To Punchistown races, yer riverence," said Mick. "You are going to hell then!" exclaimed the priest. "Musha faix, if I am, what matter?" replied Mick; "for I've a return ticket, and here it is."

Some years ago an exceedingly funny dramatic hitch occurred in the Queen's Theatre, Dublin. The piece was a *Faust* extravaganza. In one of the scenes Mephistopheles—who happened to be a very portly devil—had to "go home"; but as he sank through a small circular trap in the stage, he stuck fast. The demons below tugged at his crimson legs; the mortals above tried to stuff him down. But all was in vain. And then over the delighted din which arose from the whole house, came a still, small voice from the gallery: "Well, bhoys, that's a comfort anyway: the lower regions is full!" The delight given by this droll remark is complete. It is fully satisfying. One feels that a happier comment on the ludicrous stage *contretemps* is impossible. The following story also affords an excellent example of the side of Irish humour which I am now illustrating—the incongruous association of things or ideas quite dissimilar, or not usually connected. A well-known temperance advocate, while waiting for a tram in Dublin, said to a man under the influence of drink, who was going into a neighbouring public-house, "Do you know, my friend, that the devil is going in there with you?" "Faith, thin, he needn't, for I've only tuppence," said the man.

The native humour of Ireland is like the national character—it is impulsive, sympathetic, and mellow. It is not dry and caustic like the Scottish humour; unlike the English it is rarely sententious or sarcastic. A man was observed staring intently after an old gentleman who was tripping up Grafton-street, Dublin, with all the jaunty elasticity of youth. "What's the matter with the old gentleman?" he was asked. "What's the matter with him! Yerrah, look at the walk of him!" was the reply. "Begor, he only touches the ground in an odd place!" A crack hussar *corps* was recently stationed in Dublin. After a levee at the Castle one summer evening, an officer, in full military dress, walked down Dame-street. Two men standing at a corner seemed quite bewildered by the gorgeous and glittering apparition clanking towards them; but when the officer passed from their dazzled eyes, one said to the other, "Oh, shouldn't I like to pawn him!" During the Land League agitation a tenant farmer, who occupied a conspicuous part in the movement in his own locality, returning from market one evening, not very steady in his walk, fell into a bog-hole by the side of the road, where he stuck fast. His landlord, chancing to pass on horseback shortly afterwards, saw the tenant's dilemma, and laughingly cried, "Well, James, you've got fixity of tenure now." "Yes, begor, yer honner," ejaculated James; "and shure 'tis I would be moightly obliged to yer honner if you'd be after evictin' me."

Of the good-humoured drollery of the Irish people, there is a happy illustration in an incident which recently occurred in a Dublin infirmary. "Well, my man," said the visiting physician to a patient, "how do you feel this morning?" "Purty well, sur," was the reply. "That's right. I hope you like the place?" "Indeed, and I do, sur," said the man. "There's only wan thing wrong in this establishment, and that is, I only get as much mate as wud feed a sparrow." "Oh, you're getting your appetite, are you?" said the doctor. "Then I'll order an egg to be sent up to you." "Arrah, docther," rejoined the patient, "would you be so kind as to tell thim at the same time to sind me up the hin that laid it!" Another instance of the same quality is afforded by a story told of a Killarney guide. The late Mr. A. M. Sullivan, M.P., who was an ardent temperance advocate, hurt his ankle while climbing a hill in the Irish lake district. The guide who accompanied him produced a flask of whiskey, and rubbed a portion of the spirits on the injured part. It had the desired effect, for Mr. Sullivan got up and walked. "Faix, sur," said the guide, "'twould be a long time before soda wather would do that for you."

An English tourist, who visited Ireland a short time ago, told in a letter to a London newspaper an amusing experience he had of the quick-wittedness of the peasantry. In the west of Ireland he met a farmer driving some young cattle to a local fair, and encountering him again in the evening, asked him how much he had got for his stock. "Four pounds a head," replied Pat. "Only four pounds a head!" said the tourist. "Why, if you brought them to my country you would have got at least £6 each for them." "Och, maybe so, yer honner," rejoined the farmer, "an' if I cud bring the lakes of Killarney to Purgatory I'd get a pound a drop." Pat, indeed, is never at a loss for a rejoinder. A reaper, of a rather small stature, applied to a farmer for work on the harvest. "I'm afraid you're too small," said the farmer. "Wisha, now, and do you cut your corn at the top?" asked the labourer.

A friend of mine told me that while he was

standing one day at the door of a hotel in a little village in County Cork, two of the villagers met, and one said to the other, "What time might it be now, Tom?" The second man gave the questioner, in playfulness, a smart crack on the head with a stick, and said, "It's just struck wan." "Troth, thin," said the other good humouredly, as he rubbed his skull, "it's a lucky job I wasn't here an hour ago." An example of the quaint and fantastic power of expression of the Irish people was afforded at a dinner given by a temperance society in Limerick, to celebrate the centenary of Father Mathew's birth, a few years ago. The proposing of the toast of the memory of the great apostle of temperance was entrusted to a local shopkeeper who had spent several years in America. "Gintlemen," he concluded, "I ask ye to toast, in wather, the Mississippi of men, the father of wathers—Father Mathew."

A faculty for giving expressive nick-names is also a feature of Irish humour. I knew a flour dealer in Limerick, who, being an old soldier, was known as "Marshal Saxe" after the great French general of the eighteenth century. One day, as he was driving a cart full of sacks of flour from a local mill to his shop, I heard a man, lounging at a street corner, cry: "There goes Marshal Saxe at the head of the flower of Limerick!" There was also in Limerick a well-known character, who spent most of his days in a certain public-house, and ran up a rather long score there, which was marked on a big slate hanging in the bar. One night a fire occurred at this particular public-house, and the fire-brigade was called out. While the men were pouring a flood of water into the blazing shop, a voice was heard from the crowd: "Arrah, Captain, whatever you do don't fail to play on the slate." It was the voice of the man who had the long score to his account! Charles Lever used to tell a very good story of a hotel domestic, which, contrary to his usual custom, he never made use of in any of his novels. During a visit to Mayo, he stayed for a time at the Sound Hotel, Achill. As the woman brought in the tea-pot her hand shook violently; and Lever, noticing the infirmity, said, "I'm sorry to see, Biddy, that you have a weakness in your hand." "Faix, yer honner," said the domestic, "you'll soon find it isn't in my hand the weakness is, but inside, in the tay-pot." And, sure enough, the decoction in the teapot was not remarkable for its strength. "Yes, Biddy," said Lever subsequently, "the tea was decidedly pale. How was that?" "Oh, thin, I don't know, yer honner," replied Biddy, "except it saw a ghost"!

Fantastic exaggeration is another quality of Irish humour. The wonderful progress of the science of optics was being recently discussed at a meeting of a learned society in London. One gentleman said he believed that a telescope would soon be invented by the aid of which the interior of the moon could be observed as clearly as if the spectator were actually in the planet itself. Sir Robert Ball, Professor of Astronomy at Cambridge University, who spoke subsequently, said the town of Wexford possessed the most wonderful telescope imaginable, if an Irish friend of his who lived in that town was to be believed. He recently got a letter from that friend, from which the following was an extract:—" I have a telescope at my house here in Wexford that beats anything you ever heard of, for it brings the Church of Enniscorthy, twelve miles distant, so near to my view that during the Sunday service I can distinguish the psalms sung by the congregation and hear the sermon."

Here are some other amusing instances of the same quality of happy exaggeration. The people about Enniskerry were, and probably are now, great poultry fanciers. One day on "the long car" plying between Bray and Enniskerry, two gentlemen were deep in discussion respecting the sizes and merits of certain famous Cochin China fowls which they had seen at Lord Monk's. A Munster cattle dealer who was listening attentively to the conversation, at last remarked—" Well, I never heard tell before of the like of thim Coachin fowls, but I seen Tim Deegan's turkey down in Tipperary, that I think wud be a match for any of 'um." On being pressed to mention what were the valuable attributes of Tim Deegan's fowl, he gravely told the following humorous story. "Tom Deegan's turkey was the gratest baste of a bird I iver seen. They used him six days of the week cartin' manure to the farm, and on Sundays he drew them to Mass in the jauntin'-car. Last winter they wor forced to kill the poor thing, and with that they salted him down, and they axed Father McGrath to dine with thim; and begor, when the dinner was over his riverence said, 'Tim, where did ye get that beautiful beef?'" The gentlemen admitted that Lord Monk's Cochin China did not equal that wonderful bird. "'Deed, thin, 'tis hard to bate Tipperary," said the cattle jobber. As I was travelling to Athlone one day, there happened to be in the carriage an English agriculturist and a Westmeath farmer. The conversation turned on the productiveness of the respective soils of England and Ireland. The Englishman boasted that nothing could beat the richness of the soil of his native Devonshire; and he quoted several instances of the abundant crops his farm yielded. "Oh, that's nothin'," said the Westmeath man, with a twinkle in his eye. "I've a few acres of ground the like of which isn't in creation. One evenin' I put down into me land a twelvepenny nail, with a shovel full of manure, and I'm blest if be the followin' mornin' it hadn't grown into a kitchen poker!"

The late Mr. Lefanu, chairman of the Irish Board of Works, used to tell a laughable story illustrating the humour and readiness in reply of the Kerry peasantry. A farmer from "The Kingdom," as Kerry is called, went into the adjoining county of Limerick, where the land is richer, looking for a farm. He saw one which he thought would suit; but he could not agree with the landlord as to the amount of the rent. "Get away," cried the landlord at last. "This land is not like your miserable Kerry land, where a mountain sheep can hardly get enough to eat. The grass grows here so fast and so high, that if you left a heifer out in the field there at night you would scarcely find her in the morning." "Bedad, yer honner," replied the Kerryman; "there's many a part of my own county where if you left a heifer out at night the divil a bit of her you'd ever see agin."

The quick-wittedness of the Irishman gets him out of many a "tight place." I was told the following story of an Irish M.P. who owned extensive estates, and was a conspicuous figure in public life some years ago. He was spending a few days at Castle ——, the residence of an Irish nobleman. There were several interesting and accomplished young ladies in the family, to whom the M.P., who was a bachelor, showed, as in duty bound, every attention. Just as he was about to take his leave, the nobleman's wife, whose sole remaining ambition was to make "good matches" for her daughter, said she desired to consult him on a matter which, she alleged, was giving her no little distress. "It's reported," she said, "that you are to marry my daughter Letitia. What shall we do? what shall we say about it?" "Oh," replied the M.P. quietly, "just say she refused me." Many stories have been told of the nimbleness of wit displayed by the late Father James Healy, of Bray; but the following story is, I believe, fresh, and is also a very good example of the amusing way in which he parried awkward questions. As he was dining with Earl Spencer at the Viceregal Lodge, an A.D.C. of an inquiring turn of mind said to him, "As you are, no doubt, well up in Biblical points, Father Healy, will you tell us the difference between the two orders of angels, the Cherubin and the Seraphin?" "Well," replied Father Healy, "I believe there *was* a difference between them a long time ago; but I am glad to say they have since made it up." I overheard on the pier of Kingstown, one summer day, a reply in which humour and sarcasm were equally blended. A man was fishing at the end of the pier. Up to him came rather a pompous individual who said,

"Well, my man, what sort of fish do you catch here?" "Well, to tell you the truth, you niver can tell till you pull 'em up," was the sharp rejoinder.

Cardinal Manning was fond of telling the following story:—"One night I was returning to my residence in Westminster when I met a poor man carrying a basket and smoking a pipe. I thought over this Aristotelian syllogism—'He who smokes gets thirsty; he who is thirsty desires to drink; he who drinks too much gets drunk; he who gets drunk is lost.' This man is in danger of mortal sin, let me try to save him. I affectionately addressed him: 'Are you a Catholic?' 'I am thanks be to Heaven!' 'Where are you from?' 'From Cork, yer riverence.' 'Are you a member of our total abstinence society—The League of the Cross?' 'No, yer riverence.' 'Now,' said I; 'that is very wrong. Look at me, I'm a member.' 'Faith, maybe yer riverence has need of it,' said the man. I shook hands with him and left him."

The sense of humour is highly developed in the Irish peasant. He finds in it the anodyne for much of the misery of his earthly lot. He can even knock a lot of fun out of his misfortunes. "Will you have it raw or well done?" said the waiter, in a Dublin *restaurant*, to a poor countryman who asked for a plate of beef. "I'll have it well done for a change," said the countryman. "It's rare enough we get it down in County Mayo." An Irish country gentleman of a very obliging disposition, who thinks that personal favours do not cost much, while they make friends, was applied to some time ago by a labourer for a certificate of character. The gentleman, taking the applicant into his study, wrote out a very flattering recommendation, which he handed to the man for perusal. The latter took it, spelled through it, scratched his head, and remained silent. "Well," said the gentleman, puzzled at the man's behaviour, "don't you consider it favourable enough?" "Oh, no, sur, not that; shure it couldn't be better, but—but——" "But what?" angrily inquired the gentleman. "Begorra, sur," was the reply, "I was jist thinkin' that yer honner might give me somethin' to do yerself on the stringth iv that recommindation." The unexpected and droll turn given to the situation by the quick-witted reply of the labourer is characteristic of Irish humour. Here is another anecdote in which ideas, as wide apart as the poles, are ludicrously brought into association. A Galway landlord, who was ill, went to London to consult an eminent specialist. The physican, having examined him, said, "I should like to know whether your family have been long-lived." "Well, doctor, I'll just tell you how it is," replied the patient thoughtfully. "My family is a

West of Ireland family, and the age of my ancestors depended entirely on the judge and jury who tried them."

Whimsicality, as these stories show, is a strong point in Irish humour. A hunting party in Meath went out to look for a fox which was noted for its 'cuteness. Reynard could not be found, and the party had to turn home disappointed. "Faix, I'm not surprised," said the whipper-in, noted in the locality for his drollness, "Shure, I came across the fox the other day in the cover near Daly's, readin' a newspaper to find out where the hounds wor to meet." In this anecdote, too, the emotional shock which causes laughter is produced by things utterly different: a fox, and the reading of a newspaper, being brought into intimate and absurd association. A witty Irishman, popular in London society, was a guest at a large and fashionable musical party. Suddenly, by some mischance, the electric light went out, and there was profound darkness. During the momentary silence which followed upon the accident, the Irishman was heard to exclaim in pathetic tones, with a touch of the brogue, "This would be worth a hundred pounds a minute if we were rightly sorted." At a private dance in a Dublin mansion, a buxom lady was very *décolletée*. "Did you ever see anything like that?" said a gentleman to an eminent Irish judge. "Not since I was weaned," was the reply. A monk of the

Cistercian Order told Father Tom Burke, the Dominican Preacher, of his fasts and mortifications. "My dear fellow," said Father Burke, "if it should turn out that there is no hereafter, what a sell you'll get." At a British Association dinner, Father James Healy, of Bray, was sitting next Professor Huxley, who told him a long story of a certain Catholic priest who had examined and cross-examined him about the alleged existence of mind in monkeys. Huxley asked Father Healy what position the Catholic Church would take on such a question, and what object the priest could have had in questioning him so closely as to whether he had found in monkeys any glimmering of real human intelligence. "Depend upon it," said Father Healy slyly, "he was hoping to find a cheap curate among the monkeys."

In conclusion, two characteristic stories may be told to show the sense of humour of the "Fathers O'Flynn" of the priesthood. The Catholic bishop of Limerick was examining some school children preparatory to Confirmation. "What is the sacrament of Matrimony, my child?" he asked one little girl. "'Tis a place or state of punishment, me lord," she replied, giving the Catechism's description of Purgatory, "where some souls suffer for a time before going to Heaven." "Oh, oh!" exclaimed the bishop, "that is very bad, Father Fahy," he added, addressing the parish priest.

"Sure, me lord," said he, "for anything you or I know to the contrary, the child may be perfectly right." The second story is told of Father Tom Maguire, who was well-known, some years ago, as a theological controversialist and a humourist—though the two characters might seem incompatible. He was asked by a rather simple-minded farmer what a miracle was; and he gave a very full explanation, which, however, was not quite satisfying, for the man said, "Do you think yer riverence could be after givin' me an example of a miracle?" "Well," said the priest, "walk on before me and I'll see what I can do." As the farmer did so, Father Tom gave him a knock on the head with his stick. "Did you feel that, Mick?" said he. "Wisha, why wouldn't I feel it, yer riverence," replied Mick, surprised that the priest should ask him such a foolish question. "Faix, I felt it hard enough." "Well, Mick," said Father Tom, "it would be a miracle if you didn't."

Chapter X

IRISH REPARTEE AND SARCASM

REPARTEE, or readiness in smart, witty, and sarcastic retort, is said to be the highest form of wit. These immediate and felicitous replies, these answering thrusts in mental fencing, these illuminating flashes of quick and lively imaginations, are common among all classes in Ireland. On old Carlisle Bridge in Dublin there was a fruit-stall, the keeper of which, "Biddy, the apple-woman," was a better-known figure than even the Lord Mayor. She had a ready and glib tongue, and never allowed a verbal assailant to retire with all the honours. An American visitor, thinking to take a "rise" out of the old woman, took up one of the water melons she was displaying for sale, and said, "These are small apples you grow over here. In America we have them twice the size." Biddy slowly removed her "dudheen" from her lips, and coolly surveying the joker from head to heel, said, in a tone of pity, "Yerra, what an *amadawn* ye must be, whin yez take our gooseberries for apples!" The Irish people are perhaps unequalled for concentrating into a phrase an amount of bitter sarcasm. A Dublin jarvey, seeing a man of fashion, who prided himself on his skill in handling the reins, driving down Grafton Street said, "That fellow looks like a coachman, but drives like a gentleman."

John Philpot Curran was noted for his powers of repartee and sarcasm. Many of his good things in that line have come down to us through the century. There could not be a better testimony to their worth, but, as most of them are too well known to need repeating here, I will simply give a few that I have picked up in out-of-the-way places. At a dinner-table in London the conversation turned on speaking. Curran stated that he could never speak in public for a quarter of an hour without moistening his lips. "I have the advantage of you there, Curran," said Sir Thomas Turton, a pompous and pretentious Member of Parliament. "I spoke the other night in the House of Commons for five hours on the Nabob of Oude, and never felt in the least thirsty." "That is very remarkable, indeed," replied Curran, "for every one agrees that it was the driest speech of the Session." One day he was walking past the Parliament House in College Green, before the Bank of Ireland got possession of it, with a nobleman who had promoted the Legislative Union by his vote. "I wonder what they intend to do with that useless building?" said the nobleman. "For my part, I hate the sight of it." "I do not wonder at that, my lord," returned Curran. "I never yet heard of a murderer who was not afraid of a ghost." Curran, as will be seen from these anecdotes, could say mordant and cutting things; but perhaps no man was ever insulted with such dialectical neatness and ingeniousness as Curran once was by the famous maker of "bulls," Sir Boyle Roche, in the Irish House of Commons. "The honourable gentleman says he is the guardian of his own honour," said Roche, in reply to a speech of Curran. "But on other occasions I have heard him boast that he was an enemy of sinecures."

Curran was once defeated in a conversational contest with Lady Morgan, one evening, in the lady's drawing-room, when the hostess, exaggerating the prevailing fashion in short sleeves, wore only mere straps over her shoulders. Curran was walking away from the little party who witnessed the conflict of the two wits, when Lady Morgan called out, "Ah, come back, Mr. Curran, and acknowledge that you are fairly beaten." "At any rate," said he, turning round, "I have this consolation, Lady Morgan, that you can't laugh at me in your sleeve."

O'Connell's sarcastic and graphic description of a lady of stiff, cold, and formal manners is very happy: "She has all the characteristics of a poker —except its occasional warmth." This recalls the story of the two Irish servants, who, discussing the stiff and unbending manners of the young lady of the family, agreed that "when she was a baby, her mother must have fed her upon boiled pokers, underdone." Another happy and humorous example of sarcasm—as apart from repartee—is afforded by the following anecdote. I quote it on the authority of a friend, who, I am afraid, was the villain of the incident. A most imperturbable man was followed from Westmoreland Street, Dublin, over the O'Connell Bridge to the General Post Office, by two little street arabs, who importuned him for the end of his cigar. "Throw us the butt, sir"; "Ah, sir, throw us the butt," cried the youths; but as the man did not betray the slightest consciousness of their existence, they gave him up at last in despair and disgust. "Arrah, let him alone," said one, with the most scorching scorn; "shure it's a butt he's picked up himself." I once heard a bumptious little man, who, acting as steward at athletic sports in Dublin, was very assertive in keeping back the crowd, thus addressed by an angry spectator, "If the consate was taken out of yez, ye'd be no bigger than a green gooseberry; and ye're as sour as wan already."

The *omadawns*, or half-witted fellows, who are to

be met with occasionally in Ireland—but not so commonly now as formerly—are noted for their bitter and sarcastic sayings. A fool was standing with some labourers cutting turf in a bog, when an unpopular land-agent, who had acquired by his passion and vindictiveness the significant name of "Danger," was seen driving along the high-road. "Ah! ha!" cried the fool, "there you go, Danger, and may I niver break bread if all the turf in this bog would warm me to ye." A fool, known as "Jim the omadawn," was some years ago a well-known character in Kilkee, the sea-side resort in Clare. "Now, Jim," said an upstart to him one day, "tell me the biggest lie you ever told, and I'll treat you to a pint of stout?" "Be me sowl, thin," cried Jim, "I say yer honer's a perfact gintleman."

A very happy example of a man falling into the pit which he had dug for somebody else is afforded by the following well-known but always fresh story of a famous repartee. John Parsons, one of the first Irish Commissioners of Insolvency, was travelling in a coach with Lord Norbury. Passing a gibbet, Norbury said with a chuckle, "Parsons, where would you be now if that gallows had its due?" "Riding alone, Norbury," was the quick reply. The neatness and felicity of this retort afford unmitigated surprise and delight. Parsons does not hold a conspicuous place in the band of brilliant, witty, and humorous lawyers and politicians who lived in Dublin at the close of the last century, but he was the sayer of two or three of the most perfect "good things" which that age produced. During the rebellion of '98 a country gentleman, who was suspected of being a rebel, met Parsons in Dublin. "I hear it is rumoured that I sympathise with disloyalty; but it is quite untrue," protested the squire. "It is well known that I have a stake in the country." "Faith, if you have," exclaimed Parsons, "I'd swear there's a pike at the end of it." The memory of Sir Boyle Roche has been kept green principally by his "bulls"; but, as his retort on Curran proves, he could say bitter things as well. Then his invitation to an Irish nobleman was amusingly equivocal and sarcastic. "I hope, my lord," said he, "if ever you come within a mile of my country house, you'll stay there all night." There is a well-known repartee which has been "fathered" upon many a wit, but whose real parentage I should like to set clear here. The Rev. Arthur O'Leary was a famous Irish priest, preacher, controversialist, politician, and wit, who died in London in 1802. In a polemical controversy with Bishop Woodward he wrote: "His lordship says he does not believe in the Papist purgatory. Well, perhaps he may go farther and fare worse."

Repartee and sarcasm are most wisely and

skilfully used when they are employed in ridiculing humbugs, exposing shams, rebuking rudeness, punishing bullies, and pricking the windbags of self-conceit. Chief Baron O'Grady, subsequently the first Lord Guillamore, had a dry humour and a biting wit. The latter was so fine that its sarcasm was often unperceived by the object against whom it was directed. A legal friend of his, who was extremely studious, but in conversation exasperatingly dull, showed the judge over his newly built house. The lawyer prided himself especially on a library that he had contrived for his own use, so secluded from the rest of the building that he could pore over his books in private, quite secure from disturbance. "This is splendid," exclaimed O'Grady. "My dear fellow, you could read and study here from morning till night, and no human being would be one bit the wiser." This recalls the capital story told of the late Father Healy, of Bray. A very pompous friend was showing Father Healy and other guests through his new house, on which he had spent a good deal in furnishing and decorating. In the library, the host, waving his hands towards the book-shelves, exclaimed, " Here, surrounded by these best friends, I feel most happy." "And I notice," said Father Healy, examining some of the volumes, "that, like a true friend, you never cut them."

During the famine of 1847, the local relief committee in Limerick had for one of its members a county landlord who had the reputation of being rather exacting with his tenants. "The people asked for bread, sir, and you gave them a stone," said a priest at one of the meetings of the committee. "Not at all, sir," replied the landlord; "they asked for potatoes and I generally gave them half a stone." Potatoes are sold in Ireland by the stone weight. At a meeting of another of these local relief committees, the question of a substitute for the potato was considered. "Don't you think, sir," said a member of the committee, addressing the chairman, "that turnips would be a wholesome and nutritious food for the people?" "Certainly," replied the chairman, "very wholesome and nutritious—with mutton, of course."

Charles Lever, the novelist, was once the guest of Dr. Whately, the Archbishop of Dublin, at his country seat. Among the other guests were some of the expectant clergy, who paid submissive court to their host. While the Archbishop and his guests were walking through the grounds, the prelate plucked from a bush a leaf which he declared had a most nauseous flavour. "Taste it," said he, handing the leaf to one of the clergymen. The latter smilingly obeyed, and then with a wry face subscribed to the botanical orthodoxy of the

Archbishop. "Taste it, you, Lever," said the gratified prelate, handing the leaf to the novelist. "No, thank you," said Lever, laughing; "my brother is not in your Grace's diocese." Michael Joseph Barry, one of the "Young Ireland" poets, was appointed, long after 1848, a police magistrate in Dublin. During the Fenian troubles an Irish-American, arrested in Dublin on suspicion of being in Ireland with seditious designs, was brought up before Barry. A constable swore that the suspect when arrested was wearing a Republican hat. "A Republican hat!" said the counsel for the prisoner; "does your worship know what that means?" "I presume," said Barry, "that a Republican hat is a hat without a crown."

A committee was formed to erect a monument over the grave of a popular Dublin physician, who died some years ago and was buried at Mount Jerome. A witty citizen who was asked to suggest an inscription for the memorial recommended the use of the famous allusion to Sir Christopher Wren, the architect, on St. Paul's Cathedral, London: *Si monumentum requiris circumspice*—"If you seek his monument, look around; if you doubt his merit, behold his works." An eminent Dublin doctor was a member of a house party in the district in which he had begun his career. One day he was observed in a neighbouring churchyard. "What is he doing among the graves?" asked one of the party. "Paying a visit to some of his old patients," replied another.

There is one good old story of Irish repartee which has done duty for many years. It turns up again and again, but as there is real humour in it, those who have often heard it must smile when it comes their way again. An English tourist, under the guidance of a peasant, was admiring the scenery of the Galtee Mountains. Pointing to a gap in the hills, the guide said it was known locally as "The Devil's Bit," and a low hill hard by was called "The Devil's Chair." "Indeed," remarked the Englishman; "the devil seems to have a good deal of property in these parts." "Yes, sur," rejoined the Irishman; "but he is an absentee landlord and lives in England."

Peabody, the philanthropist, and John Bright often visited Ireland together to fish the Shannon, making the pretty little village of Castleconnell, about six miles from Limerick, their headquarters. One day they went up for a turn on Lough Derg, at Killaloe. Two of the chief boatmen of the town joined forces in order to row these distinguished visitors. Late in the evening, after a hard day's work, the party arrived at the landing-stage, and Bright, accosting the inevitable policeman on the bank, said, "What is the proper price to pay these boatmen, constable?" He replied,

"Seven shillings and sixpence, yer honner; but some gintlemen give them ten shillings." Bright, turning to his companion, said, "I have no change, Peabody; have you three half-crowns?" The millionaire produced the coins and gave them to one of the boatmen. "Is that all ye're givin' me?" asked the latter. "That's all," said Peabody. Holding the coins in the open palm of his hand, and slowly scratching his head with the other, the man said: "An' they call ye Paybody, don't they? Well, I call ye Paynobody." Walking in Hyde Park, one Sunday afternoon, I was attracted by a crowd round a man who was attacking the movement for Home Rule. The speaker had only one leg; and his maimed condition was made the subject of chaff by some hostile Irishmen who were in the group. "Arrah, how did yez lose your leg, me ould bhoy?" said one. "Well, I'll tell you," said the man, interrupting the discourse. "On examining my pedigree, I found there was some Irish blood in me; and, becoming convinced that it had settled in my left leg, I had it cut off at once." "Wisha, thin," said the Irishman, "I'm sorry it wasn't in your head it settled."

Father Healy, of Bray, found himself at dinner beside a pompous and rather patronising Protestant clergyman. "Do you know, Father Healy," said the latter. "I've been sixty years in this world and I've never been able to find any difference between a good Protestant and a good Catholic." "My dear sir," replied Father Healy, "you won't be sixty seconds in the next world when you'll know the difference." On another occasion a Protestant of a polemical turn of mind got a similarly sarcastic answer to a rather unfortunate question. The eternity of punishment was under consideration, and purgatory, of course, figured in the argument. "Now, which would you rather go to, Father Healy," said the Protestant, "to hell or to purgatory?" "To the latter on account of the climate," replied the priest, "but to the former on account of the company—I'm so fond of Protestants."

Chapter XI

WILD FLOWERS OF SPEECH FROM IRELAND

ONE of the quaint mental characteristics of the Irish people, which so distinguish them from other races, is the odd and unexpected view they take of things. This habit of mind must not be confounded with the confusion of thought to which "bulls," or blunders in words or actions, are to be ascribed; and it is also quite distinct from the native wit and drollery of the race. The peasants who are endowed with this curious mental peculiarity are absolutely unconscious of the delightful quaintness and oddity of their views. They do not mean to be funny. They simply use the expressions which come naturally to their lips.

The points of difference between the native humour, the unconscious "bulls" or blunders, and this unexpected and surprising view of things—with which we are now concerned—will be more clearly illustrated by examples than by any attempt at elaborate definition. I was once present at a discussion among friends on the virtues or evils of smoking. One Irish lady in the party insisted that the habit shortened the lives of people who indulged in it. "I don't agree with that," said a gentleman. "There's my father, who smokes every blessed day of his life, and he is now seventy years old." "That proves nothing," cried the lady impulsively. "If he hadn't smoked he would probably be eighty by this time." The amusing retort of the lady is not a bad sample of that incongruity of ideas commonly known as a "bull." It was due, not to stupidity, but rather to excessive swiftness of thought and expression. Here, on the other hand, are instances of natural wit and repartee. An old peasant woman, overhearing a "squireen"—or upstart—complaining proudly of an attack of gout, remarked, "Bedad! some people are so consated that whin their corns bite them they say it's the gout." A gentleman, not liking the way in which some work on his property was being done by a labourer, gave vent to his indignation in some rude language. "Well, long life to yer honner," said the labourer, after the storm of passion had subsided, "and I'll be prayin' that if yer honner does die you'll go to heaven." "Indeed," said the gentleman, touched by this unexpected prayer from one whom he had consigned to eternal perdition a few moments before. "Yes, indeed, yer honner; for if yer honner gets to heaven it's a sure thing that we'll all go there." The Irish mental characteristic, to which I now particularly desire to draw attention, is illustrated in the following anecdote. A maid slipped as she was carrying a valuable tea-service on a tray, and the cups and saucers were—as she would express it—"smashed to smithereens." "Oh, Bridget, what have you done!" cried the mistress, in her grief for her ruined tea-set. "Oh, ma'am, there's nothin' to be onaisy about," said Bridget. "The Lord be praised! I didn't hurt meself in the laste." The humour of this story lies—it is needless to say—in the unexpected nature of the servant's answer.

Every one who has mixed freely for any time with the Irish peasantry must have experienced many such delightful surprises of an absolutely unstudied word play. Carriages, or enclosed vehicles of all kinds, are in Ireland often called "insides," to distinguish them from the "outsides," or public conveyances. On the night of a Vice-regal ball at Dublin Castle, there was a block of carriages in Dame Street, and a policeman, who was asked the cause of it, replied, "There was a collision, and Lady Brady's inside is scattered all over the street." A Limerick gentleman was discussing with his coachman the character of a noted "rowdy" named Jim MacKeown, who lived in an adjacent village. "I don't like to see that MacKeown about here, at all," said the gentleman.

"I should think that if he were well vexed he would not mind murdering a man." "Murthering a man, yer honner!" exclaimed the coachman. "Faith he would not stop at that. 'Pon my sowl, sir, if Jim were well roused he'd murther a bull!" The humour of this reply lies, of course, in its evidence of the odd point of view from which the coachman regarded Jim MacKeown's ferocity. It was the physical, rather than the criminal, side of the fellow's wickedness which the remark of his master brought to his mind. I remember hearing in the Police Court, Dublin, a quaint instance of incongruity between question and answer. Two women were charged with disorderly conduct, and a "naybour" was called to give evidence for one of them. She was asked what she knew as to the character and veracity of the accused. "Since ever I knew her, yer worship, she has kept her house clane and dacent," was the reply. The same lack of agreement in the view taken by two persons of the same subject might be illustrated by several amusing anecdotes. Some time ago the newspapers contained a tragic story of a drunkard who had filled himself with so much whiskey that on attempting to blow out the candle before going to bed his breath caught fire, and he was consumed in a few minutes. The report was read to a man who was "fond of a drop"—as they say in Ireland—in the hope that it would prove a salutary warning to him. "A warnin'!" he cried. "Faix, it will be a warnin' to me. I'll never blow a candle out again the longest day I live." A priest called on a farmer who had given way to drink, and lectured him on the evils of intemperance. "Just look at that poor cow, there at the stream," said his reverence. "You may be sure she won't drink too much." "Who'd thank her, when it's only wather?" replied the farmer.

A crier in the Assize Court at Galway was ordered by the judge to clear the building of all persons but the lawyers, whereupon he shouted, "All ye blackguards that isn't liars quit the Coort!" A reply of a somewhat similarly mixed character was given by the gamekeeper of an estate near Tralee to a gentleman of the town who requested leave for a day's shooting. "Shure, yer honner may as well do the poachin' as any other blackguard out of Tralee." Of course the gamekeeper meant that the gentleman might as well enjoy the advantages of the preserves as "the bhoys from Tralee," who were in the habit of surreptitiously coursing the estate for hares and rabbits. Writing about poaching recalls the comic answer given by a country girl who, on offering a salmon for sale to a fishmonger in Limerick, was questioned as to how she had obtained the fish. "Shure," she ingenuously replied, "my father is poacher to Lord Clare." A lady took her Irish maid to task for carelessness and forgetfulness. "Why is it, Mary," said she, "that you keep on making the same mistakes over and over again? Why don't you try to remember what I tell you?" The day happened to be very warm, so Mary returned the quaint reply, "Shure, ma'am, I can't be after aggravatin' me moind this hot weather." Two men were fighting in the streets of Cork. One got the other down, and was administering to him a severe punishment, when the man below cried out to the onlookers, "Oh, tare us ashunder, or we'll murdher ache other!"

A gentleman of humane feelings and religious principles witnessed, with deep pain, a man lashing his horse along a country road, and heaping curses on the unfortunate brute. "Stop, stop, my man!" he cried. "Don't you know it is not only very cruel to whip your horse like that, but also very absurd to be making use of those oaths to him, for the poor animal does not understand a single word of that language." "Shure, yer honner, it's his own fault if he doesn't understhand it," said the man, "for he hears enough of it every day." Another whimsical mis-interpretation of a reproof is the following. A priest arranged with a car-driver to call for him at the house of a friend after a dinner-party and drive him home. The jarvey was "fond of a drop," and manifestly had a quantity of drink taken when he called for his parish priest. "Drunk again, Jim," said Father Tom reprovingly, as he mounted the car. 'Well, to tell ye the truth, yer riverence," replied Jim, "I'm a bit that way meself." An amusing instance of misplaced compassion is recorded in the biography of Thomas Moore, the poet. As Moore, when a boy, was walking with his uncle from Sandymount into Dublin early one morning, they saw lying dead on the road a highwayman, who had evidently been shot during the night by some one whom he had attacked. There was a small bullet hole in his right temple, and an old woman pointing this out to Moore and his uncle, said, "Wasn't it the blessin' o' God, gintlemen, that the bullet didn't hit him in the eye?"

Smoking is very prevalent among old women in Ireland. They take to the habit as a solace in their declining years. I once asked an old woman at what time of her life she first began to indulge in tobacco. Her reply was, "I tuk to it as a bit of divarshion after me poor old man was tucked under the daisies." This was her way of saying that she took to the pipe as a comfort after the death of her husband. I remember helping to her feet an old countrywoman who had slipped and fallen heavily on the pavement one frosty day in Limerick. "I hope you are not hurt," I said. She made no reply, but fumbled excitedly in the folds of her dress. "What's the matter?" I asked anxiously. "I hope there are no bones broken." "Bones bruk!" she cried. "I was more concarned to know whether my ould *dudheen* was bruk;" and she produced from her pocket a little black pipe, happily intact.

The love of the Irish people for their native land perhaps never found quainter expression than in the reply of an Irishman in America as to how he was faring. "Pretty well, pretty well; but, faix, I'd rather be a gas-lamp in Dublin than President in the United States." A woman, in the slums of Cork, who had a portion of her ear bitten off in a fight at close quarters with another virago, told the story to a crony. "Oh, glory be to God to think she'd ate the mate raw!" was the absurd comment of the crony. A peasant who was about to emigrate was given a box by a lady who took an interest in him. "And what is the box for, ma'am?" he asked. "To put your clothes and things in, of course," said the lady. "Arrah! ma'am, do you wish me to go naked?" exclaimed the peasant in all simplicity. A navvy who had his leg cut off in a railway accident was advised to bring an action against the company for damages. "For repairs, you mane," he replied. "Shure, I've damages enough."

For combined extravagance and audacity nothing could beat the reply of a Galway farmer, who was told by his neighbours that he should be proud of his mare, who had won a race. "Proud of her!" he cried. "Why, I couldn't be prouder of her if she wrote the Holy Bible!" I heard a Mayor of Limerick tell the following whimsical anecdote at a municipal dinner in that city. A man came to him for a testimonial of character, as he was about to seek employment in Dublin. "But I have never seen you before," said his worship. "Faix, sir, that's the very reason I came to you," said the man. "I've niver been summoned before you. Indade, your worship niver had the laste bit of trouble with me." A man who was too fond of a glass of whisky was strongly recommended by his priest to drink nothing but water. "Arrah! Father," he replied, "shure, the carcases of these wather-drinkers grow only rushes, like Pat Nolan's low-lyin' fields." The land in question was marshy ground, suffering from excessive moisture. An old woman, very poor as well as very old, was condoled on the loss of her teeth. "Time for me to lose 'em," she replied, "when I've nothing for 'em to do."

Two women were discussing the merits of a certain blend of "tay." "Oh, it's shuper-excellent," said one; "it takes such a fine grip of the second relay of wather." There could be no better recommendation of a tea in Ireland, where, families being large and money scarce, and tea a favourite drink, "a second relay of wather" in the teapot is often necessary.

Sayings like these—deliciously quaint or delightfully extravagant—rise naturally and spontaneously to the lips of the Irish peasants. A gentleman noted for his bulk of person fell ill, and was kept alive only by the occasional administration of a teaspoonful of brandy. One of the servants of the house mentioned this circumstance to a friend. "A tayspoonful, is it?" said the other contemptuously. "An' what good would a tayspoonful be, sthrayin' about in such a wilderness of a man?" A beggar man was brought into a workhouse, got a good washing, which relieved him of many years' encrustation of dirt, and was then discharged in a new suit of clothes. As the old man was leaving the institution the master said, "Well, Mick, how do you like your fine new suit?" "Oh, thin, the duds is rale illigant," said he; "but the washin' took more hate out of me than is in four shutes of clothes." A proof that, to an Irishman at least, there are different ways of looking at things is afforded by this reply of a peasant to his priest. "Ah, Mick, Mick," said his reverence, "coming from the public-house again." "Of course, Father," said Mick; "shure I can't always stay there." An old countrywoman, visiting the dairy show at Dublin, saw an incubator for the first time. "Ah, thin, won't it be a grate aise to the hins entirely!" was her whimsical comment. A steward of an Irish estate was asked by a visitor whether certain trees were old. "Well, sir, thim that planted thim mustn't have the toothache any longer," was the mysterious reply. A horse dealer while examining a restive animal at Ballinasloe Fair had a narrow escape from a bad kick. "Faith, I'll have nothin' to do with that boyo," said he. "He's as handy with his hind legs as a pugilist."

During the Crimean War the supply of tallow was limited, and, as a consequence, candles went up in price. A woman was charged a halfpenny, instead of a farthing, for a tallow candle at the village shop. "Now, how is that, Mr. O'Brien?" she inquired. "It's due to the war, ma'am," said the shopkeeper. "Well," exclaimed the woman, "I niver thought they fight by candle-light before." A gentleman once said to a milkman—who admitted that he went with his pail occasionally to the pump—"How do you know, Tom, when to stop watering the milk?" "Begorra! yer honner, I go on watherin' till the customers cry out agin it," was the candid reply. A farmer's wife bought a box of matches in a shop in Limerick on her weekly visit to the city. On the next market day she returned the matches, as they were damp. "They're all right, ma'am," said the shopkeeper; "look at this," and he lit one of the matches by rubbing it on the leg of his trousers. "Arrah! get out with you!" cried the countrywoman. "When I want to light the fire must I come in six miles from Ballyneety to strike a match on yer ould britches?" There is a classic locality in Dublin known as Pill Lane. The way to the Four Courts from the northern part of the city lies through it. As a distinguished member of the Irish Bar passed down the Lane one day the following conversation took place between a fishwoman and a man: "Faix, if ye had all the larnin' that that gintleman has got undher his hair ye might consider yerself a wise man," said the woman. "Oh, thin, I'd sooner have the money he has in his purse," replied the man. "More fool you, thin!" said the woman; "shure 'tis with their brains the likes of him fills their pockets."

I think it will be admitted that these expressions,—absurd, quaint, audacious, whimsical, and extravagant,—which rise spontaneously and incessantly to the lips of the Irish peasantry, have a charm just as subtle and just as delicious as the most brilliant flashes of wit and humour.

An old peasant woman, who spoke little English, was examined by her priest, who told me the story, as to her knowledge of the doctrines of the Catholic Church. She was asked, among other questions, to repeat the names of the Trinity.

"Father, Son," she replied, and then, after a pause, added, "Faix, yer riverence, I forgit the name of the other gintleman." A friend of mine found two countrymen in the dust of the highway. The uppermost was thumping the lowermost. My friend said, "Let him get up. 'Tis a cowardly thing to hit a fellow when he's down." The victor panted, "Yer honner 'd never be after askin' me to let him up av ye knew the thrubble I had to down him." The governor of a prison in Limerick told me an amusing story of a refractory prisoner with whom he had once to deal. The man refused to work on the treadmill, and was brought before the governor for disobedience of the warder's orders. The governor asked him what objection he had to working on the treadmill. "Me go on the thread-mill!" he cried. "Niver, sur!" and, proudly drawing himself up, he added, "I'd rather lave the jail first!"

The boy being father to the man, the same quality of unconscious humour is to be found among the youth of Ireland. A Roman Catholic bishop was examining a class of schoolboys in the doctrines of the Church preparatory to the administration of Confirmation. "What is cursing?" he asked one youth. "Wishing ill to a neighbour," came the stereotyped reply. "Can any boy give me a better definition?" said the bishop. "Go to the divil! me lord," cried a bright little boy at the end of the class. A youth in another Confirmation class was asked the meaning of "a clear conscience." "It manes a clane inside," was the reply. A school inspector told me that while examining a class of small boys in geography in a national school in a remote part of Ireland, he put the question, "What is a lake?" "Shure 'tis the hole in a kittle, sur," said one of the youths. It was the only "lake" with which he was acquainted. A little boy was caught by an irate farmer up in one of his apple-trees. "Come down this instant!" roared the farmer, "and I'll give you a sound box in the ear, you bla'guard!" "Troth, sur, I wouldn't come down if you'd give me a dozen," said the youth.

Irish domestics are widely noted for their simplicity and their quaint remarks. A lady desiring to make the most of her choice tap of table-beer, the merits of which her servants had discovered, for it disappeared rapidly, thus addressed her Irish butler, "Daly, what do you think would be the best thing to do in order to save this beer as much as possible?" "Well, ma'am," replied the butler, "I don't think you could do better than to place a barrel of good strong ale close by the side of it." An Irish girl called at a house in London in answer to an advertisement for a general servant. "Have you a character?" asked the mistress. "Indeed, ma'am, I'm sorry to say

I've no character. I had a beautiful wan whin I left Ireland, but I losht it the night I crossed over to Holyhead in the steamer," was the laconic reply. An Irish man-servant was discovered in a lie. On being accused by his master of stating what was not the truth, he excused himself by saying, " Plase, sur, I lost my prisence of mind."

Father Tom Burke, the famous Dominican preacher, used to tell the following story: Pill Lane, Dublin, is an obscure fish market. The vendors of fish—in all cases old women—sit along the edge of the pavement with their baskets of herring and mackerel before them. It happened that "a mission"—or a series of devotional services, morning and evening, for a week—was given in the neighbouring Catholic Church of North Anne Street. One of the fishwomen attended it, and was consequently away from Pill Lane for some time. When she returned she was received with side remarks of a sarcastic nature from the other women, who considered her action in attending the mission as a reflection upon themselves. One took her pipe out of her mouth and remarked to the next crone, "Oh, look at the ould rip! Nothin' would do her but to go to her duty and turn religious." "Musha," said the other, "I pity the poor priest that had to listen to her story in Confession after twenty years of street-walkin'!" The devotee could no longer stand this "chaff" with equanimity. Jumping to her feet and singling out the most sarcastic of her opponents, she exclaimed, " Mag Molloy, ye're takin' advantage of me now because I'm in the state of grace, but, plase God, I won't be long so, an' thin I'll be even with yez!" As Father Burke was leaving a church in which he had preached a number of sermons, an old woman, who was sitting in the churchyard, rocking herself to and fro, saying her prayers, cried out on seeing him, " Och! shure, it's yerself that's the darlint fine man. We niver knew what sin was till ye kem among us." She alluded, of course, to his preaching.

A newly-married couple were setting up house in the South of Ireland. Being desirous of raising poultry, they bought a number of live chickens from a woman at the door, who assured them they were "dirt chape." The next morning every chick was discovered stone dead. The husband, vowing vengeance, lay in wait for the wily chicken woman, and as soon as she hove in sight greeted her warmly with, " How dare you sell fowls that were as good as dead?" "*Dead*, is it, your riverence?" with a pious uplifting of the hands and eyes. "Och! it's thankful you should be it was neither yourself nor the mistress." A gentleman and his *fiancée* were travelling in the North of Ireland some time ago. On the arrival of the train at a little wayside station, an old woman appeared at the carriage door laden with a very heavy basket. Seeing this, the young gentleman at once went to her assistance. In reply to her reiterated thanks and blessings, he made the casual remark, "Don't mention it," upon which the old lady replied in a very confidential whisper and with a sly glance at the *fiancée*, as though she would not make mischief for the world, "Begorrah, yer honour, I won't tell a sowl." When Miss Balfour was visiting the distressed districts in the West of Ireland, six or seven years ago, an old man, who had been calling down blessings on her head and on the head of her brother, walked away saying, "By the powers, if it hadn't been for the famine it's starving entirely that we'd be this day." A domestic was asked if she had a good mistress. "Good!" she exclaimed. "Shure, if she murdhered you, you couldn't but like her."

A lodging-house in Cork took fire during the night. One of the inmates being aroused by the noise, asked what was the matter. "The house is burning. Get up," he was told. "Arrah, what's that to me? I'm only a lodger;" and turning over, proceeded to go to sleep again. A peasant woman in the north was asked by a tourist if the people in that part of the country spoke the Irish language. "No, yer honner, none of thim do around here." "But," he went on, "when they get excited and angry don't they then use the

Irish language?" "Faix, yer honner," said the woman, "whin they're angry it's very bad language they use."

An Irish dispensary doctor told me of an old woman who, being dissatisfied with another local practitioner, transferred the care of all her bodily ailments to him. "So you prefer my medicines to those of Dr. Delany?" he said to her once. "Och! indeed, doctor dear," she replied, "ye're a dale betther than that other ould humbug and imposther." A drunken man was staggering home with a sober friend. "Come on, Pat," said the latter, "come on; the road is long." "I know it's long," said Pat, as he lurched from side to side; "but it's not the lingth of it, but the breadth of it, that's killin' me." A beggarman called on a shopkeeper in Tralee, and having told a pitiful tale of children starving at home, asked for a copper. The shopkeeper, suspecting that the man wanted the money for drink, exclaimed, "Be off out of that! I know your game. You're collecting subscriptions for a public-house." The newly-wedded wife of a Westmeath landlord, desiring to act the part of a Lady Bountiful, had a school-house erected on the estate, and supplied the erstwhile barefooted children with shoes and stockings. One day the lady met a woman who asked her for some favour which she was unable to grant. "An' is that the thanks I get for makin' me childer wear shoes and go to school to plase ye?" was the woman's indignant comment. A priest who was an enthusiastic advocate of the blessings of temperance succeeded in inducing a worthy, but not very abstemious, parishioner to take the pledge. Shortly afterwards his reverence met his convert in a condition of advanced intoxication. "How is this, James?" asked the amazed priest; "I thought you were a teetotaler?" So I am, yer riverence," replied James, "so I am a teetotaler; but I'm not a bigotted wan." Another priest, being successful in getting a parishioner, who was arrested for being drunk and disorderly, discharged with a caution, said to the man, " Now remember, Pat, what brought you to the dock." "Faith, I will, yer riverence," said Pat. "I'll be even wid that bhoyo, Constable Feeney, yet." A well-known Dublin temperance advocate was standing near a public-house waiting for a tram, when a man, in a rather intoxicated condition, approached the tavern. "Stop!" said the temperance advocate; "the devil is going in there with you." "He needn't, thin," said the man, "for I've only tuppence."

One of the most incongruous remarks I ever heard was from the clerk to a chapel in Limerick. One Sunday, during Mass, a number of boys were playing in the yard of the chapel, when the clerk rushed out and shouted at them angrily. "Go in to the divil out of that, and say yer prayers!" Kilkee is a delightful little sea-side resort beside the Atlantic on the Clare coast. A resident, during a visit to Dublin, complained to a friend of the loneliness of the place. "Ah," said the other, thinking of the Atlantic in its many moods, "but you have a beautiful view." "Sorra a bit," said the Kilkee man; "shure there's nothing but the say betune us and America." At a Viceregal ball, in Dublin Castle, a young military officer approached a pretty young lady from the provinces, who was sitting with her mother, and asked her whether he might have the pleasure of a dance, but before she could reply the fond parent hastily broke in, "'Deed, and you can't then have a dance with Molly. She's keeping herself cool for the Earl of Clanfarly!"

Chapter XII

LOVE-MAKING IN IRELAND

A SONG called "The Sprig of Shillelagh," which has been very popular with the Irish peasantry since it was written, close on a century ago, says,—

> "Love is the soul of a neat Irishman;
> He loves all that's lovely, and loves all he can."

But, though there seems to exist a widespread impression that strong, passionate, masterful love is a characteristic of the Irish temperament, love-making in Ireland is really a very calm and placid business; and the old song I have quoted, notwithstanding, the average Irish peasant takes unto himself a mate with as clear a head, as placid a heart, and as steady a nerve, as if he were buying a cow at Ballinasloe Fair. The peasantry of Ireland are very emotional and very sentimental. And yet, with that singular contrariness of character which makes them so uncomprehensible as a race, love by no means decides all the marriages that are made in Ireland. The match is often arranged in a ludicrously cool, business-like, and

mercenary fashion, between the parents of the
"boy" and the "girl," the young people themselves
rarely being allowed, and indeed rarely expecting,
any voice in the matter. But if there is little
romance in the origin of most of the matrimonial
contracts made in rural Ireland, they are as a rule
entirely successful. The marriages thus prosai-
cally arranged are as happy as happy can be.
Pat and Mary fall fondly in love with each other,
after they are made husband and wife; children
quickly spring up around their hearth, and the
older they grow the more passionately do they
cling to each other. Their domestic felicity is
rarely, if ever, disturbed by jealousy, for Pat makes
the faithfullest of husbands and Mary the fondest
and truest of wives; and as there is little or no
illicit passion, the crimes which spring from that
source, and make desolate so many a home in
other countries, are almost unknown in Ireland.

The great marrying season in Ireland is Shrove-
tide. During the forty days of Lent the Irish
peasantry, in accordance with the ordinances of
the Church, abstain from matrimony, as well as
from eggs, butter, and milk. Some time before the
approach of that holy season a farmer with a
marriageable son or daughter whom he desires to
see settled tells his friends and neighbours of the
fact. He usually conveys the intelligence in an
indirect, offhand manner. He meets a friend at

the fair or market, and says with a laugh, "Whisper here, Jim; I'm trainin' up me little Maggie for your Johnny." "Ah now, Jim," the other says, "you do me a grate favour entirely. But mind you, my little Johnny is very particular. The boy do be sayin' what a grate fortin he'll want with his wife." The subject having thus been broached the parents discuss it whenever they meet, and it often happens that a long time elapses, and many a discussion and wrangle takes place, before the terms are finally settled. The farm generally goes with the boy, and the great difficulty in the arranging of matches is the fixing of the girl's dowry, which consists partly of money and partly of furniture and culinary utensils, as a set-off to the land. Often the affair is broken off because the girl's father resolutely refuses to throw into the scale another "tin-pound note," or a kitchen table, or it may be a pot. Sometimes "the Matchmaker" —an old woman who undertakes these delicate negotiations for a consideration—induces the parents to "split the differ"—that is, to come to an agreement on half the value of the additional articles of furniture, or half the amount of the additional sum of money, in dispute; and occasionally the point is referred for arbitration to some old and substantial farmer or trader of the district who is held in esteem by both parties. It is a curious circumstance that the priest, to whom the Irish peasant flies for advice in all his other troubles and difficulties, is rarely or never consulted in regard to a marriage. There is a superstition that "a priest's match" always leads to an unhappy marriage.

A funny story is told of the parents of a couple in Cork who met together to arrange a match. All had nearly been settled, when the father of the girl objected to parting with a kitchen table. "An' won't you give me the table, Tim?" said the proposed bridegroom's father. "No, Pat," replied the other. "Thin the divil a bit of me son your daughter will get!" cried the angry parent, and the negotiations were suspended. Another amusing anecdote, current in Ireland, throws further light on these interesting parleyings between the fathers. At Irish fairs there is a curious custom known as "dirtying the baste." When the terms of the purchase of a pig or a cow are agreed upon, after a long and vehement haggling between buyer and seller, the former picks up a piece of mud on his finger, or stick, and rubs it on the hind-quarters of the animal, to indicate that the bargain is concluded. Two wealthy cattle-buyers met to arrange a marriage between their children. The fortune of the bride was, as usual, fiercely disputed. "Look here, Mick," cried the father of the young man, "give me another hundred pounds, and be me sowl you may dirty the bhoy!".

But it is only when the affair is satisfactorily

settled by the parents that Pat and Bridget are informed of their fate. They rarely demur to the arrangement. They know it is the custom of the country; and custom makes people everywhere do things which to outsiders seem amazing and incomprehensible. Pat and Bridget, if neighbours' children, are, of course, acquainted; but if the parents reside in different districts, it is probable that they may have never even seen each other until it has been arranged that they are to become man and wife.

One Shrove Tuesday—the eve of Lent, during the forty days of which marriage is prohibited—a large number of peasant weddings were being celebrated in a chapel near Mill Street, Co. Cork. In the front rows or pews of the chapel sat the brides and bridesmaids, in gay attire, waiting their turn to go to the altar steps for the marriage ceremony, while some little distance down the aisle sat the bridegrooms and their male friends. One of the young men was congratulated by an acquaintance. "An' where is yer intinded, Joe?" asked the friend. "Bejob, Mick," said the bridegroom unconcernedly, "I couldn't tell ye, but I believe she's up there among the feathers and ribbons in the front row of sates." In fact, in this particular case it was not until the clerk who was assisting the priest at the altar cried out, "Joe MacSwiney and Margaret Dunphy will now come forward," and the parties met at the altar-steps, that the bride and bridegroom saw themselves for the first time!

I believe it was Lord Beaconsfield who cynically observed, "Early marriages are to be deprecated, especially for men." That is a maxim which does not prevail in Ireland. A favourite proverb of the peasantry in regard to matrimony is, " Either marry very young, or become a monk very young." Early marriages are the rule in Ireland, and the poorest marry the earliest. Farmers marry later in life than the agricultural labourers. Those who are accustomed to comparative comforts are as a rule more prudent, and exercise greater self-restraint in the matter of matrimony than the very poor. The fairly well-to-do form for themselves a standard of comfort below which they will not very willingly descend. But with the poor, especially in Ireland, it is otherwise. Their position is comfortless, their earnings are precarious, and with that resignation and fatalism which is so characteristic a trait in the Irish nature they will say, " Shure, whatever we do we can't be worse off than we are." In a word, no prudential motives seem to exist to counteract the natural promptings of the human passions.

And yet many of the Irish poor enter into matrimony as a sort of provident investment for old age. A very intelligent Irish peasant once said to me, "A poor man ought to marry young that his children may be able to assist him when he grows old." When Pat and Biddy begin housekeeping, their little cabin is soon filled with children; and the more their flock increases the more they say, "Shure the childer will be a grate support to us in our ould age." And, happily, this investment for old age never fails them. In no country in the world is the affection between children and parents so strong; in no country in the world is the duty of children to provide for their aged parents held so sacred as in Ireland. Four generations may be seen in many of the poorest cabins in the west—the children, the young father and mother, the old grandparents, and an ancient great-grandmother or great-grandfather. The thousands of pounds which have been annually sent by children in the Colonies and in America to parents in Ireland during the past half-century is another striking demonstration of this intense filial affection.

This, then, explains the early marriages in Ireland. But, of course, in some cases the step does not turn out to have been wise. I once met an old peasant who had married when he was nineteen, and thought he had not done well. "I'll niver marry agin so young if I wor to live to the age of Methuselah!" he exclaimed. And he kept his word; he was eighty when he married the second time.

Many humorous stories might be told to illustrate how marriage is regarded in Ireland—as in every other country, alas!—simply as a means of retrieving broken fortunes, or of obtaining an improved position in life. A small farmer went into a bank in Limerick, when the following conversation took place between him and the manager. "Good-mornin', yer honner; I called about a little business, and though there's other banks in the town, I thought I'd give yer honner the compliment." "Well, Tom, I'm glad to see you; and what's the business?" "I hear the interest in Widow Brady's farm is to be sould soon, yer honner; and I want to 'rise' five hundhred poun' to buy it." "Nonsense, Tom; how could you ever pay the money back, if I lent it to you?" "Oh, there's nothin' asier in life. Shure me young Jim 'ud get it in a fortune when he marries." "And may I ask, Tom, what age is the young fellow?" "He's just three year ould, yer honner." Needless to say Tom was unable to raise the money on that remote security. The wife of an Irish landlord was once censured by a friend for bringing her second son up in idleness, instead of putting him to a profession or a business. "Oh," she replied, "he's a fine, handsome boy, and when he grows to be a young man I'll send him to England, and, take my word for it, some rich English lady will treat herself to him." A gentleman who had married well gave some assistance to a poor peasant. "Well, yer honner," exclaimed the thankful countryman, "the blessin' o' God on ye. An' shure it is on ye, for haven't He given ye a lady that cud keep ye widout doin' a sthroke of work all the rest of yer days." A farmer who was told he would find it difficult to get a daughter off his hands, as she was not very pretty, laughed the idea to scorn. "Not very purty!" he cried " Faix, I'll make her purty with cows!"

Further light is thrown on this mercenary mode of regarding matrimony by the following story which was told me by a member of the Irish Bar. Some years ago my friend was standing outside the bank at Tralee, talking to the manager, when a peasant approached, and took off his hat to indicate that he had a communication to make. "Well, what is it?" asked the manager. "A deposit-note, sur," said the peasant, handing him the paper. "One hundred and twenty pounds," said the manager, looking at the note. "Your wife must sign it, for it is in your wife's name." "She's dead, sur," said the peasant. "When did she die?" "Ere yestherday, yer honner." "Faith, you haven't lost much time," said the manager. "And now that I come to look at you, didn't you bring me another deposit-note of your wife's, about a year and a half ago?" "'Tis true for you, sur," said the peasant. "That was my first wife.

'Tis the way wid me, that I'm very lucky wid the wimmin."

"Pat, is this true that I hear?" said a landlord to one of his tenants, whom he met on the roadside. "An' what's that, yer honner?" asked Pat. "That you are going to marry again." "Oh, that's so, yer honner." "But your first wife has only been dead a week, Pat." "An' shure she's as dead now as she ever will be, yer honner," was Pat's unexpected and inconclusive reply. "Yerra!" said an old woman, in tones of amazement, to a young peasant girl newly married. "What did ye see in Jim that made ye tie yerself to him?" "Shure, he was tormintin' the life out o' me, followin' me everywhere, an' I just married the *omadaun* (fool) to get rid o' him," was the reply. But it was a peasant woman who advanced perhaps the quaintest reason for marrying the third time that I ever heard. Her parish priest met her and said, "So you have married again, Mary? There was Tom Whelan and Mick Murphy, rest their souls, and now there is Tim Maloney. "Och, yer riverence," said she, "it wasn't for the fun or the divarshion of it I married the third time, but I thought it wud soften me poor ould cough, which I'm kilt wid ivery winther."

But, happily, many of the marriages in rural Ireland have their spice of romance. The match is made by the boy and girl themselves. An Irish peasant-maid in the heyday of her youth, with her pretty figure, her abundant black hair, her large blue eyes, with their indescribable half-alluring, half-shy expression, and the soft, lulling intonation of her coaxing and beguiling brogue, is quite irresistible ; and the boy has too often an impressionable heart and a " deludhering tongue " to render it always necessary that the parents should " make the bargain." The youthful couples met at dances, or on Sundays after Mass,—even a wake is turned to account for a little courting,—and they are in hearty accord with the boy who said, " It is a grate pleasure entirely to be alone, especially whin yer sweetheart is wid ye." " Do you drame of me, Mike ? " said the girl to her lover as they walked arm-in-arm down the lonely glen. " Drame of you, is it, Kate ? Shure, 'tis the way wid me, that I can't sleep dramin' of you, me darlin'." Yes, they have the flattering tongue, those Irish boys. " And I wish I was in jail for stealin' ye," was the compliment one of them paid to a pretty *colleen*. Even when they get a refusal they have a " soft word " to say. Eileen was engaged to another boy, and so she had to say " no " to Tim when he asked her. " Wisha, thin," said Tim, with a sigh, " I wish you'd been born twins, so that I cud have half of yez." An amusing instance of the fascination of Irish girls occurred some years ago at Dingle, Co. Cork. During a period of agrarian disturbance some of the well-to-do residents petitioned the authorities to send them a military force. But there happened to be no accommodation in the town for the soldiers; and so the Government sent a small cruiser to the bay. The friendliest relations were quickly established between the ship and the people. Several marriages between the sailors and the girls of the town followed. Then the officers caught the infection. The commander and the purser married two sisters, daughters of the Protestant rector; and the lieutenant found his better half in the daughter of the local landlord. A most delightful state of things prevailed till one sad Saturday a communication was received from the Admiralty, ordering the commander to leave the bay, the very next day, under sealed orders, which were to be opened when he had got twenty miles out to sea. A terrible commotion prevailed in the town. The wives of the sailors were distracted at the thought that they were to be so suddenly parted from their husbands, and perhaps not see them again for years. But the commands of the Admiralty are inexorable and must be obeyed. Accordingly, on Sunday the cruiser steamed out of the bay, and was soon lost to the view of the heart-broken wives and their relations assembled on the shore.. Early next morning, guns were heard in the bay, and the inhabitants of Dingle, on rushing to their windows, saw with amazement the cruiser at her old moorings! The commander, on opening the sealed orders, found instructions to return again to the bay. The Lords of the Admiralty stated they had been informed that the crew of the cruiser were having more balls, and excursions, and wives than were good for discipline; and they expressed the hope that after this lesson the commander would be more careful in future!

"Ah," said a girl shyly to a boy who was slow in making up his mind, "if you wor me, Jack, and I wor you, I wud be married long ago." But the girls in Ireland are not disposed to do the wooing in that fashion. Times have changed since an old woman in the West of Ireland used to impress upon all the rising female generation in her district that "E'er a man is better than ne'er a man." "Marry him, is it!" exclaimed a peasant girl to whom her parents were suggesting an old man as a husband. "Faix, I'd rather be tied be the neck to a milestone." The girls in Ireland can afford just as well, if, indeed, not better, than the girls of any other country to take up this independent position in regard to matrimony. Two old servants were discussing the matrimonial prospects of the young lady of the house. "Oh, the Lord love her and send her that she is not an ould maid," said one. "Ah, hould yer whist!" exclaimed the other. "Is it the likes of Miss Norah left an ould maid? Shure she can get heaps an' heaps o' min."

The boys, therefore, have often a great deal of difficulty in inducing the girls to agree to "getting the words said," as the marriage ceremony is colloquially described. In one case I have heard of, a farm-servant was told by the girl to whom he proposed that she was too much attached to her mother and her mother to her to think of getting married. "Arrah, shure, no husband could equal me mother in kindness," said she. "Oh, thin!" exclaimed the boy, "be me wife, and shure we can all live together, and see that I don't bate yer mother." He could not have meant that he would ill-use the mother—that was only his Irish way of putting things—for his declaration induced the girl to yield to his wishes. A bashful youth (a rather rare person in Ireland, be it said), who was in love with a girl, entrusted his proposal for her hand to his sister one day that the maid visited his father's cabin, while he, with anxious heart, hid behind the door, awaiting the result. The girl, who did not care to be wooed at second-hand, replied with a saucy toss of her head, "Indeed now, if I'm good enough to be married, I'm good enough to be axed." The boy then stuck his head into the room and exclaimed, with a sob in his voice, "Mary, *allanah*, will yez do what Maggie axed ye?" In another case an exasperated rural lover was driven, as he said himself, "beyant the beyants" (beyond the beyonds—that is, to extreme desperation) with the carryings-on of the girl with another boy. "I'll never spake to you any more, Peg!" he cried, with excusable vexation. "Oh, thin, keep yer spake to yerself," said the provoking girl coolly; "I'm sure I cud get along very well widout it, or you ayther." "I'm sure so can I, thin," was the lover's wrathful rejoinder. The parents also often stand in the boy's way. "Well, Mr. Hickey," said a young labourer to the father of his heart's desire, "any chance of gettin' Mary this Shrove?" "Arrah, take your time, Pat Meehan; shure the heifer is young," said the cruel, matter-of-fact father. "In any case, I couldn't spare her till I get in the praties."

When the day has been named, whether by arrangement between the boy and girl themselves or through the intermediary of their parents, preparations are made, on the most extensive scale, for a grand wedding. It is considered essential in the humblest circles that, for the honour of the family, the guests at the wedding, which include sometimes the whole of the country-side, should have lots of eating and drinking,—"lashin's and lavin's of iverything." Closeness on such an occasion is the unforgivable social sin. "Arrah, if I wor gettin' married," I have heard a woman indignantly exclaim when she saw a poor display at a wedding, "I'd sell every stitch to me back, and go naked, in order to get married dacently!"

To make a "gran' match" and have a "grate weddin'" is the ambition of Irish parents in regard to their daughters. Sometimes a strange notion prevails as to what is a grand match. I once asked an old woman what had become of a certain young girl, "Faix, she made a gran' match, entirely; for a rale gintleman married her," was the reply; "but it turned out he was married before." "And the poor girl—where is she now?" I inquired. "Oh, shure, she's at home. She hasn't put her fut outside the dure for months, ashamed to show her face to the naybours." A pitifully grand match, surely!

A pretty Irish servant-maid, who had got married, called to see her mistress. "I hear you are going to Australia with your husband, Kitty," said the lady. "Are you not afraid of such a long voyage?" "Well, ma'am, that's his look-out," said Kitty. "I belong to him now, an' if anything happens to me, shure it'll be his loss, not mine." But there is not always that complete loss of the wife's identity in the husband which the above anecdote suggests. It is the wife that rules the household in rural Ireland. The title the husband gives her is "herself." "Shure herself wouldn't allow me," is the excuse he usually advances when he is asked to do something which, perhaps, it would be better that he should not do. "How is herself?" and "How is the woman that owns ye?" are greetings commonly heard between husbands in Ireland. The husband surrenders to her all his earnings, to the uttermost farthing; an excellent arrangement for Pat, who, feeling the money burning in his pocket, as he says himself, is disposed to get rid of it rapidly; and a still more excellent arrangement for the sake of the children. Bridget is, indeed, Pat's guardian angel. On many a Saturday, when a boy in Limerick, have I seen the long line of country cars returning homewards from market in the dusk of the summer evenings, the wives driving, and the husbands, with a "drop taken," perhaps, lying quietly in the straw behind.

There is a story told of a young Cork lady who was presented at the Vice-regal Court, Dublin, shortly after her marriage. The Viceroy has the pleasant duty of kissing on the cheek the ladies presented him at a drawing-room; but when his Excellency was about to give this young lady the regulation salute, she cried, "Oh, no! that privilege is exclusively reserved for Mr. O'Mahony." And so it is with most Irish wives in every class of society. Husbands rarely have occasion for jealousy; and, as I have before said, there are few countries in the world where, as a rule, the marriage state is so happy.

Of course, there are exceptions to the general serenity of the domestic hearth and the fond attachment between husband and wife. I knew at least of one Irishman in Limerick whose life was made miserable by a drunken wife. She had sold everything in the home for drink; and, as a last resource, she threatened to commit suicide if money, to procure more liquor were not forthcoming. Next morning, before proceeding to work, the husband, driven to desperation by his wife's conduct left his two new razors lying on the table, telling her to "select the best wan ov thim." At night when Pat came home, trembling with apprehension, he found his wife huddled up in a corner, not dead—but dead drunk. By her side was a pawn-ticket, and on it was written, "*Two razors, 1s. 6d.*" There is another story of the exception which proves the rule. Some years ago, as the mail-boat from Ireland was entering Holyhead harbour, a lady fell into the water. One of the sailors, an Irishman, jumped overboard and rescued her from death by drowning. When she was safe on deck again the husband, who was a calm spectator of the accident, handed the brave sailor a shilling. The spectators did not hesitate to express their indignation of the man's meanness, when the sailor, with native shrewdness, threw a new light on the matter by saying, "Arrah, don't blame the gintleman; he knows best. Maybe if I hadn't saved her he'd have given me half a crown." I am disposed to think that the husband in this case was not an Irishman. History, certainly, does not indicate his nationality.

A party of English tourists at Killarney, whi st partaking of their luncheon, animatedly discussed the vagaries of courtship. "Let us ask our guide for his opinion," suggested one of them. "Here, Pat," he continued, "what's your idea about courting?" "Well, ladies and gintlemin," replied Pat, rubbing his chin and grinning as he spoke, "Ye've oftin h'ard it said that ivery cloud has a silver linin'; but I think some people's coortin' brings the silver to the fore, wid the cloud hangin' behind like a thief in the dark. Now, gintlemin and ladies, when I was coortin' the ould woman I'm married to, I was that fond of her I could have ate her; an', upon me conscience, I'm sorry I didn't ate her, for I've had to swolly a lot since." A woman named Mrs. Flynn was placed in the dock of one of the Dublin police courts, a few months ago, charged with having assaulted her husband. The police applied for a remand, as the husband, being confined to hospital, was unable to appear. The woman seemed also to be in a very battered condition. Her face was bruised, one eye was closed, and she had a bandage over her head. "What an awful condition the poor woman is in!" said the magistrate pityingly. "Och, yer worship," exclaimed the woman, with a ring of exultation in her voice, "just wait till yez see Flynn!"

However, marital relations in Ireland are, as I have said, of the most harmonious character; and if a husband and wife do fall out occasionally, and even resort to blows, like Mr. and Mrs. Flynn, they think nothing the worse of each other in the end. "It's seldom you hear of an Irishman staining his own hearthstone with blood," said an Irish girl who was being "chaffed" by some English friends about agrarian murders in Ireland. "In Ireland," she went on, "if a wife offends her husband, a few hard words, or at most, blows, is her punishment. But if the English boor's wife offend him, very likely she'll go to bed to-night to rise in the morning and find her throat cut." Yes, a blow is the Irish wife's worst punishment. "That's a fine black eye you've got, ma'am," said a man to a woman sitting over her basket of fish in Pill Lane. "Fightin', I suppose, agin?" "No, I wasn't fightin'," replied the fishwoman. "Himself (her husband) it was that gave me that;" and, facing fiercely round on her questioner, she added, "and I'd like to know who had a better right!" A labourer out of employment applied for outdoor relief for himself and his wife, at the North Dublin Union. "Well, my good fellow, we must have evidence that you are legally married," said the chairman of the relief committee. "Begor, sir,

I've the best proof in the wuruld," said the applicant, and bending his head he displayed a scar on his skull. "Does yer honner think," he added, "I'd be after takin' that abuse from any wan but a wife?"

Having such happy homes and faithful wives, is it any wonder that Irishmen are loth to leave them behind? An Irish car-driver was wrapping himself up carefully before starting on a journey on a cold winter's day. "You seem to be taking very good care of yourself," said the impatient fare. "To be shure I am, sur," replied the driver. "What's all the wuruld to a man when his wife's a widow?"

Chapter XIII

THE HUMOURS OF IRISH POLITICS

WITH all its seriousness, and oftentimes its tragedy, there has ever been a whimsical side to Irish agitation. Every political movement in Ireland, no matter how intense and bitter the party or sectarian passions it has aroused, has, happily, been relieved by many humorous incidents at which all Irishmen, without distinction of politics or faith, have laughed. A delight in fun is the one touch of nature which makes the warring political sections in Ireland kin.

As long ago as 1759, when a report was circulated through Dublin that Parliament contemplated passing an Act of Union with Great Britain, some whimsical and characteristically Irish scenes took place in front of the Parliament House in College Green. A large anti-Union mob took possession of the Green, and as the members of Parliament appeared, on their way to the respective Houses, they were compelled by the people to take an oath "to be true to Ireland and to vote against the

Union." Just as the Lord Chancellor had taken the oath, the Lord Chief Justice drove up in his carriage. The idea took possession of the mob that perhaps their administration of the oath was not quite proper and legal, and that, therefore, it might not be considered binding by the Lord Chancellor. They consequently compelled the Lord Chancellor to repeat the oath in the presence of the Lord Chief Justice; then they administered it to the Lord Chief Justice in the presence of the Lord Chancellor; and, as a further precaution to ensure the legality of the entire proceeding, they detained the Lord Chief Justice, so that he might be a witness to the taking of the oath by other Peers and members of the House of Commons as they arrived. Those members of Parliament—Peers and Commoners—who were known to be in favour of the Union were rolled in the gutter. Finally, the House of Lords was invaded by the mob, and an old woman, with a clay pipe in her mouth, was placed on the Woolsack.

Edmund Burke's only son, Richard—he whose early death brought bitter sorrow to the great statesman in his old age—was appointed by the Catholics of Ireland in 1792 to act as their agent in forwarding the movement for Emancipation. He visited the Irish House of Commons one evening to present a petition on behalf of his clients. Ignorant of the rules of the House, he thought the document should be presented at the table, and not at the Bar. Accordingly, he crossed the Bar and walked up the floor of the Chamber. Loud and angry cries of "A stranger in the House!" was raised on all sides. The Speaker roared, "Sergeant-at-Arms, do your duty!" The Sergeant-at-Arms drew his sword, and advanced to meet Burke, who was now retreating with agitated and frightened looks to the Bar; but, catching sight of the cold steel in the hands of the Sergeant-at-Arms, he lost his head completely, and, returning up the floor again, passed the Speaker's chair at a run, and ultimately got out of the building by a back door. When his escape was reported to the House, the Sergeant-at-Arms was censured by the Speaker for not having succeeded in arresting Burke in the building. It was on this occasion that in extenuation of the shortcomings of the Sergeant-at-Arms, Sir Boyle Roche delivered his famous dictum, "No man could be in two places at the one time, unless he was a bird." "How," he continued, "could the Sergeant-at-Arms stop him in the rear, while he was catching him in the front?" Toler said the incident reminded him of "a printer's mix" of two items of news, which he had seen shortly before in a Dublin newspaper: "Yesterday a petition was presented to the House of Commons—it missed fire, and the villain ran off."

The first time the motion for the Union was moved in the Irish Parliament, in 1799, it was defeated by a small majority; and as the members came out they were cheered or groaned—according as they had opposed or supported the motion—by a great crowd assembled in College Green. Mr. Foster, the Speaker of the House of Commons, was the leader of the anti-Unionists. The mob unyoked the horses from his carriage, for the purpose of hauling him to his residence, when Lord Chancellor Clare, the leader of the Unionists, was observed coming down the steps of the Parliament House. There was a shout of "Harness the Lord Chancellor to the carriage!" and immediately a rush was made for him, but before the mob could reach him he retreated into the building, and thus narrowly escaped the ludicrous and humiliating position of having to pull home the Speaker of the House of Commons. About the same time a popular songstress was singing nightly, in the Dublin Theatre, a favourite song, the refrain of which ran, "My heart goes pit-a-pat, pit-a-pat." One night an occupant of the gallery interrupted the singer with the cry—"A groan for Pitt and a cheer for Pat!"

Wolfe Tone, the chief organizer of the United Irishmen, wrote a pamphlet, in 1797, advocating the establishment of an Irish Republic. An Irish Protestant bishop picked up the work in a Dublin book-shop, and having glanced through its pages, exclaimed, "Dear me! if these awful revolutionary doctrines were to spread we would have to pay £5 a ton for our coals!" The simplicity of the good bishop was excelled by one of the rebels in the subsequent insurrection of '98. During the hotly contested battle of New Ross, a peasant who led a charge of pikemen to capture a cannon shoved his hat into the gun's mouth and shouted, "Come on, boys! her mouth is stopped!"

One of the cleverest political poems ever written was the work of Arthur O'Connor, the friend of Lord Edward Fitzgerald, and, like him, a prominent figure in the Rebellion of '98. He was arrested at Margate that year when on his way to France on a secret mission. After being detained in Kilmainham Gaol for some time, he was at length removed, with other political prisoners, to Fort George, in Scotland. It was while on his way thither that he distributed copies of the following poem, which was regarded as a proof of his return to loyalty :—

> "The pomp of Courts and pride of Kings
> I prize above all earthly things;
> I love my country, but the King,
> Above all men his praise I sing;
> The Royal banners are displayed,
> And may success the standard aid.
>
> "I fain would banish far from hence
> The "Rights of Man" and common-sense;

>   Confusion to his odious reign,
>   That foe to princes, Thomas Paine!
>   Defeat and ruin seize the cause
>   Of France, its liberties and laws!"

If the above lines be read continuously, they seem to express very loyal sentiments. But if the first line of the first verse, and then the first line of the second verse, are read, and so on, it will be found that they breathe the spirit of rampant rebellion :—

> "The pomp of Courts and pride of Kings
>   I fain would banish far from hence;
> I prize above all earthly things
>   The "Rights of Man" and common-sense.
> I love my country, but the King—
>   Confusion to his odious reign!
>
> "Above all men his praise I sing,
>   That foe to princes, Thomas Paine!
> The Royal banners are displayed;
>   Defeat and ruin seize the cause!
> And may success the standard aid
>   Of France, its liberties and laws!"

Arthur O'Connor ultimately made his way to France, where, in 1807, he married the daughter of the Marquis de Condorcet. He entered the French Army, and rose to the rank of general. His death took place in April, 1852, when he was eighty-seven years of age.

One of the fiercest agitations which ever swept over Ireland was that in the early Thirties for the abolition of the tithes paid to the clergy of the

Established Church. The tithe-proctors—the men who collected the impost, or, in default of payment, seized the stock of the Catholic peasants—were objects of intense popular hatred. As an old, simple priest sat in the confessional of a country chapel, awaiting penitents, a rough youth entered to confess his sins. What he had to relate to the priest was very sanguinary indeed. "Four murthers!" exclaimed the good father, in horror. "Now, will ye have me believe ye've been killin' all yer family?" "No, yer riverence, they wasn't me own flesh and blood at all," said the penitent. "And who wor they, thin?" inquired the confessor. "Well, Father, they wor tithe-proctors." "Tithe-proctors is it ye say?" exclaimed the priest. "Now, why didn't ye tell me that at first, and not to be takin' up me time that way? Get out of here! Ye don't come here to gossip, but to confess yer sins."

This story, which was told me by a priest, is said to have been a favourite with Cardinal Wiseman. Many a dinner-table roared over its recital by his Eminence. The same clergyman related an amusing anecdote of another priest, who was an earnest advocate of teetotalism. One Sunday at Mass he addressed his parishioners on his favourite topic—the fearful effects of drink: "What is it that degrades us to the level of the bastes of the field?" he asked. "I'll tell ye. It's the drink.

What is it that deprives ye of yer nerves? The drink. What is it that makes ye shoot at yer landlord—and—and—miss him? It's the drink, and nothin' but the drink." These anecdotes of olden times recalls a story which is told of the late Father James Healy, of Bray. He was a Conservative in politics; and one evening at a dinner some young priests chaffingly asked him when he would join the Bray branch of the Land League. "Ah," said he, "that work is all very well for young fellows like you. But I'm too old to lie in a wet ditch of a night with a blunderbuss, waiting for the landlord or the agent to come along."

Some years ago the War Office authorities sent a distinguished officer to Ireland to inspect the militia regiments. At Limerick, after the inspection, he sent for the drill sergeant. "These men of yours, sergeant," he said, "could hardly hit a target as big as the Tower of London. You cannot have taken any pains to teach them to shoot." "Tache thim to shoot!" cried the sergeant, in astonished tones. "Of coorse I didn't tache thim to shoot, yer honner; for, bedad, if I did there wouldn't be a landlord left in Munsther." After the great famine of 1847 a man who had made money in business bought one of the numerous heavily-mortgaged properties which were compulsorily sold in the Landed Estates Court. He was small of stature, very thin and wiry-looking;

and the tenants, after they had met him for the first time, began to discuss him. "I don't think much of him," said one. "Shure, that little *gossoon* would be as hard to shoot as a jacksnipe!" So it is always in Ireland. However tragic a thing may be, it is always certain to yield a good story.

The unhappy disposition of the Irish peasantry, in times of political or agrarian excitement, to take that which they consider to be summary justice into their own hands has been ascribed to various causes,—their "brutal ignorance," their "natural savagery," for instance,—but it remained for a London newspaper to point out, in all seriousness, that it might be due to the bloodthirstiness of the names of their towns and country districts! Many of these places are named "Kil" something or another,—"Kil" in Irish meaning church,—such as Killarney, Killaloe, Kildare, Kilkenny, Kilrush, and Kilruddery. This reminds me of the story of an Englishman who went over to Ireland to assist an old college chum who was standing in the Unionist interest for a constituency in the South of Ireland, and who, in his ignorance of this geographical nomenclature, was considerably startled on hearing, at a railway station, the following conversation between two wild-looking peasants: "I'm just afther bein' over to Kilpatrick," said one. "An' I," replied the other, "am afther being over to Kilmary." "What murderers they are!" thought the Englishman; "and to think they talk of their assassinations so publicly!" "And where are ye goin' now, Jim?" asked assassin No. 1. "I'm goin' home to Kilmore," was No. 2's reply. The Englishman's blood curdled. "Kilmore, is it?" said the other. "Faix, you'd bether be comin' wid me to Kilumaaule." The story goes that the frightened Englishman went no further on his journey. He waited at the station for the next train back to Dublin, and returned to England by the first boat!

During the Land League agitation a landlord called on the widow of a neighbouring landowner to give her his condolences on the death of her husband and his friend. "Well, glory be to God!" said he, "it's a fine thing for a man to be allowed to die in his bed these troubled times."

Several amusing stories are told of that great demagogue, Daniel O'Connell, as a political agitator, but they are too familiar, at least in Ireland, to bear repetition here. But one of his most faithful henchmen, during the agitation for Repeal of the Union, was an eccentric character named Tom Steele, who contributed not a little to the humours of that movement. Steele was a Protestant, a graduate both of Dublin University and Cambridge University, and a landlord in reduced circumstances. O'Connell appointed him "Head Pacificator of Ireland," and to the office with this high-sounding title there was a small salary attached, but what its duties were no one was ever able to understand. Tom, however, was very proud of the office, and in virtue of it he strutted about in a gaudy, semi-military uniform, which made him the laughing-stock of Dublin, the people of which—however stoutly they may hold their opinions—have a keen sense of the ridiculous in political movements. At one of the weekly meetings of the Repeal Association, Steele attacked a prominent Dublin tradesman named Peter Purcell, a Repealer who had quarrelled with O'Connell on some minor question of political tactics. "Say no more on the subject, Tom," said O'Connell, who was in the chair. "I have forgiven Peter from the bottom of my heart." "You may forgive him, liberator and saviour of my country," rejoined Steele, in a characteristic burst of his amazingly fervent rhetoric. "Yes, you, in the discharge of your ethereal functions as the moral regenerator of Ireland, may forgive him; but, liberator and revered leader, I also have functions of my own to perform; and I tell you that, as Head Pacificator of Ireland, I can never forgive the diabolical villain that dared to dispute your august will!"

Steele was one of the traversers with O'Connell

in the famous State trials of 1843. This distinction nearly turned the head of poor Tom altogether. The Attorney-General, who conducted the prosecution, was Mr. T. B. C. Smith—"Alphabet Smith" he was called by O'Connell, who had a genius for nicknames; and Archbishop Whately said of him, "He is a man of more letters than learning." During the trial Tom Steele interrupted the proceedings several times by audibly contradicting statements of the Attorney-General, and by frequent gestures of impatience and disapproval. "If you do not keep quiet, Steele, I shall have your name struck out of the indictment," said the Attorney-General, who knew Tom's little weakness. And sure enough the Head Pacificator of Ireland remained as quiet as a mouse for the remainder of the trial! Sir James O'Connell, the elder brother of Daniel, and a man who, though he kept clear of politics, was of Conservative opinions, was once asked how his famous relative came to appoint a half-madman like Tom Steele Head Pacificator of Ireland. "And who the devil else would take such a job?" was the reply.

One of the secrets of the great hold which political leaders like O'Connell and Parnell had on the people was the implicit confidence in their powers which they were able to inspire. Mr. Aubrey de Vere relates that in 1848, after the death of O'Connell, the tenants on an estate in Limerick refused to pay the full rent, as there was to be a " new Act," called " tenant right," under which rent would be greatly reduced. " How do you know that ? " asked the astonished landlord. " Shure," said they, " ould Dan left an order on the Government in his will to have the Act passed at wanst." The late Mr. Lefanu, who was chairman of the Irish Board of Works, stated that in his time the Board received many amusing letters, particularly from farmers who were borrowers under the Land Improvement Act. Here is one which came from a man who had been refused a second instalment of a loan because he had misapplied the first :—

" Sir,—I spent the money all right. Send me the rest, and don't be humboling me any more. Send it at once, I tell ye. Hell to your souls! send me the money, or I'll write to Mr. Parnell about it.—Yours affectionately, JAMES RYAN."

When the Crimes Act of 1887 had, after a determined struggle in the House of Commons, been at length passed, a well-known Dublin timber merchant, and a Unionist in politics, met Father Healy, of Bray, and said, " I'm glad this Coercion Act is safely through." " Yes," said the wit ; " it's a good thing for your business : plank beds will go up." About this time Mr A. J. Balfour, who was Chief Secretary for Ireland, met Father Healy at a dinner in Dublin. " Tell me, Father

Healy," said Mr. Balfour, "is it true the people of Ireland hate me as much as the Nationalist newspapers represent?" "Hate you!" replied the priest; "if they hated the devil more than they hate you, Mr. Balfour, my occupation would be gone." And yet, such is the whirligig of Irish politics that before many years had elapsed Mr. Balfour—thanks to his Light Railways and Congested Districts Board—had accomplished the no small achievement towards the pacification of Ireland of giving a new name to the national animal of the country. A gentleman, writing to *The Times* in 1892, stated that, driving into the town of Westport, Co. Mayo, a pig went careering in front of his vehicle, when an old peasant shouted across the ditch to a boy who was on the road lazily contemplating the animal, "Arrah, Mick, will ye stir yerself? Don't ye see Arthur James runnin' away?" Struck by the oddness of the name, the gentleman pulled up, and, on inquiry, discovered that the peasants, in thankfulness to Mr. Balfour for being the means of obtaining them pigs, had called the animals after him!

The "voices" at political meetings in Ireland are often very laughable. Shortly after "the split" in 1890, I was present as a reporter at an open-air meeting in Tipperary, in the Anti-Parnellite interest. During the speech of a well-known member of Parliament, a donkey in a neighbouring field began to bray. " Boys," exclaimed the M.P., " I'm interrupted by a Parnellite ; " but the roar of laughter excited by the sally had hardly died away, when a man on the fringe of the crowd shouted, " No, thin, ye're not intherrupted be a Parnellite. 'Tis yer brother that's spakin' to yez, and askin' yez to hould yer whist ! " I remember at a Land League meeting in Limerick, in the early Eighties, the arrests of the chief leaders of the movement as "suspects " was denounced by one of the speakers. " How should you retaliate ? " he asked ; " I will tell you. The landlords will never get a penny of rent from you until our brave leaders are released." " Wisha may they niver be let out, thin ! " cried a " voice " from the crowd, rejoicing at the prospect of escaping the payment of rent for ever.

Some of the sayings of the speakers at these meetings are also very funny. I heard one " suspect," who was arrested on suspicion of being concerned in agrarian outrages, described at a meeting as " A man whose heart would be touched by the bleatin' of a bruised worm."

William Smith O'Brien, the leader of the revolutionary Young Irelanders, belonged to an ancient Celtic family. He was, in fact, a direct descendant from the Kings of Thomond—one of which was the famous Brian Boru—and his brother, Lord Inchiquin, still retained in Clare a portion of the old ancestral dominions. His manners were cold and formal, and, having been brought up in England, he had the English accent. He was as unlike an Irishman as it was possible for an Irishman to be. "What do you think of Smith O'Brien?" one of his chief followers was asked. "Well, to tell you truth, I think the amalgam is unskilfully made," was the reply; "there is too much of the Smith, and too little of the O'Brien." But, for all that, he was not free from the Irish propensity to make "bulls." In a speech at Limerick, which he represented in Parliament, he said: "The new Irish flag is orange and green. It shall henceforth be the Irish tri-colour." At one of the public receptions he received in Limerick, on the eve of the insurrection of 1848, he was presented by the brushmakers of the city with a monster sweeping-brush, inscribed: "To William Smith O'Brien, Esq., M.P. To sweep the English Government out of Ireland." "Williamsmithobrienbrushboru" was the designation given him by Clarence Mangan, the poet, after that droll incident.

But subsequent events proved that the English Government was not to be swept from Ireland by a huge sweeping-brush. They also showed that Smith O'Brien—one of the kindest and most humane gentlemen that ever lived—had not in him the stuff to realize his grand ambition of being "the Washington of Ireland." The rebellion which he headed in Tipperary, in June, 1848, was a complete failure. Followed by an undisciplined crowd, armed chiefly with pitchforks and other farming implements, Smith O'Brien approached the police-station at Mullinahone. The door was wide open, as if nothing unusual was going on in the district. A big policeman put his head out of an upper window, and exclaimed, "Yerrah! shure the time isn't come yet to surrendher our arms. Do ye wait till the right time comes." The " rebels," moved by the grotesque humour of the scene, laughed heartily, and, amid cries of "Och ! let the dacent man alone!" they marched away. At another police barrack, which was occupied by a sergeant and six constables, Smith O'Brien, who was accompanied only by a few comrades, called upon the men to submit and deliver up their arms. "Oh, sir," said the sergeant, "if we give in to three or four min, we'll be disgraced for iver. Bring a force, and we'll submit." The insurgent leader, the most courteous and considerate of men, willingly agreed to furnish this solace to the honour of the constabulary; but, when he returned an hour later with twenty men, the barrack was empty. The constables had gone off with their arms!

After the "troubles" of 1848, one of the rebels who escaped to the United States inserted the following business advertisement in a New York newspaper :—"Watches and Watchmaking! Warranted to outlast the British Empire! Edward

Butler, late President of the Tipperary Confederate Club, now a fugitive from British despotism, has commenced his business as watchmaker at 403 Pearl Street, and earnestly solicits the patronage of the public. Watches, clocks, jewellery, etc., promptly and accurately cleaned and repaired on very reasonable terms. John Mitchel, the rebel, said of him 'He is a good man, and true as the time of his watches.'"

The Fenian Conspiracy in 1864-67 was a much more formidable affair, but even that had its amusing side. There is a story told that an Englishman, who was having a drive in Dublin in 1867, asked the car-driver whether he thought the Fenians would fight? "Fight is it?" exclaimed the car-driver, indignant that any doubt should be thrown on the bravery of his countrymen. "Faith, they wud fight, sur, only they're afraid they'd be tuk up by the police." A popular Dublin doctor, who was the medical attendant of the Constabulary Depot in the Phœnix Park, spoke at a public meeting in Dublin in aid of a local charity. As he approached to the front of the platform a voice cried out, "Three cheers, bhoys, for the dochter! Shure he kilt more policemen than all the Fenians put together."

In 1867, Mr. Wilson Barrett, the well-known actor, went as a young man to fulfil his first engagement in Dublin. He had heard much of the love

for the theatre and the generous warmth of the
Irish race, and looked forward to pleasant times,
but little did he expect the perfect storm of cheers,
stamping of feet, whistling, and waving of hats and
handkerchiefs which greeted him from the pit and
gallery on his first appearance in the Queen's
Theatre; and every speech of his during the play
was the signal for a fresh outburst of enthusiastic
applause. Needless to say, the young actor was
highly delighted with this magnificent reception.
After the first act, he had a conversation with the
property man. "A very enthusiastic audience to-
night," said he. "Yis, sir, a grand audience entirely," replied the property man. "Are Irish
audiences always as warm as this?" asked the
actor, feeling his way cautiously. "Och, not at all,
sir," said the property man. "Well, they seem to
like my acting very much." "Your actin'!" exclaimed the property man; "faix, it isn't that at
all, at all. Shure, they're after takin' you for a
relation of Barrett, the bhoy that was hanged the
other day!" A man named Michael Barrett had
just been hanged at Newgate for complicity in the
Fenian explosion at Clerkenwell Prison. The object of this outrage was to effect the escape of two
of the Fenian leaders, who had just been captured
and lodged in the prison.

In the same year three Fenians, named Allan,
Larkin, and O'Brien, were hanged at Salford Jail

for the murder of Police-sergeant Brett, who was shot during the rescue of two other Fenian leaders from a Manchester prison van. These men are known as "the Manchester Martyrs" in Nationalist circles. Shortly after the affair, Dr. Moriarty, the Roman Catholic Bishop of Kerry, who had strongly denounced the Fenian movement, was examining some children preparatory to Confirmation. "Who are the Martyrs?" he asked one youth. "Allan, Larkin, and O'Brien, me lord," replied the boy, without hesitation, to the consternation of the Bishop.

Chapter XIV

ON THE WAY TO ST. STEPHEN'S

PERHAPS in no phase of Irish politics is the humorous element so conspicuous as in the wooing of the Irish electors. It is often said that Parliamentary elections have lost all their fun since the Ballot Act of 1872 substituted secret voting and several polling booths in each constituency for open voting at one polling station for the borough or county, with its hustings, or temporary platform, from which the rival candidates addressed the electors during the stormy three or four days, or week, the polling lasted. However that may be true of England and Scotland, it certainly is not the fact, I am glad to say, in the case of Ireland.

Even at the last General Election of 1895, two laughable incidents occurred in Ireland, which are hardly surpassed for humour by anything that has come down to us from the old rollicking, boisterous and practical-joking days. In the city of Cork the contest lay between Parnellite and Anti-Parnellite. Four voters were married to ladies who were not in agreement with the political views of their lords; and early on the morning of the polling day these gentle dames secretly left their respective homes, carrying away every article of male attire and locking in their husbands, in order that they should not be able to go to the polling stations. Fortune, however, was against the ladies. They had reckoned without the canvassers, who are sent out in the interest of the candidates to bring voters to the poll. The predicament of the clothesless electors was discovered, an entry was forced into their homes, and, wrapped in blankets, they were conveyed in carriages to the polling booths just in time to record their votes! Another comic incident happened at the election in Londonderry. The contest was very close. Every weak and decrepit voter with life in him was brought to the poll, in a bath chair or in a bed. A workingman executed a smart manœuvre. A warrant for his arrest, to undergo two months' imprisonment for wife beating, had been out against him for a week past. But though he illused his better half, he was a good party man. He, therefore, lay in hiding until the day of the polling, when, huddled in bedclothing and wearing a false beard, he was carried as an invalid to the booth and voted!

But, despite mirthful incidents like these, which are never absent from Irish Parliamentary contests, and occasional fierce encounters between the supporters of the rival candidates, elections in Ireland now-a-days are models of sobriety and peaceableness, compared with the wild, whiskey-drinking, skullcracking contests of yore. Lord Charles Beresford, M.P., has related an experience in connection with his political campaign in the county of Waterford in 1874, where he was first returned to Parliament. He met an old peasant who boasted that he could remember the famous Waterford election of '26 which was fought on the question of Catholic Emancipation, and was one of the bloodiest electoral fights on record. "Ah! ye're no man, Lord Charles," remarked the old fellow. "Shure, ye're no man." "I don't agree with you, Paddy," said the jovial sailor; "but what makes you think so?" The old peasant replied—with the air of one who really disliked to find fault with a Beresford— "Arrah, thin, the lasht time wan of yer family stud for the county, it's up to me ankles I was in blood, and up to me brains in whisky; but sorra a dhrop av ayther I seen this time."

I do not think that abnormal whiskey-drinking has been a feature of any Irish Parliamentary contest since the Great Famine of 1847, which, as I have already said, divides Old Ireland from New Ireland. But there is a story told of an election for the borough of Dungarvan as recently as 1868 which, if true—and the story is said to have the authority of the successful candidate, the present Lord Llandaff—beats anything to be found even in the novels of Charles Lever. There were only about 300 electors in Dungarvan, but wooing their suffrages was, in accordance with the general custom of the times—especially when the candidate was a Saxon stranger, as in this case—attended by considerable expense. Mr. Henry Matthews (as Lord Llandaff then was), therefore, expected a heavy bill from his agent when the contest was over and he was M.P. for Dungarvan, but he was taken aback, on looking through the account, to see the item—"Whiskey, £547." "What does this mean?" he inquired of his agent. "Ah, shure, the bhoys needed a dhrop o' the crature," was the reply. Mr. Matthews ventured to suggest that the thirst of "the bhoys" was somewhat abnormal, and that possibly they had been swimming in the spirit; but the agent cut him short with the indignant remark, "Begorra, if ye want to squeeze a pippin like that ye'll never do for Dungarvan!" Mr. Matthews paid the bill.

In those old hotly-contested elections it was the custom of the candidates to engage on their side barristers who were known as "fighting counsel" —men who were not only learned in the law, and could use their tongues effectively, but were also adepts at the use of the pistol. At an election at Cork, a famous fighting councillor, named Tom O'Brien, conducted the business of his client in a style so pacific as to excite the astonishment of his friends. "Why, Tom," said one of them, on meeting the councillor in Dublin, after the election, "you were marvellously quiet. How is it that you did not get into any rumpus?" "Because O'Leary did not pay me my fighting price," replied O'Brien, with the most business-like air in the world. There were two scales of payment for election counsel—the "talking" price and the "fighting" price.

Many humorous experiences are obtained in the work of canvassing, when, from house to house, the candidate—attended by some of his most influential supporters—threads his way, soft of speech and profuse of promises, to solicit the votes of the electors. A gentleman who contested an Irish county many years ago used to tell an amusing story of the embarrassment caused him on one occasion by a too blunt and outspoken supporter. The candidate was driving with this friend from one district to another when they met a voter on the road. They pulled up, the candidate jumped off the car, and courteously approaching the voter, asked him in the blandest of tones for the honour of his support. "Faix, sir," replied the man, "I'd like to know your principles first." "Look at that for impudence!" cried the candidate's fiery friend from the car. "You ask a gentleman like Mr. Foley what are his principles! Get along with you! A nice pass we're come to when Mr. Foley must stop on the high-road to tell his principles to the likes of you! Come along, Foley. Pitch the fellow, his votes and his principles to the devil altogether; and don't waste your time!" Another candidate, on paying a second visit to the house of a doubtful voter of the peasant class, was very pleased, but somewhat surprised, on hearing from the elector that he would support him. "Glad to hear it," said the candidate; "I thought you were against me." "Shure, I was at first," rejoined the peasant. "Whin the other day ye called here, and stood by that pig-stye and talked for half an hour, ye didn't budge me an inch. But after ye was gone away, sur, I got to thinkin' how ye reached yer hand over the rail and scratched the pig's back till he lay down wid the pleasure of it. I made up me mind thin that whin a man was so sociable as that wid a poor fellow-crathure, I wasn't the bhoy to vote agin him."

But it must be said that Irish voters, as a rule, are not so easily influenced as the peasant in the preceding story. The voters have firmly made up their minds, one way or the other, and it is almost impossible to shake them in their convictions. The "wobbler"—the voter with no pronounced opinions, who, holding the balance between parties, decides the issue of elections in England—is unknown in Ireland. The term was used in a recent Parliamentary contest in Ireland, and, naturally, was puzzling to many of the electors, who had never heard of it before. "What do they mane by a wobbler?" asked a peasant of the local schoolmaster. "Well, thin," replied the schoolmaster, "a wobbler's a sort of bosthoon that wastes a dale of his time makin' up his mind what he should do. Whin he's gettin' up in the mornin' he shtands for half an hour wid his trousers in his hand, considherin' which leg he should put in first"!

The bantering and chaffing of opponents was an entertaining feature of Irish contested elections in the old days. As the existence of the Irish Parliament was drawing to a close there was a contest for the representation of Tallaght—then a small borough outside Dublin—in which the Government nominee was the noted duellist, "Bully" Egan. One very warm day in the course of the polling, John Philpot Curran, who was on the other side, met Egan mopping with a handkerchief his perspiring forehead. "I'm sorry for you, my dear fellow," said Curran. "Sorry! why so?" asked Egan; "I'm perfectly at ease in the matter." "Alas! Egan," rejoined Curran, "it's too visible to every one that you are losing tallow (Tallagh) fast."

O'Connell was a great adept at chaff of this kind, and often did that gift of ready retort help him out of a difficulty. During a contest in Tralee he spoke from a balcony of the Chamber of Commerce. Immediately opposite were the committee rooms of the Knight of Kerry (the Tory candidate), the windows of which were crowded with opponents of O'Connell. In the midst of the agitator's speech a donkey began to bray. The effect was most ludicrous. Of course, the supporters of the Knight of Kerry were boisterous in their mirth, and even the crowd, who were on O'Connell's side, could not keep from laughing. "Hear him! hear him, boys!" cried the agitator; "'tis the chairman of the Knight of Kerry's committee!" In the historic Clare election of 1828, which resulted in the election of O'Connell—a Catholic, and, therefore, disqualified from sitting in Parliament—and led to Catholic Emancipation, the Government candidate and former representative of the county, Vesey Fitzgerald, whose acceptance of the office of President of the Board of Trade had led to the contest, quitted Ennis, the chief town of the county, where the polling took place, when the issue was no longer in doubt. O'Connell opened his speech on the hustings, returning thanks to the electors, in the following characteristic fashion:—

"Boys, where's Vasy Vigarald? Och, hone! Vasy, but it's me that's dull and lonely widout yez! *Righi, mavourneen, righi*; sind the bell about for him. Here's the cry for yez:—

> 'Stolen or strayed,
> Lost or mislaid,
> The President of the Board of Trade.'"

In Ireland—as everywhere else—voters in the days of bribery and corruption expected a favour, in some shape or form, from the candidate they supported. "I have just heard, Michael Molloy, that you sold your vote for £2 at the election," said a priest indignantly to one of his parishioners. "Aren't you ashamed of yourself?" "Shure, Father, 'twas all I cud get," was the voter's candid reply. The late Sir William Gregory, who was at one time Member for Dublin, used to tell a story that one of his supporters requested him to get him "something undher the Government." "Faix, I voted for yer honner undher thirteen different names, and could I do more for ye than that?" said the claimant. O'Connell once told the House of Commons an amusing Irish story of bribery. A farmer in the county of Wexford was promised a position for his son in return for his vote for a member of the Loftus family. The father's ambition for the boy aimed at a sergeantcy in the artillery; but Lord Loftus, on applying for this post for the youth, was informed that it was totally impossible to grant his request, inasmuch as it required a previous service of six years to qualify a candidate for the position. "Does it require six years to qualify him for a lieutenancy?" demanded

Lord Loftus. "Certainly not," was the answer. "Well, can't you make him a lieutenant then?" rejoined Lord Loftus. "Whereupon," said O'Connell, "the fellow was made a lieutenant, for no better reason than just because he was not fit to be a sergeant."

The following is a genuine election account. The contest out of which it arose took place in the borough of Trim over 80 years ago. It was presented to Sir Mark Somerville, one of the candidates, by a hotel keeper of Trim, for the accommodation he afforded to supporters of Sir Mark. A copy of the document was found in 1826 among the papers of the Very Rev. Archdeacon O'Connell, Vicar-General of the diocese of Meath:—

"16 April 1826

My Bill

To eatin 16 freeholders above stairs for Sir Mark at 3s. 3d. a head is to me £2 12s.

To eatin 16 more below stairs and 2 pints after supper is to me £2 15s. 9d.

To 6 beds in one room and 4 in a nother at 2 guineas every bed and not more than 4 in any bed at any time cheap enough God knows is to me £22 15s.

To 18 horses and 5 mules about my yard all night at 13s. everyone of them, and for a man who was lost on the head of watchin thim all night is to me £5 5s.

ON THE WAY TO ST. STEPHEN'S

For breakfast or tay for every one of them and as many more as they brought as near as I can guess is to me £4 12s.

To raw whisky and punch widout talkin of pipes tobacco as well as for porter and as well as for breakin a pot above stairs and other glasses and delf for the first day and night I am not sure but for the three days and a half of the election as little as I can call it and to be very exact it is in all or thereabouts as near as I can guess and not to be too particular is to me at least £79 15s. 9d.

For shavin and croppin off the heads of the 49 freeholders for Sir Marks at 13d. for every head of them by my brother had a Wote is to me £2 13s. 1d. For a womit and nurse for poor tom Kernan in the middle of the night when he was not expected is to me ten hogs.

I don't talk of the piper or for keepin him sober as long as he was sober is to me £o.

The Total

2	12	00	
2	15	09	
22	15	00	Signed
5	5	00	in the place Jemmy Cars wife
4	12	00	his
79	15	09	Bryan X Garraty
2	13	01	Mark
10	10		
	0	0	

£110 18s. 7d. you may say £111 0s. 0d. so your Honour Sir Marks send me this eleven hundredh by Bryan himself who and I prays for your success always in Trim and no more at present."

Cashel, which once enjoyed the privilege of returning a member to Parliament, was disfranchised about forty years ago for corrupt practices. £20 was the fixed price of a vote. At the last election held for the borough, one of the candidates was comparatively a poor man; and having the parish priest on his side, he got his reverence to preach a sermon at Mass, on the Sunday before the polling, on the heinousness of the sin of trafficking in the franchise. The next day the candidate met one of the voters, and asked him what he thought would be the effect of the sermon. "I think it will make the election run very close," said the voter. "How so?" inquired the candidate. "Why, we always got £20 a vote before we knew it was a sin; but as Father Buckley says we will be damned for selling our votes, we can't for the future take less than £40." Some time after the disfranchisement of Cashel it was referred to, in the course of a debate in the House of Commons, by an Irish member as "Cashel of the Kings," having been in ancient days the capital of Munster. "Cashel of the Kings!" cried another Irish member. "Nay, rather Cashel of the sovereigns!"

Chapter XV

AT ST. STEPHEN'S

THE debates in the House of Commons are often very dull; and members of Parliament, being, after all, only human, welcome not only flashes of genuine wit and those incongruous expressions popularly known as "bulls"—which are often deliciously humorous—but any trivial incident or saying out of which they can possibly raise a laugh to relieve the monotony of the proceedings at St. Stephen's. For most of the humour of Parliament we are indebted to the representatives from Ireland.

The capacity for making "bulls" is not, however, monopolized by the Irish members. Mr. Gladstone was the author of one of the most amusing "bulls" I have ever heard at St. Stephen's. In the course of a speech he imputed to a member an intention which the hon. gentleman referred to denied by a shake of his head. "No, no," exclaimed Mr. Gladstone; "it is no use for the hon. member to shake his head in the teeth of his own words." A short time ago Mr. A. J. Balfour indulged in another very laughable incongruity of expression. Some of the Scottish members urged that they should be allowed time to discuss a Bill in which they were interested; and Mr. Balfour, in reply, commented on the fact that Scottish debates were carried on, as a rule, in a thin House, which he described as "an empty theatre of unsympathetic auditors." Lord Randolph Churchill on one occasion spoke of a sum of money which was under discussion as "a mere fleabite in the ocean of our expenditure"; and it was only recently that a Welsh member concluded a categorical denial of a statement which had been made in the course of a debate by saying, "It gives me great pleasure to have nailed that lie to the mast." A few years ago the House was in Committee discussing the Civil Service estimates. In the vote for mining inspectors there was an item for "clerical assistance." To this an English member representing a mining constituency objected. He was not aware, he said, that mining inspectors were such wicked people that they required clergymen to be kept to look specially after their spiritual condition. The House roared with laughter, and the hon. member himself joined as heartily as any one in the merriment when it was explained to him that by "clerical assistance" was meant the assistance of clerks, and not of clergymen.

But, undoubtedly, expressions like these—so far

at least as they are due to confusion of ideas, or rather to the thought being too rapidly uttered to be correctly and adequately expressed in words— are used most frequently by members from Ireland. "Now that the Chancellor of the Exchequer has let the cat out of the bag, it is time to take the bull by the horns," exclaimed an Irish member a short time since. Another said, "The Government by this proposal are opening the door to the thin end of the wedge." A prominent Conservative member, who represents a constituency in Ulster, speaking on a Bill which proposed to extend the franchise in Ireland, said, "You should refrain from throwing open the flood-gates of democracy lest you should pave the way for a general conflagration." This amusing specimen of mixed metaphors was equalled, if not excelled, by Sir Patrick O'Brien, who had a wide reputation as a maker of "bulls," when he described the author of a certain political pamphlet as "an understrapper; a mere political fly, who is acting the part of a snake in the grass; a backstairs assassin of the people who has the audacity to appear before them in the light of day and stealthily stab them in the back." On hearing the Royal Assent announced to the Act for the Disestablishment of the Irish Church, in 1870, he exclaimed, "Thank God! the bridge is at last broken down that has so long separated the English and the Irish people." On another occasion Sir Patrick gave expression to another whimsical involution of phase, during a debate, in 1880, on a Bill to suspend the Habeas Corpus Act in Ireland. He said, "The suspension of the Habeas Corpus Act would merely leave the rotting sword festering in the wound." It was in this debate also that Mr. Dwyer Grey (at one time proprietor and editor of *The Freeman's Journal*) said, referring to the outrages reported from Ireland, "Three-quarters of them are exaggerated and half have no foundation in fact."

I have heard another Irish member, in an eloquent peroration, speak of "the primæval forests of America, where the hand of man has never set foot." During a debate on party riots in Belfast, a Nationalist member exclaimed, "Well may we call the orange the apple of discord in Ireland." "We live," said another Nationalist member, "in a country where the police are always with us, behind us, before us, and in our midst."

A ready retort is also highly appreciated at St. Stephen's. The happiest and most crushing one I ever heard was given about ten years ago. In the course of a rather acrimonious political debate an Irish member taunted his opponents on the other side of the House with their want of knowledge. "At least we are not stupid," said one of the members subsequently. "Can that be said of the hon. gentleman? For my part, I do not believe he could say 'boo' to a goose." The Irish member at whom this taunt was cast immediately sprang to his feet, and in a loud voice shouted across the floor, "Boo, boo!" There is a good story told of a smart repartee by Lord Charles Beresford in his early Parliamentary days. His lordship had a Chinese servant called Tom Fat; but, though "childlike and bland," like his race generally, Tom had made himself proficient in copying his master's signature, and, having access to the cheque-book, had made away with a couple of thousand pounds in the course of a few years. Shortly after these doings of Tom Fat were made public in the Criminal Courts, Lord Charles Beresford made a speech in the House, in the course of which he deprecated the prominence given to questions of religion in discussions of primary education. For his part, he thought a Mohammedan or a Buddhist had just as good a chance of getting to heaven as a Roman Catholic or a Protestant, if he only acted conscientiously, according to his beliefs. "But what about Tom Fat?" interjected Mr. James Lowther. "That Fat will certainly be in the fire," was the prompt reply of Lord Charles; but, in deference to Parliamentary decorum, he refrained from designating the particular fire which he had in mind. A Gladstonian member, talking to Colonel Saunderson, M.P.—the well-known leader of the Irish Unionists,—said, "Do you know, the Nationalists are great admirers of you ? If you were one of them, they'd soon raise you to the top of the tree." "Yes," replied Colonel Saunderson, "I am sure they would; but it would be by means of a rope!"

Lord Monck, at one time Governor of Canada, sat in the House of Commons for an English constituency. An Irishman himself, he was very patronising to the Irish members. Meeting Vincent Scully, the Member for Tipperary, in the Lobby one night, he slapped him on the shoulder, and said familiarly, "Well, Scull, how are you?" The other, annoyed by this form of address, rejoined: "I will thank you, my lord, not to deprive my name of the last letter. Or, if you do, pray add it to your own and call yourself—Monkey." This recalls an amusing story of the great Daniel O'Connell. A certain member, named Thomas Massey, who had his eye always on the Pope, brought in a Bill to obliterate the Popish affix "mas" or "mass," and substitute the good old Saxon word "tide" in all such instances as Christmas and Michaelmas, so that they should read "Christ-tide and Michael-tide," respectively. O'Connell listened attentively to all the member had to advance in favour of his scheme, and then got up and said, "Since the honourable gentleman is so anxious to wipe out the obnoxious 'mass' from the English vocabulary, why does he not make a commencement by Saxonizing his own name? In that case he would be known as Thotide Tidey." The Bill was fairly laughed out of the House.

The Right Hon. John Doherty, who was Chief Justice of the Common Pleas in Ireland from 1830 until his death in 1850, was elected member for Kilkenny in 1826; and appointed Solicitor-General for Ireland by George Canning. "When I first addressed the House of Commons," Doherty said in after life, "I was really in a great fit of nervousness, and would have given much to be back again at the Four Courts. It was a trying thing to wish to speak well in the presence of Canning, and Brougham, and Peel, and Plunket, and Tierney. When I sat down, Canning turned round and said to me: 'Well done, Doherty; very good indeed. You only made one mistake. Like every Irishman, you said "Sir" to the Speaker too much. You should say "Sir" only at the beginning and end.' 'Well,' I answered, 'I really don't care how I called him since I did not say, "Ma'am" to him.'"

Dick Martin (the founder of the Society for the Prevention of Cruelty to Animals) was Member for Galway in the third decade of the century. He was one of the many unconscious humorists which Ireland has sent to Parliament. On one occasion he had to make a personal explanation in the House of Commons regarding a conversation which took place between him and Dennis O'Sweeny, whom he had defeated at Galway. The candidates had said some uncomplimentary things of each other on the hustings; and when the election was over, O'Sweeny, in the bitterness of his defeat, approached Martin "for satisfaction." Martin, relating the incident to the House, said —"He said to me, 'You charged me with something that was inconsistent with the character of a gentleman.' 'Faith, and it's yourself, Dennis, me boy, is quite mistaken in that same,' says I. 'I'm no such thing,' says he. 'Then what was it I did say?' says I. 'You know that as well as I do,' says he. 'By —— I don't,' says I." Then the Speaker interrupted the narrative with a stern cry of "Order! order!" "The hon. member," said he, "is out of order in using such an expression." "I beg your pardon, Mr. Speaker," said Martin, "and the pardon of the House, if I said anything improper. 'By —— you did, Dick,' says Dennis." "Order! order!" cried the Speaker. "The hon. member is again indulging in the same improper language." "Mr. Speaker," said Martin, amid peels of laughter, "it wasn't meself that gave that oath; it was Dennis O'Sweeny." But the story was so studded with expletives that it had to be brought to an untimely end.

Perhaps the drollest figure in Parliamentary history is Major O'Gorman, who represented Waterford in the Seventies. Disraeli, who led the House of Commons during most of the years in which the Major played the foremost part in the Parliamentary comedy, was once asked by a hypochondriacal legislator for advice as to how to raise his depressed spirits. "Be in your place when O'Gorman speaks," said Disraeli; "that will enliven you—if anything can." This genial man-mountain filled, in more senses than one, a large space in the Parliaments in which he sat. "Only say you buy your meat from me, and I'll make my fortune," said a witty Dublin butcher to the Major, as he carried his enormous proportions down Moore Street one Saturday night when the place was filled with people marketing. If he wanted to secure a place in the House of Commons on a "big night," he was allowed the privilege of appropriating two seats!

O'Gorman was by no means a buffoon. On the contrary, he was a man of culture and wit; his manners were the most courtly, and he had had a distinguished career as a soldier. But it was as an unconscious humorist that he was irresistible. One of the most amazing and amusing speeches ever heard in the House of Commons was delivered by the Major against a motion moved by Mr. Newdegate for the appointment of a Commission to inquire as to monastic and conventual institutions in Great Britain, on June

12th, 1874. The following is a report of the speech, which appeared in one of the London papers the morning after :—

"I think it would be shameful in the House to send a Royal Commissioner to inquire into these conventual establishments. Let the House suppose that a Royal Commissioner is appointed to visit them. He thunders at the door of a convent. He is admitted, and he asks the lady who admits him who she may have been and what was her quality before she entered the convent. She replies: 'I will tell you. My sire, sir, was a king (laughter); my mother was the daughter of the sixth James of Scotland, and afterwards first James of England (laughter); her mother, sir, was Queen Regent of Scotland, and Queen Consort of France, and next entitled to the throne of England (renewed laughter). She was murdered by a Protestant Queen' (loud laughter). Can any hon. member deny it? The Queen that was murdered was a Catholic, and the Queen that murdered her was a Protestant (renewed laughter). But the poor nun goes on to say: 'Sir, I had a brother; his name was Rupert, sir (laughter); he rode by the side of Charles I. until a Protestant— mind you not a Catholic (laughter), but a Protestant Roundhead of England—murdered that monarch' (more laughter). Let hon. members deny it if they can. 'Sir, I had a sister (renewed laughter); her name was Sophia (roars of laughter); she was mother to the King of England, sir. Proceed, sir, with your duties as a Royal Commissioner (laughter). My name is Elizabeth (roars of laughter). I am the abbess—the poor abbess of Ardwick' (renewed laughter). It is easy enough to go on the stage, but difficult to leave it with dignity (cheers and laughter). With what dignity can that Royal Commissioner depart from that room in the eyes of the injured Princess, and a loyal Princess no doubt (more laughter and cries of 'hear, hear')? He could not leave it except in one of two characters—either as a miserable sham or as a gentleman (cries of 'hear, hear,' and laughter). If in the former character, he is not fit to be a Royal Commissioner (cheers and laughter); if in the latter the Royal Commission is not fit for him (laughter and cheers). What is there for him to do? (cries of 'what?' and laughter). I will tell you (laughter). Nothing (laughter), nothing but to rush from the presence of that poor insulted Princess, and cover his wretched head with sackcloth and ashes (renewed laughter), put himself on his knees in front of the only god he recognises—namely, the immortal gods (roars of laughter)—and to pray that they will give him pardon. It is to be hoped he will get pardon, for he will stand in need of it (prolonged cheers and laughter)."

There was a good deal of the Sir Boyle Roche about Major O'Gorman. But it was always doubtful whether his "bulls" were not deliberate, and whether he was not laughing in his sleeve at the Legislature which thought itself laughing at him. One night in the course of a speech he referred to the old tithe system in Ireland, by which one-tenth of the produce of the holding of every Catholic peasant in every parish was taken to pay the stipend of the Rector of the Established Church in that parish. "The poor man," said the Major, "was robbed by that accursed tithe system of fully one-tenth of his hard earnings—nay, he was sometimes deprived of as much as one-twentieth." He had also the gift of witty retort. "Why are Irishmen always laying bare their grievances?" asked an irritated English member who had lost his patience during a long Irish debate. "Because they want them redressed," shouted the Major across the floor of the House.

In April, 1874, there was a debate on a motion in favour of the acquisition and control of Irish railways by the Government. Major O'Gorman said that if the project were carried out the Irish officials of the railway companies would be told by the Government to "go to hell or Connaught." Mr. Speaker Denison was evidently unaware that the Major had merely quoted an historic Cromwellian expression, for he said, "I must remind the hon. gentleman that his language exceeds the license of Parliamentary debate." "Mr. Speaker," replied O'Gorman, "the language I used was perfectly historical. It was used by the man who took the mace from off the table. But, of course, I will with pleasure beg pardon if I have gone beyond the rules." On another occasion, in 1878, a speech by Colonel Stanley, the Secretary of State for War, was punctuated by frequent irrelevant and embarrassing cries of "hear, hear" from Major O'Gorman, in his stentorian voice. At length the Speaker called on the hon. and gallant member to desist from those interruptions. "I am not interrupting!" roared the Major. "I say, I am not interrupting!" he again cried, in reply to shouts of "order! order!" and "chair!" from various parts of the House. "I am entitled to call 'Hear, hear,' he went on. "Yes, I have a right to call 'hear, hear,' after every sentence, after every semicolon, after every comma, if I think proper, and I mean to exercise it." As he persisted in refusing to apologize, he was "named" by the Speaker, and was suspended. On the morrow, however, he apologized fully, amply, and with apparently the most heartfelt expressions of regret.

Members of Parliament in those days were more interested in the movements and utterances of Major O'Gorman than they were in the sayings and doings of Disraeli or Gladstone. I have been told by a member who was in the House of Commons in the days of the Major that when the word, "O'Gorman is up," flew through the Palace, the diner dropped his knife and fork, the smoker his cigar, the reader his book or newspaper, and from dining-room, smoking-room, and library the crowd came rushing into the Chamber to catch the mellow thunder of the brogue and the random pearls of speech from the lips of the Major. It is, indeed, always thus at St. Stephen's. Any member who can relieve by his wit and humour the seriousness and monotony of debate is certain of a full House.

The Major hardly ever made a speech without telling an amusing story. During a debate on the Peace (Preservation) Ireland Bill in the session of 1875, he related a good story of the way in which a landlord's daughter secured a husband. This landlord lived in the county of Westmeath, was possessed of considerable property, and was very fond of field sports. The daughter disliked living in the country; she found it so stupid and dull: and she repeatedly asked her father to remove to their town house in Dublin. But he refused to do so; he was so fond of country life, and was so much beloved by his neighbours. Soon afterwards he received a threatening letter; a few days later he received another, but he thought little of them. Some days afterwards there came a third threatening letter, in which his coffin was delineated. He then became alarmed and sent for the stipendiary magistrate, with the result that detectives were brought down from Dublin Castle. But nothing could be discovered as to the authorship of the letters, though they still came pouring in. In the end, the landlord broke up his country establishment and removed to Dublin. "His daughter," continued O'Gorman, "was a very beautiful girl—just such a girl as could only be produced in my own Green Isle : blood, bone, and beauty, and plenty of it (laughter). She was universally admired, and was not long in Dublin before proposals of marriage were made to her by a man who was fit for her. The wedding came off, and after the usual breakfast, when the young lady came down to take her departure, she threw her arms round her father's neck and said to him : 'Go down to the country, father ; nobody will touch a hair of your head. You are beloved by everybody around you. Nobody wrote those letters but one person, and that person was myself. I wrote you every one of those threatening letters, and it was I who delineated the coffin. I found the country very dull. I asked you to leave it twenty times and come to Dublin. You refused, and as it was very fashionable, I adopted the Ribbon scheme of sending threatening letters, and it completely succeeded.'"

Here are two other stories which he told, when dealing with political affairs in Ireland: "The Protestant Archbishop of Dublin rushed one afternoon into the bedroom of the Lord-Lieutenant of Ireland at four o'clock. The Lord-Lieutenant was Lord Chesterfield, a man of great talent and of great sloth. The Archbishop called to him, 'Oh, my lord! we shall have our throats cut; the country's up! the country's up!' 'Oh,' said his Excellency, 'what time of day is it?' 'My lord, it is four o'clock p.m.,' replied the Archbishop. 'Well,' said the Lord-Lieutenant, 'it is time for everybody to be up now!'" "A certain Lord-Lieutenant—as to whose name it does not matter—was out riding a horse in the Phœnix Park in company with a man well known for his wit, scholarship, and patriotism, who had represented Knocktopher for forty years in the Irish Parliament—the late Sir Hercules Langrishe. The horse stumbled in a boggy part and threw his Excellency, who fell on the ears of the animal, but, being an Irish horse, it threw him back again. His Excellency said, 'Sir Hercules, how is it they have not drained the Park?' 'I suppose,' said Sir Hercules, 'the authorities are so deeply interested in draining the rest of the country that they have not got to this yet.'"

One hot afternoon in the middle of August, an English member complained that the House of

Commons should be asked to sit so late in the season. "I want to get away to shoot my grouse," said he plaintively. "Hear, hear!" cried Major O'Gorman ironically. "I suppose," said the English member, losing his temper, "the hon. member only shoots landlords." "Mr. Speaker," roared the Major, stung to fury by the retort, "I ask you, sir, whether I would be in order in calling the honourable gentleman a liar, an unmitigated liar, a d—— liar?"

The Major was himself the landlord of a small property in County Waterford. In the course of a speech against the Sunday Closing (Ireland) Bill, in the session of 1876, he told a story which shows the friendly relations that existed between him and his tenants. He had on his own farm a big field of hay. After the grass had been cut, and while it still lay in the field, the weather turned very wet, and he was greatly afraid his fine crop would rot. One Sunday the weather changed, and the sun shone out brilliantly. He went up to the field, and found to his surprise a crowd of tenants and other neighbours engaged turning the hay. By eight o'clock in the evening it was all dry and made up into tidy cocks. "The people would take no money for this kindly service," he went on. "What was I to do? Was I to allow them to go without some acknowledgment? No. I sent to the nearest public-house for three barrels of porter, and very soon afterwards the contents disappeared, for the people were perspiring as freely as possible, so that the porter ran out of them as fast as it went in."

O'Gorman had an importunate constituent who urged him to obtain for him a local postmastership. The Major declined, on the ground that he would never stoop to ask a favour from a Saxon Government. The man, however, persisted, and concluded a third letter with the remark, "Shure, Major, ye've only to write a line and the thing would be done." The Major thereupon replied: "Sir, I am in receipt of your letter of the 5th inst., in which you state I have only to write a line in order that you should obtain the appointment you desire. I have, therefore, much pleasure in appointing you Postmaster of Ballymahoolly.— I am, sir, your obedient servant, PURCELL O'GORMAN."

"The Major," as he was familiarly called, was the subject of some amusing verses by that racy Irish poet, Mr. T. D. Sullivan, M.P. I quote two of the verses :—

> "Of all the M.P.s
> That Parliament sees
> From session to session, I'll wager
> Neither Saxon nor Scot
> Can pretend that they've got
> A member to match the Major—
> Our portly and ponderous Major—

Our mighty, magnificent Major.
    The councils of State
    Have no man of such weight,
Or such girth, as our bould Irish Major.

"When he rises the House
    Is as mute as a mouse,
They know he's no foolish rampager;
    But soon the 'Hear, hears'
    And the thundering cheers
Are brought out by the speech of the Major—
By the powerful speech of the Major—
The roof-shaking speech of the Major.
    Be it early or late,
    The members will wait
To hear a broadside from the Major."

It would, I think, be impossible to imagine a more striking or more violent contrast between two men than that afforded by Major O'Gorman and Mr. Parnell, who, for several sessions, sat side by side on the same benches in the House of Commons, working for the same political cause. O'Gorman, of amazing girth, fond of good living, loquacious, bubbling over with fun and laughter; Parnell, spare in form, abstemious, silent, taciturn, devoid of humour. Parnell only made one joke in the House of Commons. Ward Hunt was First Lord of the Admiralty in the last Disraelian administration. He was remarkable for a propensity to fall asleep on the Treasury Bench. One session, during the consideration of the Mutiny Bill, a motion was made from the Irish benches for the abolition of "the cat" in the Navy. Ward Hunt opposed the motion on the ground that flogging was administered only in cases of serious crime. Parnell pointed out that among the offences for which "the cat" might be used was that of a man sleeping at his post whilst on duty. "Now," continued Parnell, "I should like to know whether the First Lord of the Admiralty regards *that* as a serious offence?"

The curious absence of the sense of humour in Parnell is illustrated by the following anecdote. At the original constitution of the Land League Mr. A. J. Kettle was in the chair. It fell to Mr. Parnell's lot to move a vote of thanks to the chairman, in the course of which he said: "I need hardly observe, gentlemen, that in Ireland the name of Kettle is a household word." It was plain—indeed, he afterwards confessed so much—that he had not the faintest intention of making a pun, but it was a great tribute to the personal influence which he had even then acquired that, though everybody else saw the joke, nobody dared to laugh. He often said, unconsciously, funny things of that nature. One night, in the early Eighties, when he and some of his followers were suspended for persistent obstruction in the House of Commons, he went up to the Distinguished Strangers' Gallery with a colleague to watch the subsequent course of events in the House. Noticing that he was very pre-occupied and abstracted, his colleague said, "A penny for your thoughts, Mr. Parnell." "Well," replied the Irish leader, "I was thinking with surprise how it had never struck me before that there were so many bald-headed members in the House"!

Another strange, eccentric Irishman—for many years a quaint and notable figure in the House of Commons—was Feargus O'Connor, who was elected, as a follower of Daniel O'Connell, for his native county of Cork, in 1833; and sat, as the leader of the Chartists, for the borough of Nottingham from 1847 until his death in 1855. He was a huge, boisterous, fearless creature, and always eccentric; but for some years he was a lunatic, when his freaks in the House were supposed to be only more pronounced or more insolent eccentricities. One evening he was dining at the House with The O'Gorman Mahon, M.P. On the table was some beet-root. "Mahon," said he to his friend, "give me some of that mangel-wurzel." "Beet-root, you mean," said The O'Gorman Mahon. But O'Connor insisted that it was mangel-wurzel, and finally ran into the House in order to obtain the Speaker's opinion on the matter. The Speaker, however, politely pleaded that to give a ruling on such a point was no part of his duties. The next evening O'Connor had his revenge. The Speaker was accustomed to partake of a chop, with a bottle of claret, in a room behind the chair, sometime between eight and nine o'clock, word being sent to him by the waiter when the repast was ready. On this evening it happened that a member with a long speech was in possession of the House, and some little time elapsed before the Speaker could get to his room. But when he did get there he found only a well-picked chop bone and an empty claret bottle! Feargus O'Connor, watching his opportunity, had slipped into the room and quickly put himself outside the Speaker's chop and wine. When, shortly after this incident, O'Connor gave Lord Palmerston, the Prime Minister, a hearty slap on the back, while he was addressing the House, exclaiming, "Bravo, Pam!" it was thought high time to remove the poor lunatic to a private asylum.

The Irish members do not even stop at practical joking to relieve the tedium of making laws. Some years ago there was in the House an Irish member of considerable wealth, who was very negligent in his dress, his hat especially being of a very ancient date. One night he met the Chief Secretary for Ireland in the lobby, and said, "I have got a new hat; here it is: I hope you approve of it." "It is a very nice hat indeed," said the Chief Secretary; "but I don't know why you should ask my approval of it." "Didn't you send me this note on the subject?" asked the member; and, to the Chief Secretary's amazement, he produced a note which purported to be written by him on the official note-paper of the Irish Office. The Chief Secretary was represented in the letter as expressing the hope that he would be excused for stepping beyond the privileges of ordinary acquaintance to suggest in the strictest confidence to the hon. member that his hat was not exactly what a gentleman of his position and wealth ought to wear.

Lord Charles Beresford, when he first entered Parliament, in 1874, as Tory Member for Waterford, contributed, as a young man in his "twenties," very considerably to the gaiety of Parliament. He was an incorrigible practical joker, and one of his pranks is still remembered and told in the gossip of the smoking-room. An old Tory county member, much troubled by gout, was in the habit of retiring to one of the benches under the reporters' gallery behind the Speaker's chair. His practice was to take off his boots, which he placed under the bench, lie down at full length, and doze securely under the shade of the gallery till his rest was disturbed by the call for a division, when he would slip on his boots and go into one of the division lobbies. One evening, during a division, the old gentleman was compelled to leave his seclusion and walk into the lobby with only one boot on, amid roars of good-humoured laughter. Lord Charles Beresford had carried off the other boot.

About the same time another of the Irish Tory members was an old soldier who had a grudge against Disraeli because of some imaginary or real slight. One night Gladstone made a powerful onslaught on Disraeli. The latter, who always made it a point of carefully thinking out and preparing his speeches, took elaborate notes during the attack of his great opponent. But when Gladstone had concluded, the Speaker, as it was approaching nine o'clock, interrupted the proceedings in order that he might go out to have his chop; and on his return Disraeli was to deliver his reply. The leader of the House carefully arranged in order the sheets of note-paper on which he had made the notes for his speech, and placing them under an ink-bottle on the table, went out with the other members for some refreshment. Behind was sitting the old soldier with the grievance against Disraeli watching every movement. When his leader left the House he walked down to the table, and, under pretence that he was consulting one of the books on the table, took up Disraeli's notes, disarranged their regular order, turned them upside down, and then replaced them under the ink-bottle. On the return of the Speaker in half an hour the Chamber was crowded to hear Disraeli's reply to Gladstone. The leader of the House opened with a few brilliant, general sentences, and then said, " Now I will proceed to deal with the arguments of the right hon. gentleman." He took up his notes, and, while he continued his speech, proceeded to examine them. He stopped abruptly, looked flustered, while he excitedly turned over the sheets of notepaper, and finally flinging them on the table with a gesture of annoyance, attempted to proceed without their aid. But he completely failed. To the astonishment of the House, who were unaware of the cause of his embarrassment, he quickly brought the speech—perhaps the feeblest and most impotent he ever delivered — to a speedy conclusion !

In the same Parliament sat Joseph Ronayne, the member for the city of Cork, a great humorist and practical joker. On a night that a very important division was to be taken, a large party of Conservative members went for supper to St. Stephen's Club, at the corner of Bridge Street and the Embankment, having assured the Whips that they would return immediately the division signal, which connected the Club with the precincts of the House, sounded. But they never took part in the big division, for the signal never reached them. It was found on examination that the wire was cut! Rumour had it that Ronayne was responsible for the practical joke. Well, it is said that all is fair in politics, as well as in love and war. Ronayne died some years ago from the effects of an amputation of the leg. After the doctors decided to cut off the limb, a humorous friend said to him, "Ah, Joe, when your leg is gone, you'll never be able to stand for the city again." To which Ronayne replied, "Sure, if I can't stand for the city, I can stump the county."

Ludicrous misconceptions of a speaker's words, arising from imperfect hearing, frequently occur on the floor of the House, as well as in the Reporters' Gallery. Here is an extract from a parliamentary report during the session of 1876:—

Sir George Campbell said he had some experience of the Glasgow Irish.

Major O'Gorman (indignantly)—"Mr. Speaker, Mr. Speaker, I rise to order, sir! I wish to know, sir, whether the hon. member is justified in stigmatizing my beloved country-people as 'the blasted Irish'?"

Sir G. Campbell—"Mr. Speaker——"

The Speaker—"Order, order! I did not catch the expression of the hon. member——"

Sir G. Campbell—"Will you allow me, Mr. Speaker, to explain?"

The Speaker—"Order, order! But if the expression was used, it is certainly unparliamentary and most improper" (*hear, hear*).

SIR G. CAMPBELL—" Mr. Speaker, it is an entire misconception of my remarks on the part of my honourable and gallant friend. What I said was 'Glasgow Irish,' and not 'blasted Irish'" (*much laughter and cheering*).

Mr. Swift MacNeill once quoted in the House the judicial declaration of the late Baron Dowse of the Irish Bench, that "The resident magistrates could no more state a case than they could write a Greek ode"; and it was deliciously given by a reporter as, "The resident magistrates could no more state a case than they could *ride a Greek goat!*" Baron Dowse must have immensely enjoyed this amusing rendering of his declaration. He stated in the course of a judgment in an action for libel against a newspaper, arising out of an incorrect report, that once in a speech in the House of Commons he had quoted Tennyson's line,—

"Better fifty years of Europe than a cycle of Cathay,"—

and read on a newspaper next day that he had edified the House with this statement,—

"Better fifty years of true love than a circus in Bombay"!

Mr. Swift MacNeill figured in another amusing case of mishearing in the Reporters' Gallery. He once complained of having been roughly treated by the constabulary while attending some evictions in his constituency in Donegal. "But," said the honourable member, "I took measures to put a stop to this conduct. Whenever I was hustled or knocked about by a policeman I simply chalked him, and by that means was able to identify him afterwards." This was rendered, "Whenever I was hustled or knocked about by a policeman *I simply choked him!*"

Vincent Scully once gave utterance in the House to a ludicrous confusion of thought. A landlord had been murdered in Tipperary, and during a discussion in regard to the crime, an attempt was made to prove that it was agrarian. Mr. Scully spoke of the murdered man in terms of the highest praise. "He was much beloved," said he; "he distributed food to the starving people, and no man *had a less right to be murdered!*" During the passage of the Crimes Act of 1881 through the House of Commons, which was strenuously opposed by the Irish members, the House sat on one occasion from Friday afternoon to Sunday morning. Mr. Joseph Biggar was a prominent figure in the obstruction campaign against the Bill. Though much fatigued by the continuous sitting, Mr. Biggar, who was a devout Catholic, attended mass at St. George's Cathedral, Southwark, before going home. But so tired was he that he fell fast asleep in his seat, and was not aroused until the sermon began, when, starting up and imagining himself still in the House of Commons, he loudly exclaimed, "Mr. Speaker, I beg to call your attention to the fact that there are not forty members present." Some of the members recently returned by Ireland to St. Stephen's have been simple, matter-of-fact shopkeepers and farmers. There is a story told of the comment one made when he first saw Westminster Hall. A colleague, showing him round St. Stephen's, brought him at last to that memory-haunted pile. As he stood on the broad flight of steps at the end of the Hall, and gazed down at the broad expanse of its floor and up at the height of its oaken roof, the historic associations of the Hall crowded upon his mind, and, turning to his friend, he said, "Jim, what a grand place it would be to stack hay in!"

A few years ago there occurred two amusing instances of bellicose interpretations of quite innocent observations by Irish members. Late one night, or rather early next morning, for it was long after midnight, an Irish representative made a statement which was received with a cry of "No, no," from a Conservative member. "If the honourable gentleman chooses to challenge me, we can retire," exclaimed the Irishman. Here there were roars of laughter from all parts of the House. "I mean," he added genially, "if the honourable member challenges my accuracy we can retire to the library, and I will show him, by reference to the authorities, that I am right. Being a journalist, I am a wielder of the pen, which, I believe, is mightier than the sword."

On another occasion Mr. William Field put a series of questions to the then Secretary for War (Sir H. Campbell-Bannerman) about the supply of foreign meat to the troops in Ireland, which ended in the statement by the right hon. gentleman that he had no more information to impart. "Then will the right honourable gentleman give me private satisfaction?" asked Mr. Field. There was nothing further from the mind of Mr. Field than the idea of "pistols for two, and coffee for one,"—the order usually given to the landlord of an inn in Ireland the night before an encounter in the old duelling days,—but Sir H. Campbell-Bannerman, who is one of the humorists of the House, pretended to put a bellicose construction on the hon. member's words, and said, while the House enjoyed the fun, "Oh, I earnestly trust that it has not come to that between the honourable gentleman and me!" "Oh, no!" rejoined Mr. Field, amid more laughter; "I assure the right hon. gentleman that I did not mean to challenge him to mortal combat. I am ready to admit that the Secretary for War, with the whole army at his back, would be more than a match for me in a physical encounter."

The hats of members occasionally contribute to the gaiety of life in the House of Commons. No incident is greeted with heartier laughter than the spectacle of a member spoiling the peroration of his speech by plumping down on his hat resting innocently on the bench behind him.

One session during the Parliament of 1886-92, a London member sat down, after his maiden speech, on a new silk hat which he had provided in honour of the auspicious occasion, and as he was ruefully surveying his battered headgear, to the rather unkind amusement of the crowded House, Mr. Edward Harrington (an Irish representative) rose and gravely said, " Mr. Speaker, permit me to congratulate the honourable member upon the happy circumstance that when he sat on his hat his head was not in it"! The call of "Order! order!" from the Speaker was drowned in roars of laughter.

Chapter XVI

THE ULSTER IRISHMAN

THAT Ireland is not all Celtic and Catholic, that there is in Ulster a race entirely distinct from the people of the other provinces of Leinster, Munster, and Connaught, in blood, in religion, and in character, the history of recent Irish political movements has clearly established. But, while the Southern Irishman, the ragged, careless, thriftless, humorous Paddy, is as familiar to the people of Great Britain as an old personal acquaintance, of the personality of the Northern Irishman they have only a shadowy and vague knowledge. This Ulster Irishman—this product of a mixed descent, for in his veins are mingled distinct streams of Scotch, and English, and Irish blood—is not so picturesque or so romantic as the Southern Celt, and, therefore, we never meet him in fiction or on the stage. But he is, nevertheless, an interesting character, apart from the momentous influence he has exercised on the course of Irish political events, and will repay a brief study.

How long has he been in Ulster, and how did he get there? That is an old story now, and may be told in a few words. In the closing years of Elizabeth's reign, the Celtic chiefs of Ulster rose in revolt. After a long and bloody struggle, they were defeated, driven from the country, or hanged, and their vast territories were confiscated to the Crown. Only twenty miles of sea divide Ulster from Scotland. It was this geographical fact, perhaps, which more than anything else suggested to James I.—who had become king just after the final overthrow of the rebellious Celtic chieftains—the idea of planting the confiscated estates mainly with Scottish agriculturists. Many English were also sent over, but the vast bulk of the settlers were Presbyterian Lowland Scots; and there, in that north-eastern corner of Ireland, their descendants have since then lived and thrived, constituting for close on three hundred years a separate race, with a different creed, different social manners and habits of thought, and a different utterance from the original inhabitants of the country.

There are nine counties in the province of Ulster—Antrim, Down, Armagh, Derry, Fermanagh, Tyrone, Donegal, Monaghan, and Cavan. The Scotch and English settlers penetrated into all these counties; but they concentrated themselves mainly in the first five,—the nearest to their original home,—and after the lapse of three centuries the disposition of this younger Irish race remains practically the same. Down and Antrim are the most distinctively Scotto-Irish of the Ulster counties; but in the southern districts of Down the Celtic element is predominant, as it was three hundred years ago; and in Antrim there is a district locally known as "the Glens," the population of which is, at the end of the Nineteenth Century, as it was at the opening of the Seventeenth—almost exclusively native and Catholic. There are Catholic and Celtic districts also in Armagh, Derry, Tyrone, and Fermanagh; in Donegal, Monaghan, and Cavan the ancient native race is overwhelming.

The predominant element in the younger Irish race is undoubtedly Scottish; but they differ as widely from the people of Scotland as the Americans do from the English. They are really a mixture of Scotch, English, and Irish—a racial amalgam which has been brought about by intermarriage and the influence of environment; and they combine some of the qualities and peculiarities of the three races—the energy and grit of the English, the industry and thrift of the Scotch, the generous impulses of the Celt. They are proud to call themselves Irish; and they are proud of Ireland as their birth-land and home. But they are certainly more like the Scottish people in manners, customs, thoughts, and utterance than their Celtic neighbours. They have not the quickness of perception, the fine imagination, the keen sense of humour, the genial expansiveness of the Celts. In temperament they are rather dry, cold, formal, and self-contained. It is a curious fact, indeed—a remarkable illustration, no doubt, of the influence of environment—that even the pure and unadulterated Celt of Ulster has the essentially Celtic qualities in a far less degree than his kin in the South. Perhaps the Celt of the North owes his comparative sobriety and reserve of manner to his intercourse with the younger race.

But, if the Ulster Irishman is inferior to the Southern Celt in attractive manners and the art of pleasing, he has in a larger degree those qualities which the Celt so often lacks—industry, thrift, self-reliance, a practical mind, business habits—qualities which, with all his home-spun plainness of manner, and his lack of poetry and romance, make him a sterling, honest character, and have made Ulster a province of prosperous industrial and agricultural communities in a country, alas! of dead industries and decaying villages and towns.

Physically the Ulster Irish peasant is roughly cast. He is big, and brawny, and awkward. But there is a pleasing air of prosperity about him. He is well-clothed, and gives one the impression of being well-fed. One feels instinctively that he is a man of character and stake in his barony, and that he has money in the Post Office Savings Bank. If one meets him casually on the high road, and tries to enter into conversation with him, one is apt to find him slow of speech, and lethargic, and unresponsive to one's advances—a marked contrast to the genial and voluble Celt, who, in like circumstances, would tell you in ten minutes all—and, if one may use an Hibernianism, a great deal more—about himself, his neighbours, and the district. The farm he tills is small, ranging in extent from six to thirty acres; but it is, as a rule, a model of order and neatness and of how to make the most of the land. Some of the crops are specially raised to supply his own family. There is the potato-field, for instance—the potato being, in the North as well as in the South, the principal article of diet; and the wheat field—the wheat being ground at the local mill into coarse but sweet flour for home-made "griddle cakes." There is barley and flax for the market; also a little stock-raising, a little pig-breeding, a little dairying, a little dealing in poultry and eggs—from all of which sources the money is raised to pay the rent, to meet the household expenses, and to add to the little balance in the Savings Bank.

The cottage, a long, low building with tiny windows, white-washed walls, and roof of brown thatch, nestles in a shady nook of the farm. Inside the cottage everything is neat and orderly. There is the kitchen, into which you first step, with its turf fire blazing on a great wide hearth, its dresser filled with utensils and crockery ware, everything clean as a new pin ; and off the kitchen are one or two bedrooms and "the best room," or parlour. It is in "the household gods" of this latter apartment that one sees evidence of the two most conspicuous mental attributes of the Ulster Irishman—his politics and his religion : his intense loyalty to Great Britain and his staunch Protestantism. On a little round table near the window is the big, well-thumbed family Bible ; and on the walls are rude prints of "William III. crossing the Boyne" and "The Secret of England's Greatness," the latter being a representation of the Queen presenting a Bible to a negro. His politics and his religion alike have inspired him with a distrust of his Celtic fellow-countrymen, the "Papists," or the "Romans," as he prefers to call them. He is very proud of the fact that his ancestors fought behind the walls of Derry, at Enniskillen, and on the banks of the Boyne, for the Prince of Orange ; and on the 12th of July, the anniversary of the battles of the Boyne and Aughrim—the two engagements in Ireland which decided the issue of the Revolution of 1690, and placed William of Orange securely on the throne—he takes down the old fowling-piece which hangs over the mantelshelf, and, donning his Orange regalia—for, of course, he is a member of the Loyal Orange Institution—he marches in the Orange procession, with bands and banners, through the neighbouring town or village. But, in truth, the suspicion with which he regards his Catholic fellow-countrymen lasts only through the month of July, in which the Orange anniversaries occur. During the other eleven months of the year this most peaceable and law-abiding of men bids his Catholic neighbour " Good-day " when he meets him, or grasps him by the hand, and now and then has a friendly chat with him on affairs in general over a pipe and glass.

But, loyalist though the Ulster Irishman is to the backbone, he is thoroughly democratic in spirit. His loyalty is not personal, like that of the Celt, but consists rather of a respect for institutions, which make little or no appeal to the attachment or devotion of his Celtic fellow-countrymen. When he is moved to speech, he is rough and ready and unreserved in his criticism of things, especially of the relations between landlord and tenant; and though, unlike the Celt, he has never shot his landlord, he always regards him with grave suspicion, and has never been able to give him that deep, and genuine, and whole-hearted attachment which the Celt has always shown for "the ould shtock."

He has a humour, too, all his own—solid, dry, and caustic, like himself, lacking the spontaneity, and the extravagance of the drollery of the Celt. Here are a few of the best stories he tells at his own fireside, or when he meets his friends in the tap-room of a "public" on market days. A Presbyterian clergyman who was a professor in the Queen's College, Belfast, and was dry, cold, and formal in his style of address, preached a sermon to a country congregation. After the service was over an elder remarked to a neighbour, "Weel, it'll be lang afore that mon makes the deil swat." The sexton of a parish in the County Armagh was about to lose his wife. She begged him, as her last dying request, to bury her over in Tyrone, forty miles away, among her own kindred. "Indeed, Peggy," was the dry rejoinder of the husband, "I'll thry ye here first, but if ye give ony trouble I'll take ye up and bury ye in Tyrone." An old woman, who had made a good deal of money by selling whisky in a village, on fair and market days, was visited, when she lay dying, by her minister, to whom she spoke, as is usual on such occasions, about her temporal as well as her spiritual affairs. "And so, Molly," said the minister, "you tell me you are worth all that money?" "Indeed, minister, I am," replied Molly. "And you tell me," continued the minister, "that you made it by filling the noggin?" "Na, na, minister!" cried the dying woman; "I didna tell you *that*. I made maist of it by *not* fillin' the noggin!" During a dry season, when not a drop of rain had fallen for weeks to refresh the thirsty ground, a native of the Ards of Down was one day watching a cloud sailing calmly across Strangford Lough in the direction of his fields. But it took another direction, greatly to his annoyance, and he exclaimed, "Aye, if ye wor the poor-rate or the county cess, ye wad a gi'en us a call."

In rustic dialect and pronunciation Ulster also differs widely from the other three Irish provinces. The Ulster speech partakes something of the nature of broad Yorkshire, but it is more Scottish than anything else—the number of Scotch words and expressions in the dialect being very numerous—although it has also in some degree the softness of the Southern brogue. The Ulster Irishman of the peasant class always pronounces I, "a," or "aw," as "A will." He says "aye" when he means "yes," and he usually begins his sentences with "I say," pronounced rapidly "Assay." An amusing illustration of the complexity of the Ulster dialect occurred at the Antrim Assizes a short time ago. A witness in a case was asked by a barrister how he had seen a certain thing which he had described in his evidence. "I saw it by the blunk o' a caunle," was the reply. "'The blunk of a caunle'!" said the judge, who was from the South of Ireland. "What in the world is that?" "It's just what a say—the blunk o' a caunle," replied the witness. "But what is the blunk of a caunle?" asked the judge. "Well," said the witness, with the characteristic outspokenness of an Ulster peasant, "ye're a nice mon to be sittin' up there, and no' to ken what A mean by a blunk o' a caunle!" The witness meant "the blink of a candle"!

Perhaps the saddest phase of Irish politics is the sectarian animosity between Protestant and Catholic in Ulster, which flares up particularly about the time of the Orange anniversaries in July But even that, like everything else Irish, no matter how grave and serious, is not without its humorous elements. A Catholic woman went to a priest in Belfast and complained bitterly of the conduct of her husband. He drank all his wages, beat her continually, and never went to Mass on Sundays. " Is the man a Catholic at all?" asked the priest, horrified at the long litany of the husband's iniquities. "Musha, Father, it's too good a Catholic he is," was the comical reply. " If my Jim had his way he'd knock the heads off all the Proteshtants betune this and Dublin." The late Dr. McGettigan, Roman Catholic Bishop of Raphoe, used to relate that when he was P.P. of a parish in Donegal he was called one day to see an unfortunate sailor of a wrecked Derry coasting vessel, who had been cast ashore, and was lying on the beach speechless, but not quite dead. The priest stooped down and said to him, " My poor fellow, you are nearly gone; but just try to say one little word, or to make one little sign to show that you are dying in the true faith." The sailor opened his eyes just a little, and crying out with all his remaining strength, "To hell with the Pope!"—the Orange war-cry—passed peaceably into eternity.

Hatred and distrust of the Pope is the dominant passion of the Orangemen. A few years ago a small party of staunch Ulster Protestants went over on a holiday trip to London, and, among other places of interest, visited a popular Roman Catholic institution in Hammersmith, in which a poor co-religionist of the trippers had found a home denied to none who enter their portals by the good nuns in charge. "And does this place belong to the Pope now?" asked a male member of the party of one of the Sisters. "Yes," she replied; "we Sisters of the Poor are in a spiritual sense children of His Holiness: but we make no distinction between Protestants and Catholics among those who come to us for help." "Well, now, that's nice," said the spokesman of the party; "but tell me, does the Pope ever come to see ye?" "Oh no," said the nun; "he lives in Rome. But why do you ask?—have you any feeling against the Pope?" "Well," said the Orangeman slowly, "I've little aginst the mon meself, but I must tell you that he doesn't at all bear a good name round Portadown." There is another story illustrative of the readiness of the lower Protestant classes in Ulster to curse the Pope on the slightest provocation which, though it is rather well known in Ireland, is too good not to find a place here. In the County of Down an officious policeman found fault with a farmer for having his name on his cart in ordinary writing letters. "My man," he said, "those letters are very difficult to read; you should have had the name painted in Roman letters." The farmer took the rebuke in dogged sullenness until the word "Roman" fell on his ear, and aroused within him all the Protestant aggressiveness of his nature. "Roman!" he shouted, with his eyes blazing with fury. "To hell with the Pope!"

I was in Belfast during the awful Orange riots of 1886, which lasted from June to September, during which forty or fifty people were killed, thousands injured, and hundreds of houses wrecked and burned. If a person suspected of being a Catholic fell into the hands of an Orange mob, he was asked to shout, "To hell with the Pope!" and if he refused was beaten to within an inch of his life. The Catholic mob, on the other hand, asked the stranger they captured in their quarters to kneel down and "bless" himself—that is, to make the sign of the Cross—and cry, "Long life to the Pope!" in order to satisfy themselves whether his colour was "green" or "orange."

The factions reside for the most part in separate localities, known locally as "Orange districts," and "Catholic districts"; but in ordinary times they live and work peaceably together. It is only on the occasions of the anniversary days of the old battles between the representatives of the rival races and creeds, such as the Battle of the Boyne and the Battle of Aughrim, that the latent enmity of blood and faith is stirred within them. An Orange farmer was returning home one Twelfth of July somewhat unsteady from his celebration of "the glorious, pious, and immortal memory of William the Third," when he tumbled into a dyke, in which he was well-nigh suffocated. His cries for assistance were heard by a Catholic neighbour, who extricated him from his perilous position. Once more on safe ground he grasped the hand of his preserver, but on recognising him he cried, "Put me back agin! put me back agin! I wouldn't be behoulden to a Papist for onything!" The saying attributed to Oliver Cromwell, "To hell or to Connaught"—the alternative which, it is said, he presented to the Irish Catholics—is well known. At a recent Orange demonstration Cromwell was mentioned with laudation as the only man who knew how to deal with the Papists. "I'm nae sae sure o' that," came a voice, in the Ulster brogue, from the crowd; "you see, he gied them the choice!" A Catholic gentleman from the South of Ireland was staying some time ago in Belfast. On Sunday he went forth to attend Mass. He beheld crowds of people moving in all directions, evidently to Church, but he could not see the sign of a Catholic Church anywhere. "All these people, I presume, sir, are going to prayers?" he said to a man whom he met in the street. "Yes," said the man. "All Protestants, I presume?" "Yes," said the man, with a smile of contempt that the question should be even asked. "And may I inquire where do the Catholics go?" "To hell," was the reply; "where else?"

But sometimes an Orange husband and a Catholic wife can pull along very well together. During a Parliamentary contest in Belfast some years ago, a candidate visited a working-man's house, in the principal room of which a pictorial representation of the Pope faced an illustration of King William III. crossing the Boyne. Needless to say, the candidate stared from one picture to the other in amazement; and, seeing his bewilderment, the voter's wife explained—"Shure, me ould man's an Orangeman and I'm a Catholic." "And how do you get on together?" asked the astonished politician. "Och, very well indeed," replied the woman, "barrin' the 12th of July, whin me husband goes out wid the Orange procession and comes home dhrunk." "Well?" said the candidate. "Well, he always takes His Holiness down and jumps on him, and thin goes straight to bed. The nixt mornin' I gets up airly, takes down King Billy—bad scran to him!—pawns him, and buys a new Pope wid the money. Thin I gives me ould man the ticket to get King Billy out, if he plases"!

But, ah! the pity of the truth of Charles Lever's sarcastic lines:

> "A glorious nation,
> A splendid peasantry, on fruitful sod,
> Fighting like devils for conciliation,
> And hating each other for the love of God."

Chapter XVII

THE IRISH CARDRIVER

THE Irish carman—or "the jarvey," as he is styled in his native isle—enjoys a wide celebrity as a comical fellow. Sometimes his humour is absolutely unconscious. He says the quaintest things imaginable without the slightest striving after effect or the least intention of being funny. But oftenest he is consciously droll. He possesses a rich fund of natural wit and sarcasm, a readiness in good-humoured retort, and a mellifluous brogue which make him an excellent travelling companion on a long drive.

A good example of the often audacious humour of the jarveys is found in the following authentic anecdote. A few years ago there was a waiter in one of the hotels in Dublin, who was so ill that it was with difficulty he was able to go about. But he always made it a point to stand at the door to see the visitors off. A commercial traveller remarked to the carman who drove him from the hotel, "That poor waiter looks very ill. I'm afraid he won't last long." "Lasht long," exclaimed the jarvey, " shure he's dead these two months, only he's too lazy to close his eyes." A proprietor of an hotel, overhearing a cardriver in Cork asking an exorbitant fare of an unsuspecting foreigner, expostulated with him on his exaggeration of the tariff, concluding with the reproof, " I wonder you haven't more regard for the truth." " Och, indeed, thin, I've a grate dale more regard for the truth than to be draggin' her out on every palthry occasion," was the reply. The sarcasm of their rhetoric is, as a rule, deprived of its sting by the quaint manner in which it is employed. A very stout Dublin citizen, whose trade was that of a furrier, once offered a jarvey, at the end of a journey, the modest sum of sixpence. " Is that all you're givin' me?" said the car-driver indignantly. " Yes," replied the furrier, " that's your legal fare; and it's all you'll get from me, so take it, and go." The jarvey, seeing it was hopeless to extract any more money from the furrier, and determined to have it out of him somehow, concentrated all the scorn and contempt he could into his voice and facial expression, and exclaimed: ' Arrah, go lang out o' that, ye ould boa-constructor." The twofold allusion in this retort so tickled the subject of it, that he never let slip an opportunity of repeating it.

A visitor to Ireland, who engaged a car at the North Wall, Dublin, promised the driver half a crown more than his fare if he succeeded in catching a certain train at Kingsbridge terminus. This the driver failed to do, but he claimed the extra half-crown, notwithstanding. "Shure, it's no fault of me or me baste that ye missed the train, yer honner," he quaintly argued, "It's all owin' to the lateness of the boat, and would yer honner be so hard as to punish me for that?" An Englishman was being driven from Loughrea to Ballinasloe. The horse seemed both hungry and tired, and it needed the constant application of the whip to keep him going. "I think you ought to bait the horse," said the fare to the driver. "Bate the horse!" exclaimed the latter. "Shure, what else have I been doin' since we left Loughrea?"

The ways in which the drivers convey hints to fares are also often very laughable. A long car, full of passengers, was toiling up one of the steep hills in the county of Wicklow. The driver leaped down from his seat in the front and walked by the side of the horse. The poor beast wearily dragged its heavy load, but the passengers were too eagerly engaged in conversation to notice how slowly the car progressed. Presently the driver opened the door at the rear of the car, and loudly slammed it to again. The "insides" were somewhat startled at first, and then thought the driver was only assuring himself that the door was securely closed. For the second time the man repeated the same action; he opened the door and slammed it to again with a louder bang. Then one of the travellers inquired why he did that. "Whist," he whispered, "spake low, or she'll overhear us." "Who's she?" asked the astonished passenger, who began to think the driver must be mad. "The mare, to be sure," he replied, "I'm disavin' the crature. Every time she hears the door slammin' that way she thinks one of yez is gettin' down to walk up the hill, and that rises her spirrits." The "insides" took the hint.

The Dublin jarvey is said to have one unamiable quality. It is a fault which he shares with his class in all countries. He is sometimes dissatisfied with what he is given, no matter how many times it may exceed the lawful fare. There is a good story current in Dublin in illustration of this side of the car-driver's character. An American in Dublin, on being told of this circumstance by a friend, offered to make a bet that he would give a driver such a fee that he would not ask for more. "That is impossible," said the Dublin man. "I'll take the bet." They engaged a car, the first they met, and drove a distance of about two miles. "How much do I owe you?" inquired the American, at the end of the journey. "Shure, yer honner can give me whatever yez like," said the jarvey. "But I would rather you would name your charge." "Indeed, an' I won't, yer honner.

It's not for me to say what a fine gentleman like you will give me." Thus put to the test, the American handed him over a half-sovereign for a ride that should have cost a couple of shillings at the most. The driver looked at the coin, and then at the gentleman, as if doubting the evidence of his senses at this unexpected munificence, but soon recovering from his surprise, he put his hand to his hat, and said heartily, " I thank yer honner." "You have lost your bet," said the American to his friend, as they walked away. But before they had gone far the driver, leaving his horse and vehicle to take care of themselves, was by their side. " Well, what do you want now ? " said the American angrily. " Hang it ! man, you've got your fare." " So I have," said the driver with an insinuating smile ; "an' it's yourself that's the rale liberal gintleman ; but, as I don't like to change the gould, I thought that maybe yer honner has got a spare sixpence in yer pocket ! " The subject of the fare has given rise to much of the humour associated with the Irish jarvey. A military officer who passed through the Tirah Campaign was recently on a visit to the Irish metropolis. He engaged a car to drive him from the Richmond Barracks to the Kildare Street Club, and on arrival at his destination presented the driver with a shilling. Pat fixed his eye attentively on the coin, and ejaculated viciously : " Wisha, bad luck to the

Afradays!" "Why?" asked the officer. "Because, thin, they've killed all the gintlemen that fought agin 'em." The officer was so tickled by the remark that he promptly doubled the fare. It must, however, be said for the Irish jarveys, that they are more easily satisfied with what they are paid by their fares, and are more thankful for a little generosity, than the drivers of any other nationality.

They can be very sarcastic at times, these Irish jarveys. An English traveller complained at the unevenness of the roads over which he was being driven. "Arrah, sure if they wor any betther y'd import thim to England," was the ready response. Some years ago the Lord Mayor of Dublin happened to be an exceedingly superior and fidgety person, who was enormously impressed by the dignity of the office to which he had been elected for a year. One day his carriage was stopped by an ancient "four-wheeler," which impudently turned round in Dawson Street, under the very shadow of the Mansion House, and thus checked the civic dignitary's horses in their fiery career. An altercation took place between the footman and the driver of the cab, and the Lord Mayor, putting his head out of the window, cried: "Mahony, take his number, and have him summoned." The jarvey, with appalling audacity, retorted: "Arrah, go in out o' that, ye ould twelve months' aristocrat," and drove off. The drivers often vent their powers of sarcasm on themselves. A friend of mine, landing at Kilrush Pier on his way to Kilkee, gave his luggage to one of the dozen fellows who clamoured vociferously for his patronage. The others then began ejaculations like these: "May I niver, if the gintleman is not goin' with Feeney." "Faix, he'll be in Kilkee for breakfast to-morrow mornin' if no bad luck overtakes him." "Cch, Feeney, yer mother had little to do whin she rared the likes of you." "Never mind thim, sir," cried Feeney to his fare; "the divil has hard work to furnish these fellows with lies. There's not a betther horse nor a purtier wan than mine in the kingdom. We'll be in Kilkee, sir, before you're comfortably sated in the car."

The vehicle the Irish jarvey drives is as "original" as himself. The old jaunting-car, or outside car, as it is now commonly called, is indeed a curious contrivance—two wheels, a seat for two over each wheel, and a dickey, or a place for the driver in front, immediately behind the horse—should there be the full complement of fares (four in number)—on the vehicle. As you sit on the car—"travelling edgeways," as this style of locomotion has been aptly described—you see only one side of the street or road over which you are driven. Indeed, someone has said that the vehicle is like the Irish character, which limits the vision to a one-sided view of everything. However that may be, the side car has taken a strong hold on the affections of the Irish people. Several attempts which have been made to introduce the hansom have utterly failed, even in Belfast, the least Celtic of the Irish towns and cities.

No topic comes amiss to the jarveys. They will discuss any subject with you across "the well"—as the covered-in centre of the car is called—and you will find them, as a rule, racy, shrewd, and well-informed commentators on men and things; but one thing you will hardly ever discover them in, and that is a confession of ignorance. An Irish car driver is ready with some answer, no matter how wide of the mark, to your quest for information on any subject under the sun; and the only shortcoming he will plead guilty to is want of memory, or, as he himself would say, "I disremember that, sur," or he will pretend to a wise incredulity. But you will rarely hear him say. "Well, I never heard tell of that, yer honner."

It is said that, as a class, they are fond of drink. The many hours they have to spend in the open-air, the cold and wet they have to endure, and their irregular meals may be advanced in excuse for this failing. The proprietor of a shooting-box in the West of Ireland, having been driven home in a regular downpour of rain, and perceiving that his driver was almost in rags, sympathetically said: "Tim, my poor fellow, you must be wet through and through." "Faix, I'm only wet to the skin, yer honner," replied Tim; "but, plase goodness, I'll be wet inside as soon as yer honner can get out the spirrits." "There, Pat," said an English traveller to the thirsty car driver whom he had just refreshed at a roadside inn, "hasn't that made another man of you?" "'Deed, and it has, sur," was the instantaneous answer. "An' begorra, he's dry too." Who could resist the intellectual nimbleness which gave a thirst to "the other man," and insinuated that it ought to be slaked?

Sometimes the strangest reasons are given why the amount tendered by the fare at the end of the journey should be substantially increased. A gentleman, who lived at Dalkey, some years ago, was driven one dark night from Kingstown to his residence. The carman, who was discontented with the sum paid him, said, "Shure, yer honner will give me a trifle more than that?" "Not a rap more," replied the gentleman. "Faith, you would if you heard the news." "What news?" "Give me another shilling now, and I'll tell you," said the driver. The gentleman gave him the shilling, saying, "Now, what has happened?" "Sorra the harm at all," replied the driver, "only I thought you'd not begrudge a little extra for to know that I druv yez all the way without a linchpin." The unforgivable sin on the part of a fare, in their eyes, is, needless to say, stinginess. A commercial traveller told the carman he engaged at his hotel to be quick to catch the train at Kingsbridge terminus. Pat, thinking he saw an extra shilling in store, hurried along at a tremendous speed, and pulled up his panting horse at the terminus just in time for his fare to jump into the train; but the reward he got was an extra twopence. A few weeks after, Pat, on being called from "the stand" to the same hotel, recognised in the fare his parsimonious patron. This time he had to go to Broadstone terminus. On he went at a violent pace for a short distance, and then, pulling up slowly behind a big dray, pretended that he could not pass. Round he went by Henry Street, Moore Street, Britain Street—all the narrowest and slowest thoroughfares—so that when the terminus was reached the train was gone, and the fare was left lamenting, with all his luggage in a heap beside him, and five hours to wait for the next chance of transit to the West. Of course, Pat was treated to all the "blank, blanks" in the English language by the irate commercial traveller, but he coolly got up on his car, and, as he was driving off, exclaimed: "Arrah, did yez think I was going to kill my baste agin for tuppence?"

A strange request was once made by a cardriver to a friend of mine, a journalist, as he was being driven from Loughrea to Ballinasloe during the Land League agitation. The driver always sits on the left side of the car, and the fare on the right. As they approached a lonely part of the road, thickly wooded on each side, the driver pulled up and said to my friend, "Would you mind changin' places, sur?" "Why so?" asked my friend. "Well, sur, to tell you the truth," replied the driver, "there was a land agent fired at down there below a couple of months ago, and faix it was the jarvey they kilt." Mr. Thorpe Porter, a well-known Dublin magistrate, used to tell the following amusing story. On the evening of the day, in 1848, that John Mitchel, the famous young Irelander, was sentenced in Dublin to transportation for fourteen years for treason-felony, Mr. Porter was passing along Capel Street on a hackney car, when he was recognised by the crowd and saluted with a volley of stones. Not one of the missiles struck the magistrate, but the carman received a blow on the point of his left elbow which elicited from him a copious flow of malediction "Ah, well," said Mr. Porter, "the stone was not intended for you." "It hurt me all the same, yer honner," replied the jarvey. "Thim vagabonds shouldn't throw stones without havin' a good aim and knowin' who they'd hit."

A few other specimens of their wit, repartee, and powers of invention may, in conclusion, be quoted. A gentleman alighting at Bray Station was saluted with the usual cry, "Have a car, yer honner?" "No, I'm able to walk," he replied. "Musha, may yer honner long be able but seldom willin' to walk," was the witty response. A gentleman on a hackney car, in a hurry to reach his destination, was delayed by a drove of pigs on the road. "D—— them," he muttered. "Why thin, now, sir," remarked the driver, "I'd rather see them saved." A parish priest from Wicklow—a very heavy man, weighing about twenty stone—wanted to take a cab from Harcourt Street Station, Dublin, to Drumcondra, the residence of the Roman Catholic archbishop. Before he got into the vehicle he bethought him of the reputation of the Dublin jarveys for charging exorbitant fares, so he asked the driver to tell him what he would charge for the drive. "Oh, I'll lave that to yer riverence," was the reply. "But how much is it?" persisted the priest. "Whativer yer riverence plases," said the driver. "That won't do," his reverence insisted; "I shall not get into the cab until you tell me the fare." "Get in at wance, yer riverence," exclaimed the jarvey; "for if the horse turns and gets a sight of yez, the divil a step he'll go at all, at all." An English tourist, driving along a country road, drew the jarvey's attention to a wretched tatterdemalion. "What a shocking thing it is," said he, "to see a man in such rags and misery." "Begorra, thin, yer honner," replied the driver, with the characteristically Irish desire to put a good face on everything, "that's not from poverty at all, at all. The truth is that the man's so ticklesome that sorra a tailor in the counthry can attempt to take his measure." Two artistes, who were on a concert tour in Ireland, drove to their hotel in Dublin. One asked the other, in French, what he should give the driver. The other replied, also in French, two shillings, which was more than the ordinary fare. The cardriver, on hearing them speak French, immediately said, "I know what yez are sayin', sur. I speak Frinch meself." "What did I say?" asked the fare. "Don't give the poor jarvey less than four shillings on this miserable cowld day," replied the driver.

Dublin has two ancient cathedrals, St. Patrick's and Christ Church, the former of which was restored by a brewer, and the latter by a distiller. Jameson, the founder of the well-known Dublin distillery, used to tell with great glee the story of a good joke he had with a Dublin jarvey anent the restoration of these sacred fanes. Driving past St. Patrick's Cathedral during the progress of the work, he inquired of the driver at whose expense the repairs were being done. "It's Sir Arthur Guinness, the Double X Stout man, that's doin' it," replied the driver. "Oh, indeed; that's very kind of him." Later they passed Christ Church Cathedral, which was being restored at the same time, and Jameson put a similar query in regard to it. "George Roe, the whisky-maker is lookin' after that, sur," was the jarvey's reply. "But tell me," said Jameson, "they say that Jameson, the other whisky man, has piles of money. Isn't he doing any good with it?" "Faith, yer honner, it's a saycret," replied the driver; "but they do say that, on the quiet, he's building a lunatic asylum to put the other two idiots into."

The mention of whisky and stout recalls the amusing story once told by Father Mathew, the famous temperance advocate, of the inutility of using inconclusive arguments. In the course of an address to an audience of Dublin cardrivers he told them they might learn a lesson in temperance from the brute creation. "If," said he, "I were to set before one of your horses a bucket of water and a bucket of whisky, you know which the wise beast would take." Whereupon one of the quick-witted carmen replied, "Well, Father, if I wor to place before me horse a truss of hay and a beefsteak, you know which the wise baste would choose. But, Father, does it follow that the hay is the best for me?"

Chapter XVIII

THE IRISH BEGGAR

SHORTLY after the extension to Ireland of the English Poor Law system, in the Thirties, a Dublin beggar-woman was told by a gentleman, to whom she appealed for alms, to go to the poor-house. "Well," said she, "this Poor Law is a gran' thing for the souls of the gintlemin." "Why?" asked the gentleman, his curiosity aroused by the strange remark. "Because now, when we axes for alms," replied the old crone, "they only say, 'Go to the poor-house,' but before there was a poor-house they used to say, 'Go to the divil.'"

The Irish beggars have always been noted—like the Irish cardrivers—for their wit and power of retort. The genuine eloquence of some of them is also beyond question. Leitch Ritchie, the Scottish littérateur, who visited Ireland in the fifth decade of the century, talking afterwards of his experiences, stated that one man, whom he saw sitting on the ground with his back to the wall, attracted his attention by a degree of squalor in his appearance which he had not before observed in the country. But, unlike other Irish beggars, the man was strangely silent, and, struck by this circumstance, Ritchie asked him whether he was begging. "Of course, it's beggin' I am," the man replied. "But you do not utter a word," said Ritchie. "Arrah, is it jokin' yer honner is wid me?" said the beggar. "Look there!" and he held up the tattered remnant of what had once been a coat, "does yez see how the skin is spakin' through the holes of me clothes, and the bones cryin' out through me skin? Look at me sunken cheeks and the famine that's starin' in me eyes. Man alive, isn't it beggin' I am with a hundred tongues?"

But the rhetoric of the beggars reaches its highest flights in rewarding charity with blessings and good wishes, and punishing niggardliness with sarcasm and imprecations. "The hivens be yer bed!" "May the copper you gave me be a candle to light yer soul to glory!" "May ivery hair on yer honner's head become a mould candle to light ye to hiven!" "That yez may have a happy death and a favourable judgmint!" "That the prayers of the widow and orphan may meet yez at the gates of hiven and intersade for yez!" "May ye niver see yer wife a widow!" are some of the blessings which I have heard them pour with lavish tongues on the heads of those who throw them a copper. It is curious that their prayers should chiefly relate to the world to come—one exception is "God spare yez to your comforts"—and I dare say that occasionally these fall uncomfortably on the ears of those whose thoughts are far remote from the future. The wish "that yez may have a happy death and a favourable judgment" is not very exhilarating to some people; but that is better than the prayer, "May yez be in hiven in a fortnight," which I once heard an old beggar-woman address to a benefactor.

A dignified Protestant clergyman in Cork was appealed to for charity with the usual accompaniment of many sacred objurgations. "For the blessing of God, cud you spare me a copper?" exclaimed the beggar-man. "No, I will not give a copper to one who appeals to me so indecorously," said the clergyman solemnly, "but I will give you what will be of more value to you—the advice not to take the name of God in vain." "An' is it in vain I've been takin' it?" asked the beggar-man, "Whose fault is that, I'd like to know?" "You ought to ask for manners, not money," said a gentleman who was rudely accosted by one of the fraternity. "Shure, I axed for what I thought yer honner had most of," was the immediate retort.

Thackeray used to delight in telling a very amusing experience he had with a beggar-woman while he was in Ireland, collecting material for his *Irish Sketch Book*. When she saw him put his hand in his pocket as he approached her, she cried out: "May the blessin' of God follow ye all yer life"; but as he only pulled out his snuff-box, she immediately added, "and niver overtake ye." A friend of mine relates that one day, as he was walking down Grafton Street with a fair friend of ample proportions and severe aspect, a beggar woman appealed to him for alms. As he paid no attention to her, she turned to the lady, but in that quarter also her prayers fell on unsympathetic ears. Then, with a look of scorn in her face, and a world of bitterness in her voice, she sent after them this parting shot, addressed to the lady, but including the gentleman in its withering sarcasm: "Ah, thin, God help the poor man that couldn't say no to yez!"

Dr. Whately, the well-known Archbishop of Dublin, never, on principle, gave indiscriminate charity. "Go away, go away," he cried impatiently to an importunate mendicant, "I never give alms to a beggar in the public street." "And where wud yer riverince wish me to wait on yez?" asked the mendicant. But the Archbishop's resolution against indiscriminate almsgiving was nigh giving way when an old beggar-woman to whom he returned his customary reply, paid him the following compliment as she looked at his Archiepiscopal leggings : " Musha, thin, I'd never think that a gintleman with such fine calves wud have such a hard heart."

Mr. S. C. Hall stated that he heard the following exclamations from a crowd of beggars which surrounded a carriage in which he and a lady sat : " Good luck to yer ladyship's happy face this mornin'; shure you'll lave the light heart in me breast before ye go." "Oh, thin, look at the poor dark man that can't see if yer beauty is like yer sweet voice, me lady." "Darlin' gintleman, the hivens be yer bed, and give us somethin'." "Oh, the blessin' of the widdy and the five small children that's waitin' for yer honner's bounty be wid ye on the road." "Och, help the poor craythur that's got no children to show yer honner; they're down in the sickness, and the man that owns thim is at say." "They're keepin' me back from the pinny ye're goin' to give me, lady dear bekase I'm wake meself and the heart's broke in me with hunger." "Oh, thin, won't yer ladyship buy a dyin' woman's prayers—chape."

Maria Edgeworth, the novelist, was driven one day into the town of Longford. An old beggarwoman hobbled up to the carriage and asked for charity. " You know I never give you anything," said the lady. Quick and ready came the answer:

"Oh, the Lord forgive ye, Miss Edgeworth, that's the first lie ye iver told." A lady relieved a beggar who called at her door. "There, now, go away," she said, "and don't come here again." "Ah, ma'am," replied the beggar, "don't say the like of that. If we're not to go where they do give us somethin', where will we go at all?" Two old crones asked a lady for charity. She gave one of them sixpence, telling her to divide it. "I will, me darlint," said the beggar-woman, "an' may the blessed God divide the hivens wid ye." A lady gave a plate of cold meat and a glass of stout to a beggar who called at the door. The man, with a twinkle in his eye, exclaimed: "Ah, shure, me lady, if yer feet wor as big as yer heart, it wouldn't be me corns I should like ye for to be threadin' upon.

But sarcasm and not flattery is the return Irish beggars usually give to those whom they appeal to in vain. "Get along with you," said a gorgeously-dressed footman in Stephen's Green, Dublin, to a beggar-man, "and take your rags with you." "Never mind me clothes, me good man," replied the mendicant; "they're me own." A red-haired tourist was sitting on "the long car" in Eyre Square, Galway, awaiting its departure for Connemara. "Throw me a penny, yer honner," said a beggar-man. "I will not," replied the tourist emphatically. "Ah, thin," retorted the vagrant, remembering how touchy red-haired people are to any allusion to their hair, " maybe you'd lave me a lock to light me pipe with." " Get away to the poor-house," said a lady, irritated by the appeals of a beggar-woman who had called at her door. "Get away to the poor-house is it?" said the old crone with concentrated scorn in her voice. " Faix, thin, I needn't stir, for it's at a poor house I am." There is often poetry and epigrammatic point, as well as intense bitterness, in their imprecations. "May ye melt off the earth like the snow off the mountains," a beggar at Killarney was heard to exclaim. " May ye never die until ye see yer own funeral," is a favourite expression with vagrants who are refused charity. It sounds like a wish—good-natured, if extravagant — that immortality may be your portion; but it is really a prayer that you may be hanged; for a condemned man, on his way to the gallows, sees his own funeral. Indeed, hanging seems to be, in the opinion of the beggars, the most awful fate that can befall a person. It is the end of their bitterest and most epigrammatic curses. "May yer last dance be a hornpipe in the air." And again, " May ye die wid a caper in yer heel!"

The fraternity are not devoid of the native humour. A gentleman, who had the misfortune to lose his nose, had occasion, on his way to business in Dublin, to pass an old beggar-woman, who invariably saluted him with the good-natured but to him incomprehensible prayer, "Hiven presarve yer honner's eyesight." The gentleman after vainly endeavouring to suggest to himself a satisfactory explanation of this curious wish, one day put it to the old woman: "Why do you desire my eyesight preserved? There is nothing the matter with it." "Well, yer honner," replied the beggar-woman, "it will be a bad thing for ye if it iver gets wake, for you'll have nothin' to rest yer spectacles on." They are, of course, also addicted to the making of "bulls." One of them called at a house, and said to the woman: "For the love of hiven, ma'am, give me a crust o' bread, for I'm so thirsty I don't know where I'll sleep to-night." "You shouldn't beg," said a gentleman who had been asked to bestow a copper on "a poor, lone crater"; "there's plenty of work in the hay-fields." "Ah! sur, we can't all work; for thin there'd be nothin' for the rest to do," was the woman's reply.

The making of "limestone broth" was a device employed by wandering beggars to secure a good supper without seeming to ask for it. The beggar, making his way into one of the cabins—which had always their doors hospitably open for poor vagrants—would ask the *vanithee* (or woman of the house) to lend him a small pot and allow him to cook his supper upon her fire. Permission was, of course, granted, and the pot was produced. He then took from his wallet two substantial pieces of freshly-cut limestone, which he placed in the pot, and, covering them with water, put the pot upon the fire to boil. The vanithee, looking on with interest, exclaimed, " What are yez goin' to make, me good man?" "Limestone broth, ma'am," replied the beggar. "Glory be to God, look at that now!" exclaimed the amazed housewife. When the boiling had proceeded for some time the beggar-man tasted the contents, and remarked "it would be grately improved by a pinch o' salt." The " pinch o' salt" was given him, and by-and-by he suggested that all the " broth " wanted was just a couple of spoonfuls of " male" to thicken it. Next came a request for a few slices of turnips, potatoes, and onions, to give it a little substance, all of which the good woman, who continued watching the proceedings with the keenest interest, kindly supplied; nor did she refuse " a knuckle of bacon," just to give the broth " the laste taste in the world of the flavour of mate." And when, at the conclusion of the operation, she was invited to try the " limestone broth," she pronounced it " quite as good as any mate broth she ever tasted in her life."

The number of beggars in Ireland has greatly decreased within the last quarter of a century.

They are only to be found, in any large numbers, at show places much frequented by tourists, such as Killarney, and at big fairs and race meetings. But even in the streets of cities and towns begging is winked at by the authorities; and there are many mendicants who follow it, though they could do at least as well otherwise, as an easy and congenial means of making a livelihood. "Could you help a poor fellow to-day, and the Lord save yez?" said a beggar to a Dublin publican. "Get away," cried the shopkeeper, "I've had a dozen of your kind here to-day already." "Shure, and it's meself that sadly knows how the professhion is overrun," replied the beggar. Quite recently also, the following conversation was overheard between two old crones in Cork: "Good morra to ye, Mrs. Fogarty," said one. "Good morra, kindly, Judy," replied the other; "I hope I see ye well this mornin'!" "Oh, very well, entirely. So, Mrs. Fogarty, ye married yer daughter Kate. Did she get a good match?" "Divil a better, praise be to God! She got Blind Darby Driscoll on the Dyke, that makes more money than any three beggars in Cork." "Ah, thin, but it's me that's glad to hear yer news. And did ye give her anythin'?" "Faix, I did, thin! Didn't I give her the best side of Patrick Street, which if well begged is worth siven an' sixpence a week." "Upon me word, but 'tis you that was generous," exclaimed the other.

Chapter XIX

IRISH COLLOQUIALISMS AND PROVERBS

THE Irish people, in their everyday talk, use many quaint and curious idioms, phrases, colloquialisms, and turns of speech. They have not a distinct dialect like the Scottish people. It is true they use many Celtic expressions; but, as a rule, the words they employ are English words—words to be found in any English dictionary. It is the thoughts behind those words, moulded as they are, according to Celtic forms, in the speaker's mind, that gives to the conversation of the Irish peasantry its distinctive national flavour. In the talk one hears in the cabins of Ireland, in its harvest fields or market places, are to be found poetic, graphic, and expressive phrases, strange combinations of force and simplicity, humorous mingling of the ridiculous with the sublime, novel applications of words, and quaint English colloquial survivals, centuries old.

Perhaps the funniest colloquial peculiarity of the Irish peasantry is the mis-application of big, high-sounding words and expressions. A Kerry tenant giving evidence in the Land Court in support of his application to have a fair rent fixed, said, " I have rayalized siven childer, and if I wor to rayalize siven more, and God is good, I wouldn't wish wan of thim to imbibe an acre of land." When asked whether the weather in his part of the country was favourable to farming, he exclaimed, " Shure, 'tis always bad weather for wan that's immersed in land." " Wisha, how are ye at all, Mrs. Mulcahy? Ye don't look well," said one neighbour to another. " Och, thin, it's meself is the marthyr intirely," replied Mrs. Mulcahy. " Shure I was kilt all lasht week wid the infirmation in me head; an' now, on top o' that, the dochtor tells me I'm sufferin' from general ability." I once heard an old crone say, " Iver since I losht me teeth I can't rightly domesticate me food." " Ah, the poor thing was always full of sediment," was advanced as an excuse for a romantically disposed girl who had made a runaway match. While a peasant was eating his dinner in his cabin, the family pig ran in. " Judy," said he to his wife, " will you extinguish the pig." " Arrah, what am I to do to the baste ! " exclaimed Judy in astonishment. " Oh, the ignorance of some people ! " cried the husband. " I mane 'put him out,' to be shure." Talking of the pig, a gentleman was being shown over the out-offices of an extensive farm by the steward. Coming to the large and commodious pig-styes, the gentleman remarked, "Well, the pigs ought to be comfortable here." "Yes, yer honner," replied the steward, "they've ivery inconverience that any rasonable-minded pig can require." During the visit of the Duke and Duchess of York to Ireland in August, 1897, when Dublin was very crowded with visitors, a gentleman hailed a car in Westland Row to take him to his hotel on the other side of the Liffey. Great was his surprise when the jarvey replied—"Oh, begorra, I can't waste me time like that, sur. Shure, I takes no wan now only thim that wants a tower round Dublin and its inverirons."

A Mr. Burke, a native of Galway, spoke at one of the weekly meetings of the Repeal Association in Dublin, which used to assemble in Conciliation Hall. He got the following flattering paragraph in the *Galway Vindicator*:—" Mr. Burke surpassed all Conciliation Hall for Miltonic grandeur ; Addisonian sweetness ; Swift-like purity of language, and O'Connell-like vastness of ideas." I once heard an orator at a Nationalist meeting in Ireland exclaim, " The ways of Providence are, indeed, unscrupulous."

"Grate " (great) is a favourite word in Ireland. A school-teacher in Donegal was giving her pupils some elementary lessons in ornithology. Speaking on the subject of eagles, the teacher said that they belonged to "the greatest family in these parts." "Axin' yer pardon, ma'am, that's a mistake," said a little boy in the class; "they're not half as grate a family as the O'Doherty's of Innishowen."

The peasantry have the faculty of picturesque and fantastic expression. I once asked an old peasant who was noted for his good spirits and light-heartedness, what was his age. "I'm ivery wan of eighty years," he replied. "But, shure, the age of an ould hat is in the cock of it." The sayings of the people expressing good will or ill will are very remarkable for their imaginative force. "May yer undertaker never live through his teething," is a quaint way of wishing one a long life. "May you die with a caper in yer heel," means that you may be hanged. If one says to another, "Bad luck to ye," the usual retort is, "Well, thin, good luck to you, and may nayther of our prayers iver happen." "Six eggs to ye, an' half a dozen of them rotten," is the mode in which the wish that you may have a disappointment is expressed. "Bad cess to you," meaning bad success to you, is another favourite curse. It is believed that a curse is never wasted—that it must fall on some one or something. A person who has been cursed often insists on the curse being taken off him. "Take yer curse off me," he will exclaim; and if he is persistent enough he will get it transferred.

"Wisha, thin, may it fall on yer bull-pup," was the way in which I heard a peasant transfer a curse which he had in the first instance bestowed on another peasant with whom he had a quarrel. Sometimes a humorous turn is given to a wish of ill-will. "The divil go with ye, and sixpence, and thin, faith, you'll nayther want money nor company."

"Murdhered" means badly beaten. I heard a witness in an assault case say, in the course of his evidence, "I was attacked before be the prisoners, and murdhered; but I recovered. I was in bed six weeks after that." One also hears in Ireland the expression, in regard to a sick person, "He is under the *cure* of Dr. So-and-So." Edmund Burke, who, in the last years of his life at Beaconsfield, made pills for the relief of the ailments of his poor neighbours, used to tell a story which illustrates the comical use which is often made of the word "cure" or "cured." "I am," said Burke, "like an Irish peer whom I used to know, who was also fond of dealing out remedies to his neighbours. One day that nobleman met a funeral, and asked a peasant whose it was. "Oh, me lord," was the reply, "that's Thady O'Donnell, the man whom yer lordship cured." The phrase "swarms with them"—meaning there are many of the things or persons referred to in existence—is also often incongruously applied. An Hibernian in London averred that absenteeism was one of the great grievances of which Ireland had to complain. "Oh, yes," answered an unsympathetic Englishman; "that's the old stalking-horse! I don't believe in your absentees." "You don't believe in thim!" was the angry reply. "Why, the ould country just swarms wid thim." "Rotten wid thim" is a phrase that is used in a similar sense. Lisdoonvarna, a watering-place in Clare, is a popular holiday resort of the clergy. A native of the place was once asked whether it was having a good season. "Why, it's rotten wid priests!" he proudly ejaculated. There are many phrases of that character, familiarity with which effaces from the mind the incongruity of their use in certain conjunctions.

"The bhoys" means the male population of the village or country-side. But, individually, every unmarried man, no matter how old, is "a bhoy." An English family, who settled in the West of Ireland, sent word into the neighbouring village that they required a boy as a servant. Next morning a man over forty years of age called to see "the masther." "Well, my man, what do you want?" inquired the gentleman. "I'm tould, sur, you want a bhoy," said the peasant. "And do you call yourself a boy?" asked the gentleman. "Why? do I look like a girl, yer honner?" asked "the bhoy" in genuine astonishment. "The broth

of a bhoy" is another popular expression. It means the concentrated essence of a man. During a debate on the Repeal of the Union in 1834—the first time the question was raised by Daniel O'Connell in the House of Commons—Sir Robert Peel created immense amusement by reading this absurd record of the ceremonies said to be adopted at the crowning of the ancient Irish Kings:—
"The ancient Irish thus used to crown their king. A white cow was brought forth which the king must kill, and seethe in water whole and bathe himself therein stark naked; then sitting in the same caldron, his people about him, he must eat the flesh and drink the broth wherein he sitteth, without cup or dish or use of his hand." Peel did not state his authority for this preposterous record, but it is to be found in the account of Ireland written by Geraldus Cambrensis (who accompanied Henry II. in the first Norman invasion of Ireland in 1172), the historical value of which has long since been largely discounted. It has, however, been suggested that this is the origin of the phrase "broth of a bhoy." That also may safely be rejected. "I never saw the broth that was too hot for me, or met the meat that was too fat for me," is a boast of personal prowess.

The word "under" is used in a peculiar manner. "You needn't lave the hotel, sur, if ye want a drive," said the proprietor of a hostelry to me.

He meant that cars for hire formed part of the establishment. And when I gave an order for a driver, he said to " the bhoy," " Put the horse under the car, Patsy." I have also frequently heard the injunction addressed to young children in the house: "Go out under the air, childer, and play." "Overhead" is also often quaintly used. I heard an old woman, suffering from the toothache, say, "It's me overhead teeth that's aching me." A countrywoman was walking through the Dublin vegetable market. Seeing some very small potatoes, she said to the dealer, "Do ye say thim's potaties?" "How, thin, do yez call thim in your part of the counthry?" replied the dealer, annoyed by the reflection on his stock. "Faix, we niver call 'um at all; whin we want any, we go and dig 'um!" An English woman in Dublin, seeing a crowd outside a house, inquired what was the matter. "A man is going to be buried," was the reply. "I'll wait to see the sight," said the woman. "In my country we carry them to be buried." Another curious colloquialism is, "I'm after it." An Englishman said to an Irishman, "Come and dine." The reply was, "I'm after my dinner." "I hope you'll catch it," said the Englishman.

"He's a melted rogue," means that the person to whom the phrase is applied is the very essence of roguery. A person dying is said to be "booked for the down train." " I'm the heart's blood of an honest man," is the superlative boast of personal integrity. " He looks as angry as if he wor vexed," and " He has a lip on him as long as to-day and to-morrow," are phrases applied to crying or petulant children. " I was sent adrift on the waves of the world," denotes a very forlorn condition. " Whistlin' jigs to a milestone," means an absurd waste of energy or effort. During the Parliamentary session of 1898, an Irish member was called to order by the Speaker for saying, " We might as well go whistling jigs to a milestone as appeal for justice to right hon. gentlemen on the Treasury Bench." One night, in committee on the Irish Local Government Bill, during the same session, there was a loud buzz of conversation in all parts of the House while an Irish member was speaking. The hon. member paused for a moment, and then, addressing the chairman, said : " Mr. Lowther, I can't hear myself at all with all this talk." The expression, " I can't hear myself at all with the noise," is very common in Ireland ; but its literal meaning having been given to it by the House, namely, that the hon. gentleman spoke merely to hear his own voice—it tickled members immensely. The " hoight of niggardliness " is expressed by the phrase, " He'd skin a flea for its hide and tallow, and never bury its bones!" " He's a dark man," does not mean a negro or a man with a dark complexion, but a man afflicted with blindness. "Ructions" means a row or a disturbance. "Give me none of your back talk," which is used by a superior towards an inferior, is the Irish way of saying, "Don't presume to argue with me."

"Open the shutter, Mary, and let out the dark," I heard one domestic say to another in the early morning. It is said of a sharp, cute, "knowing bhoy," that "he is like the new moon, sharp at both ends." "There now for you!" is a very popular exclamation. The expressions, "That's the truth, sur, or I can't speak it"; "Without a doubt, and without a lie," and "It's the truth I'm telling you!" are used to enforce or emphasize statements. If a man, whose name is unknown is wanted for anything, he is called by the polite address, "Honest man!" "That's your consate of it," is used when you praise a thing too highly. A friend of mine heard a quaint, but very graphic, misuse of the word "transported," in its meaning of being sent to a penal settlement across the seas. He met, in a railway carriage several years ago, an old, respectably clad man, who, in the course of conversation, stated he was a returned convict from Australia on his way home to Cork. He had been concerned in some agrarian crime, was transported, and, after his release, realized a competency which would enable him to pass the end of his life in ease at home. As the train passed a field in which some miserable-looking labourers were toiling, he exclaimed, "Arrah, it wasn't I that was thransported at all, but thim poor beggars."

The trust of the Irish peasantry in the protecting care of God is uppermost in all their misfortunes. "Shure, God is good!" they say. "He sent the sore trouble on us, but praise be to His holy name; His will be done." They also use the name of the Almighty very familiarly, but without the slightest intention of being profane or irreverent. "Well, God is good, and the devil isn't bad, either," is used to point out the certainty of the good being rewarded and the wicked punished in the next world. "Shure, God Almighty's a raal gintleman!" said an old woman when some unexpected piece of good fortune had befallen her. One of the quaintest expressions I ever heard was that of another old woman in reference to some one who had done her an injury, "I'll lave him to God," said she, "an' He'll play the divil with him!"

The everyday conversation of the people is also seasoned with many apt proverbs. These pithy sayings were originally coined in the Irish language, and in them are concentrated the wisdom and satire of centuries. "However near a man's shirt is, his skin is nearer," is the Celtic variant of "Blood is thicker than water." The sentiment of "Speech is silvern, silence is golden," is expressed in Ireland by the proverb, "Melodious is he closed mouth." There is a warning against indiscretion in talk in the saying, "A man ties a knot with his tongue that his teeth will not loosen." It is said of an angry man, "Let him cool in the skin he warmed in."

> "The man that's up is toasted,
> The man that's down is trampled on,"

in Ireland as—alas for human nature!—everywhere else. Pride and pretension get a well-deserved snub in the saying—"A pig in the sty doesn't know the pig going along the road!" "You'd be a good messenger to send for death," is said to a person who loiters on an errand. Of two men dancing together, or two women kissing each other, it is said, "Butter to butter is no relish." The ancient Irish wore their hair in thick, flowing masses. What they thought of baldness is expressed in the saying—"Better be bald than have no head at all—but divil a much more than that!" "Trust him as far as you can throw a cow by the tail," is used to warn one person against another.

The Irish proverbs relating to women and marriage are, as in all nations, satiric. Here are a few:—

"Where there's women there's talk, and where there's geese there's cackling."

"Have your own will, like the women have."

"A woman's desire—the dear thing."

"A woman is more obstinate than a mule—a mule than the devil."

"Three without a rule—a wife, a pig, and a mule."

"A woman has an excuse readier than an apron."

"Not worried till married."

"The husband of the sloven is known amongst the crowd."

"A ring on the finger and not a stitch of clothes on the back," is said of an improvident marriage. When a woman marries a bad husband, it is said, "She burnt her coal, and did not warm herself." "Never take a wife who has no faults," and "Don't praise your son-in-law till the year's out!" are also two popular proverbs. How much the success of matrimony depends on good cooking is expressed by the proverb, "Out of the kitchen comes the tune."

"Sure I knew him since his boots cost fourpence!" is used when an acquaintance with a person from infancy is claimed. "He who gets a name for early rising may sleep all day"; "There is hope from the sea, but no hope from the graveyard"; "He that loses the game, let him talk away," are proverbs also often heard in Ireland. The people are fond of a fight, but they like a feast better, according to the two sayings: "Better a drop of whiskey than a blow of a stick," and "Better the end of a feast than the beginning of a fight."

Chapter XX

THE SUNNINESS OF IRISH LIFE

JAMES ANTHONY FROUDE has said many hard things of Ireland—that is, of Ireland as the battle-ground of political and social questions—but he has paid an ungrudging and eloquent tribute to the charms of Ireland, of the mountain, the lake, and the valley, and of its light-hearted and humorous inhabitants. "We have heard much of the wrongs of Ireland, the miseries of Ireland, the crimes of Ireland," he writes; "every cloud has its sunny side, and, when all is said, Ireland is still the most beautiful island in the world; and the Irish themselves, though their temperament is ill-matched with ours, are still amongst the most interesting of peoples." Every cloud in Ireland has, indeed, its glint of sunshine. Thanks to the natural charms of the country, and the kindly, genial manners of the people, there is diffused through Irish life a warm, pleasant, stimulating influence, which is best described by the expressive and picturesque word "sunny." That delightful quality of sunniness in Irish life is most appreciated by those who know the strain on mental and physical energies of living amid the perpetual rush and noise and excitement of a large and busy English city. After such an experience, one feels, while in Ireland, that there is no country in the world so fresh and reposeful as the Emerald Isle, with its perpetual touch of Spring—no race so leisurely and restful as the Irish —that there is no land and no people so well adapted to re-invigorate an overworked frame, or to restore to cheerfulness a weary mind.

What a consciousness of tranquillity, what a restfulness of spirit, one feels in Ireland! What repose and quietude is inspired, mentally and physically, by the clear, serene atmosphere of the country ; its soft lights ; its expanses of blue sky ; the refreshing green of its fields and trees ; the varied tints of its mountain ranges ; its wind-swept moorlands ; its flat stretches of bog ; its gorgeous sunset glows ; the dreamy flow of its streams ; the restful expanse of its broad lakes ; and the soothing wash of the sea on its rugged cliffs and craggy strands ! How refreshing it is to read the delightful picture of Ireland drawn by the ancient Irish student-poet in France, which Sir Samuel Ferguson has rendered into English :—

"A plenteous place is Ireland for hospitable cheer,
Uileacan dubh O !

Where the wholesome fruit is bursting from the yellow
   barley ear,
                    Uileacan dubh O !
There is honey in the trees where her misty vales expand,
And her forest paths in summer are by falling waters fanned ;
There is dew at high noontide there, and springs i' the
   yellow sand,
             On the fair hills of holy Ireland."

And if the stern rugged coasts, the heather-covered moors and mountain ranges, the vernal valleys of Ireland can vie with those of any pleasure haunt in the United Kingdom in health-giving air and pleasure-inspiring scenery, the characteristics of the Irish people are no less admirably adapted to refresh and amuse an overworked and weary mind.

A few uncongenial visitors to Ireland—people, as a rule, without a glint of humour or inspiration, to whom the complex Irish character is a hopeless enigma—have been shocked by what they conceive to be the low regard for truth which prevails in the country. They say it is very difficult to get at the Irish peasant's real opinion on any subject. But I think it will be found that the Irish peasant's occasional picturesque indifference to facts is due, not to an ingrained love for falsehood and hypocrisy—as these critics too often suppose—but partly to his powers of imagination, and partly to his amiable desire to make himself agreeable. A man, weary after a long walk, asked a peasant whom he met on the high road how far he was from a certain village.

Just four short miles," was the reply. Now the place happened to be eight miles distant, and the peasant was aware of the fact. Why, then, did he deceive the man? "Shure," said he, when reproved for the deception, "I saw the poor fellow was tired, and I wanted to keep his courage up." In this anecdote we have an illustration of the peasant's desire to say pleasant things on all occasions. This is the secret also of his general subserviency to one's expressed opinions. His sense of politeness is so fine that he positively thinks it rude to express disagreement with the views of a stranger, even though he is convinced that they are mistaken.

And who has such a pretty faculty for paying compliments as the average Irish peasant? Two young ladies stopped to talk to an old man working in a potato field. In the course of the conversation one said to him, "Which of us do you think is the elder?" "Ah, thin, each of ye looks younger than the other," replied the gallant old fellow. An aged lady, getting into a cab in Dublin, said to the driver, "Help me in, my good man, for I'm very old." "Begor, ma'am," said he, "no matter what age you are, you don't look it." No one mingles fun with flattery so genially as the Irish peasant. You are never made to blush or to feel uncomfortable by his compliments. No matter how extravagant his flattery may be, it is so expressed that you are enabled to carry it off with a laugh, while at the same time you are bound to feel pleased with the spirit which dictates it. A lady who was learning Irish in London paid a visit to a Gaelic-speaking part of Kerry, and, in order to improve her colloquial acquaintance with the language, tried to carry on a conversation in the old tongue with one of the peasants. The attempt, however, was a failure. They could not understand each other. "Ah," said the peasant at last, "how could I be expected to know the fine Irish of the grand lady from London?"

A pat answer to be given by a native of the Emerald Isle is only in the eternal fitness of things. For example:—An Irish labourer coveted a lowly municipal appointment in a certain borough, and called on one of the local town councillors to secure his influence in getting the desired job. "Is his worship at home?" inquired Pat. "He is not at home just now," replied the lady of the house, who had a very prepossessing appearance; "but perhaps I may do as well. I'm the wife of his worship," she added, repeating Pat's words quizzically. "An' sure, ma'am," said the applicant, by way of introducing his errand, "his worship isn't to be wondered at." Whether the town councillor's wife used her influence on his behalf or not, Pat never knew, but, all the same, he got the situation. A servant girl named Bridget, applying for a place, said to the lady of the house, " Yis, ma'am, I lived in me last place for three weeks." " And why did you leave ?" inquired the lady. " I couldn't get along with the misthress ; she was ould and cranky." " But I may be ould and cranky, too," said the lady. " Cranky ye may be, ma'am, for faces is sometimes decavin' ; but ould, niver!" said Bridget. And Bridget got the place. Two kinds of conveyances are commonly in use in the south of Ireland, and are known respectively as " inside " and " outside " cars. A very nice-looking lady in Cork engaged an outside car to take her to the house of a friend. As the day was rather chilly, the friend met her with the exclamation, " Have you really come on an outside car?" Instantly the driver replied, " Why, thin, ma'am, is it inside you'd be after puttin' *her*—a handsome lady that could bear inspection !"

Another characteristic feature of Irish life is the easy freedom of manners and the familiarity of intercourse between strangers. Among the people, certainly, the stranger is never received in Ireland with that cold, distant, and suspicious demeanour with which he is too often greeted in the sister countries. In Ireland the stranger is treated confidingly as a friend until he has done something wrong ; in England he is regarded with distrust until he has established his good character. I have often seen, in the south of Ireland, carters pull up their wagons or vans, and walk into a house without ceremony, beyond the salutation, "God save all here," go over to the fireplace, and take up a burning sod of turf with which to light their pipes; and then were ready, with native loquacity, to enter into conversation with any members of the household present.

There is a very humorous mediæval Irish story which I am disposed to think is a satire on the talkativeness of the race. Three hermits sought peace and quietude in a valley far remote from the haunts of men. At the end of a year one remarked, "It's a fine life we are having here." After another year the second hermit replied, " It is." When a third year had elapsed, the remaining hermit broke into the conversation with the threat, "If I cannot get peace here, I'll go back to the world!"

Simplicity is also a *trait* in the Irish character. A dispensary doctor told me that he had occasion to prescribe two pills for a sick labourer, which he sent him by his wife in a small box, bearing the directions, "The whole to be taken immediately." On visiting his patient subsequently, the doctor was surprised to learn that the desired effect had not been produced by the pills. He asked the man's wife if she had really given her husband the medicine. "I did, doctor," she replied; "but maybe the lid hasn't come off yet." The sick man had been made to swallow pills and box together! Mrs. Murphy's husband was extremely ill, so she called in a doctor, and then anxiously inquired as to the sufferer's state. " I am sorry to say, madam," replied the doctor gravely, "that your husband is dying by inches." "Well, docthor," said Mrs. Murphy, with an air of resignation, "wan good thing is, me poor husband is six feet three in his stockin'-feet, so he'll lasht some time yit." It is a grand thing to have—as the Irish peasants have—faith in the doctor! What wonders it can work is shown by the following story. An Irishman, who had a great respect for the medical profession, but had had the good fortune never to have required a doctor's services in his life before, was one day taken ill. A doctor was sent for. With eyes big with astonishment, the patient watched the doctor take his clinical thermometer from its case. As the doctor slipped it under his patient's armpit, he told him "to keep it there a second or two." Paddy lay still, almost afraid to breathe, and, when the doctor took it out, he was astonished to hear his patient exclaim, " I do feel a dale better after that, sur!"

Stories of the simpleness and artlessness of the people are very entertaining. A well-known society lady, residing at Cork, sent a letter to the militia barracks, requesting the pleasure of Captain

A.'s company at dinner on a certain day. The letter must have got into the wrong hands, for the answer rather astonished the hostess. It ran : "Private Hennessy and Private O'Brien are unable to accept, owing to their being on duty ; but the remainder of Captain A.'s company will have much pleasure in accepting Mrs. B.'s hospitality." Some years ago the keeper of the lighthouse on Tory Island (an Englishman) got married to a London girl, and his wife had, among other effects, a small light pianette sent after her to her new home. By-and-by news reached the island that the instrument was on the mainland, and two islanders were despatched in a lugger to fetch it across. The lighthouse-keeper and his wife were awaiting the arrival of the pianette, which was to brighten the long winter evenings ; but, to their disappointment, they saw the boat returning without the instrument. "Where's the pianette?" shouted the lighthouse-keeper when the lugger had got within hailing distance. "It's all right," replied one of the boatmen ; "shure, we're towin' it behind us!" The inhabitants of Tory Island are an extremely simple and primitive people. Lady Chatterton, who made a visit she paid to Ireland thirty years ago the subject of a book, describes the mingled astonishment and alarm she saw on the face of a peasant from the island as he mounted the stairs of a house on the mainland.

Another characteristic of the peasantry is their carefulness about the superscription of the letters they commit to the post. They find it difficult to believe in the capability of the post office authorities to safely deliver a letter, outside their own immediate postal district, unless it is addressed with the utmost fulness of detail. The manager of a large hotel in Dublin showed me the envelope of a letter received by one of the maids of the establishment from her old mother in County Mayo. The superscription was as follows:—

>For Margaret Maloney,
>   Rotunda Hotel.
>All modern improvements. Lift. Electric lights. Terms moderate.
>   Tariff on application to manager.
>   Sackville Street, Dublin, Ireland.

The old lady with rural simplicity had faithfully copied all the printed details at the top of the sheet of the hotel note-paper on which her daughter had written to her.

Perhaps it is only in Ireland—a country where everything is taken for granted—that an incident like the following is possible. During the meeting of the British Association in Dublin in 1871, a visit was paid by the ethnological section to the island of Arranmore, off the coast of Galway, famous for its magnificent cyclopean ruin, the Dun Angus. Amongst the other objects of interest pointed out for the admiration of the assembled *savants* was a rude specimen of those domica buildings of a beehive form, variously called oratories or *blockaunes*. They are stone-roofed structures of narrow proportions, with low entrances, and containing one or more small chambers. Whilst a famous Irish archæologist, who acted the *cicerone*, was descanting on the architectural peculiarities and the profound antiquity of the structure, which, perhaps, he said, was once the residence of Firbolg or Danaun Kings, one of the excursionists on the outside of the group sought such information about the mysterious building as he could gather from the crowd of wondering natives who were congregated around. "Isn't that a very ancient building now?" he said to an Arranite. "I suppose it's a thousand years old at least?" "Oh, no, yer honner," was the reply. "Shure, it's no more than four or five years since Tim Bourke built it for a donkey that he do be workin' in the winter."

The national characteristics are so diffused that the same *traits* are to be found in the houses of the gentry — tempered, somewhat, by education and training—as in the cabins of the peasantry. An amusing illustration of what "a ruling passion," the passion for hunting and racing is among the well-to-do classes in Ireland, occurred in a speech on the State of Ireland delivered by Lord Stanley in 1844. He pointed out, amid the laughter of the House of Commons, that an affidavit respecting the striking out of Roman Catholics from the panel from which the jury which tried O'Connell and other Repeal leaders was selected, was signed by William Kemmis, "Clerk of the Course," instead of "Clerk of the Crown." Chief Justice Doherty used to relate a strange experience which befell him during a visit to a country house. His friend, the host, sent a car to the railway station to bring him to the place. He had not gone far when the horse became very restive, and finally upset the vehicle into a ditch. The judge asked the driver how long the animal had been in harness. "Half an hour, sur," replied the man. "I mean, how long since he was first put in harness?" said the judge. "Shure, I've tould you, half an hour, sur," answered the driver, "an' the masther said if he carried ye safe he'd buy him." I was one evening in the Queen's Theatre, Dublin, during the week of the famous August Horse Show, when the Irish metropolis is crowded with visitors from every province. An elderly country gentleman, in pronounced "horsey" attire, came into the stalls; and the "gods," as is their wont, began to chaff him. He bore their remarks in silence for a time, and then, rising in his seat and looking up to the gallery, waved his hand for silence. "Gentlemen," he cried, "if you don't stop that noise, I'll lave the theatre." A shout of laughter greeted his humorous threat from all parts of the house, and he was left in peace by the "gods" for the remainder of the evening.

The Irish peasant will never confess to ignorance if he can at all escape it. This characteristic is also due to his desire to be on the best of terms with everybody. Some years ago the Fishery Commissioners held at Kilrush an inquiry into the condition of the fisheries of the lower Shannon. One old witness was very discursive, and inclined to aver everything. "Are there any whales about there?" asked one of the commissioners sarcastically. "Is it whales?" exclaimed the witness, who did not notice that the commissioner was humbugging him. "Shure ye may see thim be the dozen sphoutin' about like water engines all over the place." Another commissioner gravely inquired whether there were dogfish there. "Faix, you'd say so, if ye passed the night at Carrigaholt. We can't sleep for the barkin' of thim," replied the witness. Lastly, the third commissioner asked if flying fish abounded in the river. The old man's marvellous imagination and rapid invention were by no means exhausted, for he replied, "Arrah, if we didn't put the shutters up ivery night there wouldn't be a whole pane of glass left in the windies from the crathurs beatin' agin thim." A gamekeeper in County Waterford, who was very proud of the woods under his charge, was wont to indulge in the most extravagant accounts of the quantity of every description of game to be found there. A gentleman once asked him, for amusement's sake, "Are there any paradoxes to be found here, Pat?" Without the slightest hesitation the keeper replied, "Oh, thim's very rare in these parts, yer honner; but ye might find two or three of thim sometimes on the sands whin the tide's out."

These harmless and very amusing exaggerations may undoubtedly be traced to the fancifulness of the Irish peasantry, their excessive geniality and courtesy, and their desire to please. John Wesley, the famous founder of the Methodist sect, who visited our country about the middle of the last century, said of the peasantry that, "a people so generally civil he had never seen either in Europe or America." He also described them as "an immeasurably loving people," and declared, "I have seen as real courtesy in their cabins as could be found at St. James's or the Louvre." This, indeed, is the testimony of all fine natures who have been brought into close relations with the Irish people. Some of the *foibles* of the peasantry may have perplexed them a little; but that they are an attractive and interesting and lovable race has been admitted by all. Sir Edward Burne Jones, the renowned artist, a Welshman, has written—"I am by blood and nature and sympathy more Irish than Saxon. I do not love the English even; I admire and respect them often more than any other nation now existing; but they don't touch my heart a bit, and I often really hate them, and though the Irish disappoint, vex and confuse me, they touch me and melt my heart often and often."

I heard a very amusing story from a priest, who related it, he told me, on the authority of the clergyman who figured in the incident, which shows that this attention and courtesy to strangers sometimes leads to laughable *contretemps*. Three Protestant ladies were staying at Glengariff. Owing to the sympathetic manner in which they interested themselves in the welfare of the people, they became great friends with the parish priest. One Sunday the ladies were obliged to take refuge from a heavy shower of rain in the little chapel. The parish priest, who happened to be celebrating Mass at the time, observed them, and whispering to the simple old clerk, who was attending him at the altar, he said, "Get three chairs for the Protestant ladies." The Clerk mistaking his instructions, turned round to the congregation and cried —" His riverence wants three cheers for the Protestant ladies." They were given with a heart and a half.

The Irishman is the most approachable of human beings. There is no man with whom one can become so thoroughly acquainted in a short time, and there is no man who takes so kindly and keen an interest in one's affairs on a casual acquaintance. The Duke of Connaught had an amusing experience of this quality of the Irish character during the tour which he made through Ireland about twenty years ago. He was standing on the steps of an hotel in the west of Ireland when a peasant approached him, and with native bland and infantile assurance, said—"Welcome to Ireland, yer Royal Highness. I hope I see yer Royal Highness well." "Quite well. I'm much obliged to you," replied the Duke. "And yer noble mother, the Queen. I hope her ould ladyship is enjoyin' the best of health," said the peasant. "Yes, thank you, the Queen is very well," answered the Duke, who seemed highly amused by the easy familiarity of the peasant. "I'm glad to hear it," continued the latter; "an' tell me, yer Royal Highness, how are all yer noble brothers and sisters?" But at that moment an *aide-de-camp* appeared on the scene, and cried, "Get along there, you fellow." "What are ye interferin' wid me for?" retorted the peasant, apparently much affronted. "Don't ye see that I'm houldin' a conversation wid his Royal Highness."

But the irrepressible sense of humour of the people often leads them to the perpetration of amusing practical jokes on unwary visitors. Could there be anything more laughable than the joke played on the clever and astute Thackeray by a simple peasant? The author of *Vanity Fair* was filled with a detestation of O'Connell when, in 1843, he made that journey through Ireland which led to the production of the caustic *Irish Sketch Book*. Going along a country road one day, the eminent novelist saw at certain intervals pillar-stones bearing the mystic letters "G.P.O." The stones had just been erected by the Post Office authorities to mark the post roads. But great men do not know everything, and Thackeray happened to be ignorant of that fact. He therefore asked an explanation of the stones and their inscription from a peasant whom he met on the road. "Sure, sur," said the man; "G.P.O. stands for 'God Presarve O'Connell!'" Thackeray took a note of the explanation, and in the original manuscript of *The Irish Sketch Book* he gravely stated that so blind and extravagant was the devotion of the people to the great demagogue that they had actually erected along the highways pillar-stones with the inscription "G.P.O.," which meant "God Preserve O'Connell." The blunder was, however, discovered in the office of the publisher, and was set right before the book appeared.

Another English writer, though of far less distinction than Thackeray, went to Killarney some years ago to write a book about the place. He fell into the hands of a noted local wag, who brought him to see that extraordinary phenomenon of nature known only to the joker as "the deaf lake," across which, though it was only 300 yards wide, it was impossible to carry any sound. Placing the visitor at one side of the lake, the wag proceeded to the other, and appeared, by his contortions and grimaces, to be shouting at the top of his voice; but not a sound reached the visitor, for the excellent reason that the wag had not uttered a word. Then, joining the visitor, he gravely suggested, in order to complete the test, that *he* should shout across the lake, and roar and bellow. The visitor did; but no, not a word came across the waters to the wag—at least, so he averred—as he stood as if straining his ears to catch the expressions of the visitor.

A sporting friend told me that he went down to Punchestown races one year by train. Just as the train was leaving Kingsbridge terminus, three Dublin men, undoubtedly of the betting fraternity, jumped into his carriage. They had no tickets, for they had no time to procure them. "There will be a delay about the tickets," said one; "what will we do?" "I'll make it all right," said another. By-and-by, when the station at which the tickets were to be collected was reached, the latter got out of the carriage, and in a few minutes returned with a ticket for each of his companions. "How did you manage it?" they all asked eagerly. "Simply enough," he replied. "I went into a carriage containing some Englishmen, and said, 'Tickets, please.' They thought I was the ticket-collector, and they handed their pieces of pasteboard over to me." When the official ticket-collector reached the carriage of the Englishmen—on whom the trick had been played—there was a scene which, in the language of the poet, may be imagined but cannot be described.

The Fellows of Trinity College, Dublin, gave a dinner to a very eminent English educationist, on a visit to Ireland at a time that the Catholic bishops had condemned the Queen's colleges. In the course of the dinner, the Englishman—who had been placed, *malice prepense*, by the late Professor Houghton, between Father Healy, of Bray, and his great rival in humour, Dr. Nedley, of Dublin—remarked that although it was hardly his place to criticise the action of the Catholic bishops in condemning the Queen's colleges, yet he could not help thinking that if they had not overstepped their authority, they had at least strained it. "My dear sir," said Dr. Nedley, in the most solemn tones, but with a sly wink to Father Healy, "you can have no idea how the bishops tyrannise over us. Why, it's only the other day that Cardinal

Cullen issued an edict against fast dancing. I called on his Eminence, and went down on my knees to him, and said, 'For God's sake, your Eminence, revoke the edict against fast dancing!' but his reply was, 'I'd see you d——d first, Nedley!'" "Come, come, doctor," broke in Father Healy, apparently very indignant; "boy and man, I've known Paul Cullen these forty years, and, drunk or sober, I never heard him say the like." The eminent English educationist must have brought home strange notions as to the character of the Irish Catholic ecclesiastics.

But the practical joking is by no means confined to visitors. Some years ago the Shannon Rowing Club, Limerick, had a famous boat crew, which carried everything before them in aquatic sports in Ireland. The crew went to Cork one year, and, as usual, won the big race. Naturally there was immense excitement in the rival cities over the event, and during its height, on the day of the race, a telegram, purporting to come from the Mayor of Cork, reached the Mayor of Limerick. It was couched in the following terms:—"Your Limerick crew beat us to-day, but, for the honour of Cork, I hereby challenge you, for a stake of £50, to row a measured mile on the river Lee." Now, as the Mayor of Limerick had only one arm, he saw in this message a deliberate insult, and, remembering that the Mayor of Cork was not

complete in the matter of legs, he furiously despatched to Cork a message to this effect:—
"If you want to avenge your disgraceful beating to-day, I'll hop you over the Wellesley Bridge, in this city, for £100." The Mayor of Cork was perfectly innocent, and absolutely ignorant of the sending of the first telegram, and recognising in this message from Limerick the addition of insult to the injury done to the reputation of the city, of which he was the chief magistrate, by the ill-fortune of the Cork oars, he gratified himself by informing the Mayor of Limerick by telegraph that he was "a cowardly cad." The correspondence was subsequently continued by the solicitors of the respective mayors, and it took some days to reach a conclusion which avoided an appeal to the law courts.

The stories in circulation in Ireland are always good. There is one anecdote which is rather well known, but, as it seems to me to always retain its refreshing novelty, no matter how often I hear it, I will repeat it here. It used to be told with great effect by the famous Judge Keogh. Dr. Whately, the Archbishop of Dublin, had a large Newfoundland dog, of which he was very fond. It was a favourite pastime of his Grace to play with the animal in Stephen's Green, opposite the Archiepiscopal residence. One day two old women were observing the doings of the Archbishop and his dog through the railings of the Green. "Ah, thin, Mary," said one; "does yez know who that is playin' wid the dog?" "Troth, I don't, Biddy," said the other; "but he's a gran', handsome, riverend gintleman, whoever he is." "Shure, that's the Archbishop, Mary," said Biddy. "Ah, thin, does yez tell me so?" cried Mary. "God bless the innocent craythure; isn't it he that's aisily amused? Arrah, yez can tell the thrue gintleman anywhere." "He's not our Archbishop at all, Mary; he's the Proteshtant Archbishop." "Oh, the d—— ould fool!" exclaimed Mary. "Did yez ever in all yer life see such a charicathur of a man? To think of him playin' with a dog!"

"Peter," said a gentleman to his servant, "did you take my note to Mr. Downey?" "Yis, sur, an' I think his eyesight is gettin' very bad," replied Peter. "Why so?" asked the master. "Begorra, sur," said Peter, "while I was in the room, he axed me twice where me hat was, an' 'twas on me head all the time." But it's not often that Irish servants are wanting in good manners, and the offence in this case was unintentional. Here is another story of an Irish servant. Having carried a basket of game from his master to a friend, he waited a considerable time for the customary fee, but, not finding it forthcoming, he said: "If me masther should say, 'Pat, what did the gintleman give you?' what would your honner have me tell him?"

"Old White," the late major-domo, or house-steward of the Mansion House, Dublin—an office which he filled for many, many years—was a well-known character. Many funny stories are told of him. He was once guilty of some neglect of duty, and was summoned before the Lord Mayor, who said: "White, I have borne with you in many things, but this complaint goes beyond my power of endurance." "And does yur lordshup really cridit the sthory?" asked White. "Certainly," answered the Lord Mayor. "I've just heard it from two members of the Corporation." "Faith," retorted White, "if I believed all that twinty town councillors and aldhermin say about you, it's little I'd think you was fit to ware the gould chain of Lord Mayor of Dublin." White, as on many a previous occasion, was dismissed with a caution. He had, indeed, a hot temper and a sarcastic tongue, from the sting of which even the Lord Mayor himself was occasionally not sacred.

I often heard from "Old White" wonderful stories of "the great doings," and "the lashin's of hospitality," in the Mansion House before its civic sanctity was invaded by "the Commonalty"—as White called them—who came in when the Nationalists got the upper hand in the Corporation. A licensed vintner was Lord Mayor some years ago. A captain of a regiment stationed in Dublin called one day to see his lordship in connection with a concert for some charitable institution. The door of the Mansion House was, as usual, opened by White. "Good-morrow, White," was the salute of the captain. "Ah, thin, good-day to yez, captain, and how's ivery bit of yez? Shure you're welcome," said White. "Is the Lord Mayor in?" asked the captain. "Well, the way it is, captain, if yez want to see him at wanst, he's out; but if yez can wait a quarther of an hour, he's in." The visitor agreed to wait in the room off the hall. "Captain," continued White, "would yez be after havin' a dhrop of whiskey wid me?" "I really can't, White; but thank you very much," replied the captain. "Oh, shure, make yer mind aisy! It's none of the Lord Mayor's fusil oil I'd be after givin' ye; it's rale John Jameson. I paid me solid twenty-wan shillin's the gallon for it. You can dhrink it wid safety, captain." Then, "Whist yer sowl, captain; here's his lordshup!"

Mr. Aubrey De Vere, the well-known Irish poet, tells a funny story of a County Limerick priest to whom a young man, who had committed murder, and was "on his keeping"—that is, a fugitive from justice—came to confess his crime, and then to surrender himself to the police. "My boy, it's a very serious thing to die, and to meet one's God," said the clergyman. "I'm afraid it's a long time since you have been to Mass, and that you have forgotten your religion altogether. Let me hear now if you can say the Apostles' Creed." The youth strove to recite it, but failed. "Tut, tut, boy, you're not fit to be hanged at all," cried the priest. It was then arranged that the murderer, before submitting himself for trial, should visit the priest until he had obtained some knowledge of the doctrines of the Church, and showed a real repentance for his crime. At length the priest said to him, "I promised to let you know when I considered you fit to be hanged. Well, now, I have the satisfaction of assuring you that I never met a man fitter to be hanged than yourself." So the youth went and gave himself up.

Some of the priests were opposed to the custom, very popular at one time with the boys and girls, but now almost a thing of the past, of public dances at "the cross roads,"—a point where three or four roads meet—on fine Sunday afternoons. A blind fiddler was brought out from a neighbouring town to supply the music at one of these festive gatherings. Just as the fun was at its height, "his riverence" the parish priest, was seen approaching, and the boys and girls fled across the fields. But the blind fiddler, unconscious of the *stampede*, continued rasping out the lively strains of the jig, "The Cats' Rambles to the Child's Saucepan," when he was interrupted by the priest asking him, "Do you know the Third Commandment?" "It sounds familiar like to me, but I can't recall it," said the fiddler. "Maybe, if ye whistled a bar or two of it I might remimber it." He thought it was another jig he had been asked to play, instead of being reproved for desecrating the Sabbath!

The following good story may not be true—I certainly would not care to vouch for its accuracy—but those who know the leisurely and casual way many things are done in Ireland will admit that it is by no means improbable. A train which was slowly wending its way in the south of Ireland, suddenly pulled up outside a station. The guard, putting his head out of his van at the end of the train, shouted to the engine-driver, so that all the passengers might hear, "I say, Jim, what are ye stoppin' for? Go on out o' that, will ye?" The engine-driver roared back, "Yerra, man, how can I go on? Don't ye see the signal's agin us." "The signal's agin us!" cried the guard contemptuously. "Musha, how mighty particular yer gettin'!" I remember attending at Limerick an inquiry into the wreck of a ship in the Shannon, while it was being brought up the river by one of the local pilots. The captain stated in the course of his evidence that when the vessel struck on a rock, he said angrily to the pilot, "You said you knew every rock in the river." "Of course I do, sur, and that's wan o' thim," replied the pilot!

Ireland has also produced very simple-minded

men, even among the dons of Dublin University. Every one remembers the story of Newton, who cut a large hole in his room door to let his big cat out and a small one for the use of the kitten. That anecdote is told in Ireland of the Rev. John Barrett, D.D., who was Vice-Provost of Trinity College, Dublin, at the beginning of the present century. Dr. Barrett, who was known in Trinity as "Jackey," was remarkable for his eccentricity and want of knowledge of the world, and had, it is stated, for half a century never wandered outside the walls of Trinity College. He was an accomplished divine of blameless life, and a celebrated Hebrew scholar. His language, however, was uniformly profane, and his favourite method of commencing a conversation was "May the devil admire me." On being asked on one occasion how he was, he replied "Between lectures and chapels, chapels and lectures, h—l to my soul, I have no time to say my prayers." A student was summoned before the college authorities for shouting "Sweep! sweep!" after the Vice-Provost, who was not marked for cleanliness of attire. The student's defence was that he was merely calling a sweep, whom he required to clean the chimneys of his rooms. The Vice-Provost met the explanation thus: "May the devil admire me, but I was the only sweep in the quadrangle at the time." He was a notorious miser, and lost heavily in Irish canal shares. He was told his money was "sunk in the canal," and immediately asked in the simplicity of his heart why could it not be fished up. When his attention was directed to the fact that the big hole in the door would be available for the kitten as well as the cat, he immediately exclaimed, "Well, may the devil admire me, but I never thought of that before." At a meeting of the College Board, at which the question of getting rid of a heap of rubbish lying in the College Park turned up, Barrett suggested that a hole should be dug, and the stuff buried in it. "But, Dr. Barrett," said some one, "what shall we do with the stuff that comes out of the hole?" "Dig another and bury it," was the ready response. An old woman who attended Barrett went out one frosty morning with a penny to bring him a halfpenny-worth of milk for his breakfast. As she was returning to the College, she slipped, severely injured her leg, and was conveyed to Mercer's Hospital. Her master visited the poor creature, and was affected to tears when he found her writhing in pain. But his penurious feelings at length getting the upper hand, he said, "Catty, what about the jug?" "Ah, sure, sur, it was smashed on the pavement," she replied. "Well, well, it can't be helped," said he; "but, Catty, what about the halfpenny change, do ye see!"

The average tourist, with his inordinate love

of personal comfort and personal well-being when holiday-making, often finds it hard to bear with the shortcomings of some of the hotels in the remote parts of Ireland. But the genuine, heartfelt welcome which is given to visitors at these primitive hostelries—a welcome which is not at all inspired by mercenary motives —and the quaint and homely experiences to be met with in them, undoubtedly add to the charm of touring in out-of-the-way parts of Ireland. Thackeray relates in his *Irish Sketch-Book* that once when dining in a rural hotel in Ireland, he asked the waiter for some currant jelly with his roast mutton. "There's no jelly, sur, but I'll give you some fine lobster sauce!" was the waiter's answer. We may be sure that this quaint and unexpected reply lent more piquancy to the novelist's dinner than all the currant jelly in the world could have imparted.

A traveller staying at one of these out-of-way inns found his boots still lying uncleaned outside his bedroom door in the morning. He summoned the landlord, to obtain an explanation of this remissness in the service. "My boots have been lying there all night untouched!" he exclaimed. "Yes, yer honner," said the landlord, proud of the honesty and good name of his house, "an' they might lie there for a month, and no wan wud touch thim!" The excuses given for deficiencies at these hotels are always diverting. "Bring me a hot plate, waiter," said a visitor to a Mayo hotel as he sat at the dinner-table. "The hot plates is not come in yet, sur," replied the waiter. "Then hurry up and get them in," said the hungry visitor. "I mane, sur, they're not in saison," explained the waiter. "Hot plates come in in October and goes out in May." A friend of mine who visited the backward parts of Kerry last summer, told me that he stayed one night at an humble hotel in Cahirciveen. His bedroom was on the ground-floor. During the night he was awakened by a noise in the room, and to his consternation saw a rat prowling about for something to eat. Next morning he reported the matter to the landlord. "Look at that, now," said the landlord; "it's all that Johnnie's fault. Johnnie, Johnnie!" he cried, and on the appearance of a bare-legged youth, who acted the part of "boots," he exclaimed, "You bla'guard, why didn't ye put Biddy into the room wid this gintleman last night?" "Biddy" was an Irish terrier!

The Irish waiters in country hotels are, as a rule, very comical and amusing. Lord Carlisle used to relate a laughable experience he had with a waiter at an agricultural dinner in Galway during the time he was Lord Lieutenant of Ireland. This waiter, who happened to be a droll person, was specially appointed to attend to the wants of the Viceroy. He passed remarks on every dish with which he supplied his Excellency. Handing him a dish of peas, he said, "Pays, yer Excellency," adding in a whisper, "an' if I was you, the divil a wan iv thim I'd touch, for they're as hard as bullets!" A barrister told me that during an Assize at Nenagh he and some friends played cards one night at the hotel where they were staying. He dropped a pound note under the table; and discovering his loss as he was going to bed, returned to the room immediately. The waiter said to him, "Did you lose anything, sur?" "Yes, a pound note," replied my friend. "I found it; and here it is," returned the waiter, adding, "Begor, wasn't it lucky for you none of the gintlemen found it!"

A Dublin gentleman was travelling in the West of Ireland. He asked for a bath the morning after his arrival, and a pail of water was brought to his bedroom. "Why don't you have a proper bathroom constructed?" he said to the "bhoy" who attended him. "What would be the use of it?" was the ready retort. "We are not accustomed to thim dirty gintlemin from Dublin that wants a bath ivery day!" Whatever may be said of Irish hotels, it cannot be written of them what Dr. Magee, Archbishop of York, a witty Irishman, wrote in the visitors' book of the hostelry in a popular holiday resort in England: "I came here for change and rest. The waiter has the change; the landlord the rest."

Heinrich Heine has described Ireland as an ethereal young lady, "with her heart full of sun, and her head full of flowery wit." A happy and poetic description, truly. It is not, alas! all flowery wit in the head of Ireland, nor all sunshine in her heart; but she has as large a share of joyousness and humour as any nation in the world. She also rejoices in the passionate devotion of her children. Wherever they may be, Ireland is always in their thoughts. An Irish exile was at a dinner in Paris. Some one proposed the toast of " The land we live in." "Aye, with all my soul," cried the Irishman, raising his glass, " Here's to poor old Ireland ! "

Chapter XXI

AT THE GATES OF DEATH

THE Irish gaze with a look of drollery even into the eyes of death. A dying Irishman was asked by his clergyman if he was prepared to renounce the devil and all his works. "Oh, sir!" he exclaimed, "don't ask me that. I'm going to a strange country, and I don't want to make myself enemies!" Another Irishman, who lay on his death-bed, did not seem quite reconciled to the long journey on which he was about to depart. A friend tried to console him with the commonplace reflection that we must all die once. "Yes," rejoined the sick man, "that's the very thing that vexes me. If I could die half a dozen times I should not mind!" When the doctor told Richard Brinsley Sheridan, during his last illness, that he seemed to cough with greater difficulty than on the previous day, the wit exclaimed, "Do I? That's odd enough, for I've been practising all night!"

It is hardly necessary to add that the Irish

people, who can thus joke in the face of death, accept the inevitable with resignation. An English medical doctor, who has a very extensive general practice in a working-class portion of London — including a large number of Irish patients of the poorer classes—told me that, in his experience, the Irish receive the announcement that a patient is beyond hope of recovery in a totally different manner from the English. The humble Irish have a profound belief in the professional capacity of every medical doctor; and so, when this London practitioner told the relatives or friends of an Irish patient that there was absolutely no hope of recovery, his word was never in the slightest degree questioned. It was accepted as absolute. What the relatives or friends did on receiving the announcement was to send for the priest at once, to administer to the patient the last rites of the Roman Catholic Church. But very different, indeed, was the conduct of English people of the poorer classes. When they were told by the doctor that the end of a patient was near, and that nothing more could be done, they, as a rule, replied that it must be so, and that they had perfect faith in the skill and judgment of the medical attendant. But as soon as he had left the house, they sent in haste for another doctor, to see what he could do. Often, indeed, when my friend has said that a patient was past hope, he has been peremptorily ordered out of the house, and told that he did not know his work, which they should show by fetching another and a cleverer doctor, who would effect a cure.

The old Irish custom of "waking" the dead has given rise to much misrepresentation of the Irish character. And yet in its intention it is a kindly and humane custom. To those who do not understand the Irish nature, or the impulses which move it, the drinking, smoking and conversation which go on at wakes appear incongruous and repulsive. To the Irish people, on the other hand, there is something very cold, unfeeling, and repellent in the English custom of the corpse lying shut up in a room all alone, deserted, as it were, by the family. In Ireland we keep close company with our dead to the very last moment. "Waking" means "watching." We watch affectionately by the body of a dead relative or friend until the time arrives to depart for the burial ground. The body is laid on the bed, covered with a white sheet, leaving exposed the head and the hands crossed reverently on the breast The walls about the bed are screened with white sheets, on which are often hung bunches of flowers and laurel leaves. Seven lighted candles stand on a table near the bed; the room is frequently sprinkled with holy water to keep off the evil spirits who may be hovering around; and on the corpse is a large plate of salt, which is believed to be hygienically efficacious for the watchers.

The Irish people are gregarious in their instincts. They never like to be alone; and this feeling for companionship is strongest when death has visited them closely. A family deprived of a member by death seek consolation from the neighbours; and the neighbours, ever quick in sympathy in joy or in sorrow, crowd in to cheer up the spirits of the bereaved, to distract their thoughts from their sad loss. First entering the room where the corpse lies, they kneel and say a prayer, and shed a tear,—the women especially giving loud vocal expression to their grief. But the manifestation of sorrow is confined to the chamber of death. Outside in the wide kitchen the neighbours assemble, and snuff, pipes and tobacco, whiskey and stout are supplied to them. There are "wakes" at which stories are told, forfeits are played, and a little drollery indulged in; but, as a rule, while every effort is made by the watchers to blunt the edge of sorrow, perfect decorum is preserved, and not an unseemly word is spoken. I have been at many "wakes," and certainly I never heard a song sung, though it is often said—of course by those who do not know—that singing is a common practice at these assemblies. Moreover, there is a motive—founded upon superstition, it is true—for checking the manifestations of grief in the presence of the dead. In some parts of Ireland it is believed that the soul of a departed person is made restless by the tears and regrets of surviving friends and relatives, and that, unable to get to heaven, it hovers about the earth until the sorrow for its departure is appeased. Mourners may therefore be seen at "wakes" struggling to repress their sobs and tears. "Don't be cryin' that way *asthore*, or you'll keep him from his rest," was a remonstrance I heard kindly addressed to a young widow who was weeping bitterly over the remains of her husband.

Many, indeed, are the superstitions which are associated with death in Ireland. A good many years ago the house of Colonel Hutchinson, near the town of Macroom, co. Cork, was entered at night by a large band of burglars. The noise brought down the Colonel from his bedroom, and recognising in one of the disguised gang a man who was in his employment, he cried out, "What, McCarthy, are you here?" This sealed his doom. The burglars, seeing that they were recognised, shot Hutchinson and then fled. One of the party subsequently gave information to the authorities, six of the culprits were captured, convicted at Cork Assizes, and sentenced to be publicly hanged in the square of Macroom. On the day of the execution the criminals rode on horseback from

Cork to Macroom, a distance of fifteen miles. As the cavalcade passed through the streets of the town towards the square, an old woman threw herself before the horse of one of the culprits and cried in Irish, "John Duggan, John Duggan, you owe me sixpence." The man's arms were pinioned; but he succeeded in taking a sixpenny-piece out of his pocket and throwing it to the old woman. When she was asked subsequently why she tormented Duggan at such a time about so trivial a matter, she replied, "Troth, thin, shure I wouldn't be after letting the sixpence rest upon his soul."

There is a superstition that a person who dies as the clock strikes twelve, ushering in the Christmas morning, escapes purgatory and immediately enters heaven. A curious illustration of this superstition came to light some years ago in County Westmeath. One Christmas Eve a poor peasant lay *in extremis* in his cabin, attended by his wife and daughter. His condition was hopeless; he had, at the most, only a few hours to live, and the wife and daughter prayed fervently that he would pass away at midnight. But the clock of a neighbouring church began to strike twelve, and the husband was still living. At the stroke of six the wife seized the pillow and pressed it down on the unconscious man's face, while the daughter seated herself upon his breast. Just as the clock had ceased to strike, their purpose was accomplished. The husband and the father was dead. Was this murder? Technically, in the eyes of the law, it was; but it was inspired by affection and piety. The dying man could not have survived another hour; and these simple peasants were firmly convinced that by hastening his end by a few minutes they secured to him an eternity of joy.

Another curious superstition is that the dead of one parish graveyard play the old Irish game of hurling against the dead of another parish graveyard. They meet at night when the moon is full in one or other of the graveyards. The dead of each churchyard has a living man out of its parish to keep the goal. When a man gets a call to act in this capacity, he must go. Nothing on earth can enable him to escape the awful fate. This service is supposed to last for seven years; and it is said that if a man survive that term,—which few do,—he has power to cure diseases in the treatment of which doctors are powerless. The man who has to discharge this awful duty keeps his dread secret to himself. If he were to make it known, he would be shunned by his neighbours. Any man of a gloomy and morose disposition and eccentric manners who lives apart from the rest of the community is always suspected to be the goalkeeper for the dead hurlers. But perhaps the strangest of all the superstitions associated with the dead is that the last person interred on any day in a graveyard has to perform menial services for all the other dead in the graveyard—and some of these ancient places of burial contain mighty hosts of dead—including the service of carrying water to allay the thirst of those who are purging their sins in purgatory. These services he must continue to discharge until such time as some other person is buried in the churchyard. This superstition often leads to unseemly haste at funerals in Ireland. When two funerals approaching the same graveyard from different directions observe each other, a hotly-contested race to the burial ground takes place. At a funeral in the South of Ireland, on such an occasion, I have seen the coffin taken out of the hearse by eight stalwart men, who rushed with it to the graveyard by a short cut through the fields. Even in Dublin this superstition still prevails among the poorer classes. On Sundays, approaching twelve o'clock, the hour at which Glasnevin Cemetery is closed for interments, numbers of funerals may be seen careering along the roads leading to the cemetery, the mourners at each, animated by the desire to save their dead friend or relative from the discharge of an unpleasant task in the other world, striving eagerly to get before the others.

The wish to be buried with one's kith and kin

is another characteristic of the Irish peasantry. A new cemetery was opened near a village in County Limerick. As an old woman lay dying, her grandchildren, with whom she lived, tried to persuade her to consent to be interred in the new burial ground, instead of in the ancient, overcrowded graveyard where her husband lay, thirty miles distant. "Indeed and I won't be buried there," cried the old peasant. "Is it in that could and lonesome place ye want to lay me? Shure, I'd never be comfortable there wid not a bone nor a pinch of dust of wan belongin' to me within thirty miles o' me. No; take me to Kileely graveyard, which is full of dacent Christians."

To have "a gran' berryin," or, in other words, a large assemblage of people at the funeral, is an object of pride and ambition among the Irish peasantry. A young farmer who married a penniless girl was asked why he made so poor a match. "My wife," he answered, "has got fifty uncles, cousins and brothers; and if I was to die tomorrow, her faction could give me as long a funeral as the King of England." An English visitor said to a peasant, whom he met casually on the roadside, "What do you expect to get if Home Rule is granted?" "Iverything, yer honner," the peasant replied; "an' faix whin I'm dead it's meself maybe that'll be taken to the graveyard in a goolden hearse." Ireland is, indeed, noted for its big funerals. The whole countryside, or parish, turns out to pay the last tribute of respect to the deceased. It is the rule also in the rural districts for persons who meet a funeral to turn back, and accompany it for some distance at least "Who is it that's dead?" they will ask; and when they are told, they add, "Well, well; may the journey thrive with him"; or "Wisha, God be with him, wherever he is."

Burials are so well attended, that a lad who was asked by a sportsman whether he had seen any rabbits on his way, replied, "Yis, sur, whole funerals of thim." To him a funeral conveyed the largest possible idea of numbers. Tragedy and comedy touch each other very closely in all relations of life and death in Ireland. The loss suffered by death is often lost sight of in the family pride aroused by a largely-attended funeral. "It was a fine berryin', entirely," some friend or relative of the deceased will say after the return home. "Yes," is the reply; "there was a sight of people, and a power of cars." The coffin, in the case of rural funerals, is usually borne a long way on the shoulders of friends of the deceased. It is regarded as an honour to have carried the coffin of a popular favourite. "Ah, thin, it's I that am proud that I had me shoulder under his coffin," is a remark often heard in Ireland. The funerals of Irish politicians are usually the occasions of big popular demonstrations. A once prominent Nationalist leader, who had of late been rather neglected, cynically said to me, "Well, I'm sure of a big funeral, anyway. That's about the only thing a politician is certain of in Ireland." Another reason why funerals are so largely attended is that they afford the peasantry occasions for visiting the last resting-places of friends and relatives. The mourners disperse through the graveyard, and soon from all quarters rise wild bursts of grief from forms prostrate on mounds and flagstones. An old woman may be seen sobbing vehemently, as if for a fresh sorrow, over the grave of her infant that died forty years ago.

Douglas Jerrold relates that during a visit to Ireland he entered a cabin and found a handsome young girl busy at her needle. "I see you do some sewing," he observed. "I suppose this is for a bride," he added, seeing that the girl was working on what appeared to be an elaborate night-dress. "'Tis no wedding garment," replied the girl proudly. "It's my own shroud. Let life bring what it may, please God I'll have a decent wake." The story is apocryphal.

Though the Irish peasantry accept the inevitable calmly and resignedly, they have, at the same time, a horror of death; and it is impossible for any one who knows them to imagine a young peasant girl in the heyday of youth making her shroud. Besides, the shroud worn by peasants bears no resemblance whatever to any wedding garment. It is called "a habit," and is made of coarse brown stuff, such as is worn by some Orders of Friars. It is, however, a custom with old men or women who have no surviving relatives, to "lay up" for their interment, in order that they may escape what is considered the deep disgrace—the last and final misfortune, of a workhouse coffin and a pauper's grave. Fifty or sixty years ago it was rather a common custom among the poorer classes when they were unable to afford a coffin for a deceased relative to make the corpse beg for it. The body was laid on a bier on the footway outside the door on a Sunday, with a plate to receive the coppers of the people as they passed to Mass Sometimes this practice led to imposture. On one occasion the body of a man lay outside a cabin. The people placed their pennies or halfpennies on the plate. A poor woman came along, and, putting down a sixpence, began to gather five pennies from the plate. "Arrah, ma'am," cried the corpse; "be generous wance in yer life, and don't mind the change."

www.ingramcontent.com/pod-product-compliance
Lightning Source LLC
Chambersburg PA
CBHW032028220426
43664CB00006B/398